General Studies
for AQA B

Richard Hobson
David Walton
Victor Watton

An AS and A Level Course Text Second Edition

Hodder Murray

A MEMBER OF THE HODDER HEADLINE GROUP

The Publishers would like to thank the following for permission to reproduce copyright material:

Photo credits p.11 Illustrated London News; **p.18** Popperfoto; **p.26** Science Photo Library; **p.34** © Owaki - Kulla/CORBIS; **p.40** Eric and David Hosking/CORBIS; **p.46** *l & r* Quest/Science Photo Library; **p.52** Tobias Schwarz/Reuters/Corbis; **p.59** © Bettmann/CORBIS; **p.68** NIBSC/Science Photo Library; **p.75** Patrick Ward/Corbis; **p.84** *l* Courtesy of Apple, *r* Norbert Schaefer/CORBIS; **p.88** © Rachel Chapman; **p.127** *l* European Press Agency/Epa/Empics, *r* John Stillwell/PA/Empics; **p.131** PA/Empics; **p.147** PA/Empics; **p.151** © Larry Feign; **p.153** Popperfoto; **p.165** PA/Empics; **p.173** © Courtesy of Antony Gormley and Jay Jopling/White Cube; **p.174** Getty Images News; **p.176** Francis G Meyer/Corbis; **p.180** Tim Graham/Corbis; **p.197** PA/Empics; **p.205** Popperfoto; **p.217** Popperfoto; **p.227** Bridgeman Art Library, reproduced with kind permission of Coventry Cathedral; **p.232** © Reuters/CORBIS; **p.243** Alex Bartel/Science Photo Library.

Acknowledgements AQA for all AQA material, reproduced by permission of the Assessment and Qualifications Alliance; Associated New Media for 'Female fire fighter faces discrimination', the *Daily Mail* (Jan 02), and 'The £20 phone cover that costs £1 to make', the *Mail on Sunday* (06/01/02); Carel Press for three tables adapted from Fact File, Carel Press www.carel.org.uk; David Higham Associates for an extract from *The English*, by Jeremy Paxman, Penguin 1999; Martin Gorst for 'The truth is relative', *Guardian* (17/08/02); The Guardian for the graph 'Corporate intelligence on retailing' (01/08/99), 'Urgent need to save digital heritage', Stuart Miller (28/02/02), 'Captive audience hears Blair spell out jail to work scheme', Alan Travis (27/02/01) and 'War of pledges gives hope to world's poor', Julian Borger (21/03/02), Copyright Guardian Newspapers Limited; Her Majesty's Stationery Office for tables and figures from www.defra.gov.uk, information from the Inland Revenue website, graphs on labour market trends and social trends from the Office of National Statistics and key facts from www.camden.gov.uk. Crown copyright material is reproduced with the permission of the controller of HMSO and the Queen's Printer for Scotland; The Independent for 'Why Mr and Mrs Hashmi were right to choose life', first published in *The Independent* (24/02/02), 'Now show us a man who can run 100m in 6 seconds', first published in *The Independent* (01/10/00) and 'Why it's Bridget, Corelli or a video', first published in *The Independent* (22/04/01) © The Independent; the Independent Schools Council for information from their website www.isc.co.uk; Orion Publishing for an extract from *A Social History of England*, by Asa Briggs, 1983; Oxford University Press for an extract from *Introduction to Music*, by Richard Middleton, OUP 2002; Pearson Education for an extract from *Introductory Ethics*, by Fred Feldman, 1st Edition, © 1978. Reprinted by permission of Pearson Education, Inc., Upper Saddle River, NJ; Penguin for an extract from The Blank Slate, by Stephen Pinker, Penguin 2002; Polity Press for an extract from *An Introduction to Sociology*, by Ken Browne, Polity Press/Blackwell 1998; the Press Complaints Commission for an extract from their Code of Practice, 1997; Shadow Strategic Rail Authority for various statistics from www.sra.gov.uk; The Telegraph for 'Tourism chiefs go full tilt at windmills', Oliver Bennett, © Telegraph Group Limited (1994); The Times for 'Equal opportunities damages health of women soldiers', *The Times* (03/01/02).

Every effort has been made to trace all copyright holders, but if any have been inadvertently overlooked the Publishers will be pleased to make the necessary arrangements at the first opportunity.

Hodder Headline's policy is to use papers that are natural, renewable and recyclable products and made from wood grown in sustainable forests. The logging and manufacturing processes are expected to conform to the environmental regulations of the country of origin.

Orders: please contact Bookpoint Ltd, 130 Milton Park, Abingdon, Oxon OX14 4SB. Telephone: (44) 01235 827720. Fax: (44) 01235 400454. Lines are open 9.00 – 6.00, Monday to Saturday, with a 24-hour message answering service. Visit our website at www.hoddereducation.co.uk

© Richard Hobson, David Walton and Victor Watton 2005
First published in 2005 by
Hodder Murray, an imprint of Hodder Education,
a member of the Hodder Headline Group
338 Euston Road
London NW1 3BH

Impression number   10   9   8   7   6   5   4   3   2

Year   2010   2009   2008   2007   2006

Cover images from Ronald Grant and Corbis
Typeset in 12/14pt Garamond by Phoenix Photosetting, Chatham, Kent
Printed in Great Britain by Martins the Printers Ltd, Berwick upon Tweed

A catalogue record for this title is available from the British Library

ISBN-10: 0 340 88760 5
ISBN-13: 978 0340 88760 8

Contents

Introduction   1

Science and Technology   7
Unit 1 Scientific progress   8
Unit 2 Scientific method and its application   15
Unit 3 Religion and science   21
Unit 4 Energy   29
Unit 5 Environmental issues   35
Unit 6 Genetic engineering   42
Unit 7 Agriculture and food production   50
Unit 8 Human and animal behaviour   56
Unit 9 Medical developments   66
Unit 10 Transport issues   72
Unit 11 Computers   80
Unit 12 The relationship between science and culture   87
Unit 13 The application of maths   93

Society and Politics   105
Unit 14 The nature of society   106
Unit 15 Social change   112
Unit 16 Crime and deviance   118
Unit 17 The nature of law   123
Unit 18 Rights and responsibilities   128
Unit 19 Power and control   134
Unit 20 Politics   140
Unit 21 The British Constitution   145
Unit 22 Educational issues   152

Arts and Media   161
Unit 23 Aesthetic evaluation   162
Unit 24 The nature of culture   168
Unit 25 Creativity and innovation   175
Unit 26 The media   180
Unit 27 Censorship   187

Industry and Commerce   193
Unit 28 Economic theories   194
Unit 29 Economic issues   199
Unit 30 The European Union   209
Unit 31 Rich world, poor world   215

Beliefs and Values   223

Unit 32 The nature of religion   224
Unit 33 Why people have religious belief   230
Unit 34 The need for morality and the nature of ethical theories   237
Unit 35 Ethical issues   241

Answers to examination questions   248

Index   263

Introduction

About the specification

The second edition of this book has been revised to support your studies of the AQA B General Studies AS and A Level specification. The specification is divided into six units which are assessed in different ways. These units are shown in the table below.

The Six Unit Tests For AQA General Studies B		
AS Unit 1	**AS Unit 2**	**AS Unit 3**
Conflict	Power	Space
Four short essay questions (from choice of six) Topics covered: aggression and scientific controversy; social tensions and divisions; popular and performing arts; market forces and employment; stereotyping and public and private values.	One compulsory written task and one structured essay (from choice of two) Topics covered: energy and physical fitness; education and voting; media influence and art and society; advertising and globalisation; social and religious power.	One set of compulsory questions on data analysis and response Topics covered: climate and environment; housing, transport and migration; architecture, sculpture and global media; land-use and access; ownership and environmentalism. Skills tested: graph construction; statistical calculations; identification of trends; evaluation of limitations; extended comment on issues.
1¼ hours 60 marks	1¼ hours 70 marks	1¼ hours 60 marks
A2 Unit 4	**A2 Unit 5**	**A2 Unit 6**
Conflict-Resolution	Power-Control	Space-Time
Problem-solving exercise: written test OR coursework assignment Topics covered: importance of science, knowledge and sustainability; politics, the social contract and equal opportunities; understanding the arts and media; workings of industry and finance; nationalism, internationalism, rights and responsibilities.	Five compulsory short essays based on question and stimulus material Topics covered: use and abuse of science; political and legal accountability; artistic standards and media control; consumerism free trade and regulation; social justice, norms and values.	Two essay questions based on stimulus material: one compulsory and one from choice of two Topics covered: understanding and exploration of the universe, progress in science and technology; social and political change and reform; cultural diversity; the new arts and media; heritage, new patterns of working, transport and tourism; history, culture and religious belief.
1 hour 60 marks	1¼ hours 60 marks	1¾ hours 80 marks

General Studies has four assessment objectives (AOs). These AOs outline the skills and abilities on which you will be assessed:

AO1 Demonstrate relevant knowledge and understanding applied to a range of issues, using skills from different disciplines.
AO2 Communicate clearly and accurately in a concise, logical and relevant way.
AO3 Marshal evidence and draw conclusions; select, interpret, evaluate and integrate information, data, concepts and opinions.
AO4 Demonstrate understanding of different types of knowledge and of the relationship between them, appreciating their limitations.

For each question in the examination there will be a number of marks allocated to some or all of these objectives according to the nature of the question and what it is intended to test. Sixty per cent of the assessment in General Studies AQA B is devoted to thinking and analytical skills and your understanding of the nature of knowledge (AOs 3 and 4). Further discussion of AO4, in particular, is needed as there will be frequent reference to it when you come to the sample examination questions at the end of each unit.

Different types of knowledge

'Different types of knowledge' means in effect *different ways of getting knowledge*. We might get knowledge by fine measurement and calculation. This gives us a degree of certainty. We might get it by observation and experiment. This gives us a degree of probability. Or we might get it by examination of documents and material remains, or by introspection – that is, by canvassing our own experiences and feelings. This gives us a degree of possibility. Knowledge, like most things, is a matter of degree.

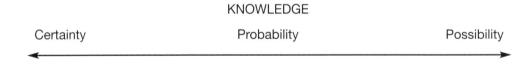

KNOWLEDGE

Certainty   Probability   Possibility

When we are talking about things, and the behaviour of things – of phenomena – we can be more or less certain about how they behave. Our evidence is less or more *hard*, and similarly we can be less or more *objective* about it. Thus, in the physical sciences, we can be confident enough to speak of *facts* and laws.

As we begin to talk about species of being, and particularly when we talk about people, our evidence is *softer*, and – since we ourselves are people – more *subjective*. In the natural and social sciences we are obliged to speak more of theories than of laws.

In the humanities, our evidence is softer still – although we might be quite scientific about how we get humanities knowledge, it is more possible than certain. We are still looking for facts. Historians, for example, must base their interpretations of what happened on publicly attested facts. When they express *opinions*, they must make it clear that this is what they are doing – and we must trust their opinions to the extent that they are supported by the facts that are available.

EVIDENCE

Hard/Objective   Subjective/Soft

←——→

Facts   Opinions
Physical Sciences / Natural Sciences / Social Sciences / Humanities / Arts

The following are facts:

- In the physical sciences that energy travels in waves of varying lengths.
- In the natural sciences that more than 95 per cent of all species that have ever lived have become extinct.
- In the social sciences that 30 per cent of couples in one-family households, in 1998/99, had no children.
- In the humanities that Robert Rauschenberg painted, and exhibited, an all-white canvas and an all-black canvas.

However, facts are not everything. Physicists and biologists express opinions, too – and these may do as much to contribute to *truth*, to accordance with reality, as facts. For example: 'Genetically modified food is not harmful to humans.' Truth is so many-sided that we may never see all of its sides. We should be aware, though, that our *values* may influence our choice of facts, and colour our opinions. Values and *beliefs* are close cousins. The value that we attach to life may, for example, be expressed as a belief in the 'sanctity' of life. Such a belief may make us *partial*; it may *bias* our opinions, so that we disregard facts that are inconvenient to our point of view. Beliefs may have rather little to do with facts at all, and rather a lot to do with emotions.

Where AO4 is concerned, therefore, the questions that we should address (in a particular context) are these:

- What are the *facts* in the case?
- Is the evidence *hard* or *soft, objective or subjective*?
- Are *opinions* well supported by facts?
- What *values* appear to influence the choice of facts and/or the opinions expressed?

Of course, we are all partial to a degree. We are all 'coming from' somewhere. There is nothing wrong with this – the important thing is to be aware of it, and to take it into account.

Here are some examples of 'second-order' (AO4) knowledge (i.e. knowledge about knowledge) in the particular context of public and private transport:

- It is an *objective fact* that 61.2 per cent of all journeys made between 1996 and 1998 were made by car. (It can be shown by means of a reliable calculation/estimate.)
- It is a *theory*, based on quite *hard evidence*, that there is an inverse, direct relationship between car-ownership and access to public transport. (The greater the number of cars per head of population in an area, the less public transport is available.)
- It is an *opinion* that it is more convenient to travel by car than by long-distance coach.

- It is a *value*, shared by many on the left of politics, that investment in public transport is a social good.
- It is a *belief*, held by many on the right, that building roads makes for economic growth.

Political bias is one thing – preference for the private car over public transport may not be pro-social, but it isn't necessarily anti-social. A racial, ethnic, or gender bias is something else, because this is always, potentially, anti-social.

The 'limitations' referred to in AO4 have to do with the abundance or the scarcity of facts available in a case, and with the degree of objectivity that is possible. We know that the proportion of children's journeys undertaken on foot fell from 47 per cent to 37 per cent between 1985 and 1998. This is a hard, objective fact – but as evidence for an overall assessment of child health, it is limited. If a qualified paediatrician was to say:

'The fact that children are walking less now than they did in the past, is a powerful factor in a general decline in child health.'

we should treat this judgment with respect – but it is still limited. It does not tell us a lot, and it tells us nothing about physical activity other than walking. If a parent said:

'My child is safer strapped in the back seat of the car than walking on the pavement beside a busy road.'

we should respect the view – but it is a view limited by the parent's concern for one child, and perhaps by that parent's preference for driving over walking with the child.

Examination questions which are designed to test AO4, focus, therefore, on such matters as:

- Analysis and evaluation of the *nature* of the knowledge, evidence or arguments, for example, used in a text, set of data or other form of stimulus material.
- Understanding of the crucial *differences* between such things as facts, opinions and beliefs, and between objectivity and subjectivity in arguments.
- Appreciation of what constitutes *proof*, what is cause and effect, when conclusions are *valid and justified*, and what the *limitations* of these may be.
- Recognition of the existence of personal *values*, value judgements, partiality and bias in given circumstances.
- Awareness of the *effects* upon ourselves and others of different physical, emotional and cognitive experiences, and the limitations of feelings as a basis for knowledge.

Analysing an argument

You can use the following flowchart to help you determine whether an argument is valid and justified.

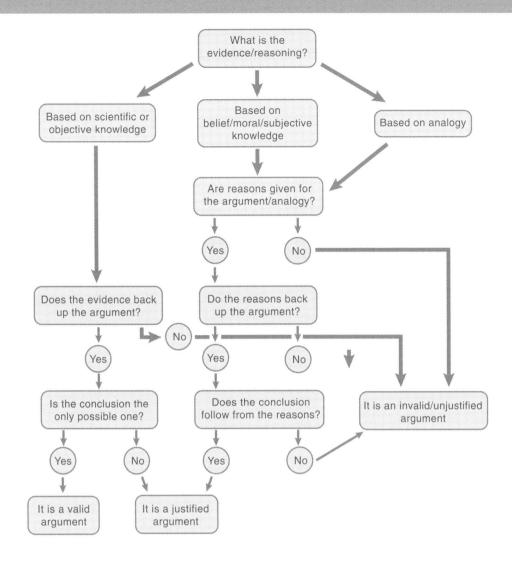

Figure 0.1 Is an argument valid?

Types of argument

Deductive argument

This is where a conclusion can be deduced from the premises – i.e. it follows automatically. It argues from the general to the particular. For example, if the angles of a triangle equal 180 degrees (general statement) and in a particular triangle two of the angles equal 120 degrees, you can deduce the other angle equals 60 degrees.

Inductive argument

This type argues from the particular to the general, for example, each time I have boiled water it boiled at 100°C, therefore water always boils at 100°C. This argument will only be probable because it is based on experience, which we can never be certain about – for example, water boils at about 72°C on Mount Everest. Some inductive arguments are better than others, depending on the amount and reliability of the evidence.

Arguing from authority

This is claiming something is true because an important person or book says it is, for example 'Murder is wrong because the Bible says so'. This is a weak form of argument

Justified argument an argument
that has reasons which are
factually correct, and the
conclusion or interpretation
follows from the reasons, but is
not the only possible
conclusion. An example would
be the film *Shakespeare in Love*,
which interprets *Romeo and
Juliet* as a product of
Shakespeare falling in love. This
is a justified argument, but it is
not the only possible
interpretation

Valid argument this is either a
deductive argument or an
argument based on scientific or
objective knowledge, where the
conclusion or interpretation
follows from the evidence and
where the conclusion cannot be
doubted

unless the authority is one that everyone recognises, for example 'Light does not travel in a straight line because Einstein said so'. By contrast, to claim murder is wrong on the authority of the Bible is not a valid argument unless you show why the Bible has moral authority and can give evidence that everything the Bible says is true.

Arguing from analogy

This is where someone quotes a similar case and argues from this that the same thing applies in a different situation. For example, William Paley argued that because a watch is a complex mechanism that could not have been made by chance, the world, which is also a complex mechanism, could not have been made by chance either. However, for an argument from analogy to work, it must be shown that two things are the same, i.e. that the world has all the order of a watch and the watch has all the disorder of the world.

Arguing from lack of evidence

This is claiming that something is true because there is no evidence to say it is false. For example, no one has ever proven that fairies do not exist, therefore they must exist. This is a false argument because there has to be evidence upon which to decide whether something is true or false.

Truth

Philosophers have argued for the past 100 years about what truth is. Some philosophers argue that the truth is what corresponds to the facts, for example the statement 'swans are white' is true because it corresponds to the facts (this is known as the correspondence theory of truth). Others argue that what is true is what has not been falsified. It is not true to say that swans are white because Australian swans are black. However, it is true to say that most swans are white.

About the book

The book is structured into the five main content areas:

- Science and Technology
- Society and Politics
- Arts and Media
- Industry and Commerce
- Beliefs and Values.

These are then split into smaller units covering the subject content. Each unit includes:

- Key terms which define the key concepts relevant to the subject.
- Activities which give you practice and suggestions to deepen your subject knowledge and skills.
- Past exam questions from the AQA B specification (both AS and A Level questions) to give you exam skills practice.
- Examiner's advice to give you guidance on how to secure high marks.

Answers to the exam questions are given at the end of the book.

Science and Techology

Unit 1 | **Scientific progress**

Unit 2 | **Scientific method and its application**

Unit 3 | **Religion and science**

Unit 4 | **Energy**

Unit 5 | **Environmental issues**

Unit 6 | **Genetic engineering**

Unit 7 | **Agriculture and food production**

Unit 8 | **Human and animal behaviour**

Unit 9 | **Medical developments**

Unit 10 | **Transport issues**

Unit 11 | **Computers**

Unit 12 | **The relationship between science and culture**

Unit 13 | **The application of maths**

Scientific progress

In order to decide how scientific progress has been made, it is necessary to define what is meant by science. The *Oxford English Dictionary* defines 'science' as 'a branch of knowledge conducted on objective principles involving the systemised observation of and experiment with phenomena, especially concerned with the material and functions of the physical universe'. This could be further defined as:

- Observing regularities in nature, for example the way in which the seasons follow each other.
- Working out a rational theory to explain why these regularities happen, for example that the Earth moves round the Sun tilted at an angle and the seasons change as the Earth leans towards or away from the Sun.
- Formulating the theory into a formula that predicts what will happen, for example when the North Pole is tilted 23.4 degrees towards the Sun, the vertical noon rays are directly over the Tropic of Cancer.

Ideas about progress in science

Science has obviously made a lot of progress since the days when people thought that rain was caused by God opening windows in the firmament, but how has this change come about?

- The traditional theory is that science has grown gradually as scholars learned a little more in each successive generation and built on what they had learned from the previous generation.
- Another view is that progress in science depends on the nature of the society in which a scientist or scholar is living. If the society is changing rapidly or encourages people to think freely and to question traditional ideas, then there will be scientific progress. If a society is settled and has a system of authority where questioning traditions is punished, there will be little or no scientific progress (see Unit 12, 'The relationship between science and culture').
- Some scientists believe that progress in science depends on technology (making tools and instruments). For example, scientists could not have made discoveries about the planets without telescopes (see Unit 12).

Thomas Kuhn, an American historian of science, suggested in *The Structure of Scientific Revolutions* that scientific progress is made in sudden jumps. He argued that, in any society, scientists accept a *paradigm* given to them by their society. By a paradigm, Kuhn meant a view of what the world is like, how it works and how it can be investigated. He argued that the paradigm tells scientists what is important in science, what questions to ask and what problems are important. Change only occurs when scientists discover problems and contradictions in the paradigm. Eventually, this causes a crisis resulting in a new paradigm. This sudden change of paradigms is like a revolution in science and brings about progress because new ideas are needed.

In order for you to have sufficient information with which to answer a question on scientific progress, it is necessary to give a brief history of science.

A history of science

Early history

Archaeological evidence, such as cave paintings and scratches on bits of bone, indicates that humans have always been close observers of nature. Indeed, the whole of agriculture must be based on early humans observing the seasons and the way in which seeds grow in order to grow crops successfully. In the megalithic structures (such as Stonehenge) found in China, Central America, Mesopotamia, Egypt and Europe, there is evidence of knowledge of a number of mathematical principles, including that of the square on the hypotenuse equalling the sum of the squares on the other two sides in a right-angled triangle, almost 2000 years before Pythagoras.

Greek science

Euclid provided a mathematical basis for science by discovering the main theorems of geometry. Archimedes developed a method for manipulating scientific observations into a scientific law in mathematical terms – such laws can then be used to predict what will happen, for example Archimedes' own laws on levers and the displacement of water.

Aristotle developed the view that science is concerned with observation followed by theorising by asking questions such as 'What is the form of the object or process being observed?', 'How did it get that form?' and 'What is its purpose?' From these observations, Aristotle determined that the world is made up of four elements: earth, water, air and fire. Aristotle's view that the Earth is the centre of the universe (the *geocentric principle*) was finalised by Ptolemy, who devised a system of small circles on top of larger ones, that enabled astronomers to predict the movement of the Sun and planets while assuming that the Earth was stationary.

The great gift of the Greeks to science was their belief that the universe works on rational, natural laws discoverable by humans.

Medieval science

The Greek scientific ideas were developed by Islamic science, especially in the field of medicine, and by the Arab discoveries of the number system, algebra and chemistry. This Islamic science and the works of Aristotle were rediscovered in Europe when Spain was recaptured from the Islamic Empire. The medieval scientists were concerned with technology, discovering such things as the crank and gears, which enabled them to harness wind and water power for the beginnings of industry. They also used experiments to help to discover the natural laws.

The rise of modern science

Copernicus challenged the basis of much early science in 1543 when he suggested that the Earth goes round the Sun. This *heliocentric theory* was backed up when the

Biological sciences those sciences that investigate the organic (living) nature of the universe (mainly biology, but also biochemistry and biophysics)

Colour spectrum a display of colours that make up a beam of white light (red, orange, yellow, green, blue, indigo, violet)

Complementary colours any two colours that produce white when mixed, e.g. red and cyan

Doppler effect the change in frequency of the sound heard when either the listener or the source moves relative to the other

Earth sciences those sciences that investigate the physical nature of the planet Earth (mainly geology, but also meteorology, geophysics and geochemistry)

Escape velocity the minimum speed required for an object to escape the gravitational pull of a planet – on Earth it is 40,000 km/h to the power of 1

Parallax the apparent movement of two objects relative to each other when seen by a moving observer, e.g. stars appearing to move when observed by people on the Earth

Physical sciences those sciences that investigate the inorganic nature of the universe (mainly physics, chemistry and astronomy)

Primary colours red, green, blue, which, mixed in the right proportion, can make all the colours in the spectrum

Science the study of the material and physical world to produce reliable explanations, e.g. physics explains the nature of electricity

Technology the application of science, e.g. technology uses the science of physics to build power stations to manufacture electricity

telescope was discovered and Galileo was able to show the phases of Venus and the moons around Jupiter (1610). Galileo's experiments on motion also showed that Aristotle's ideas were false.

Other seventeenth-century scientists built on Galileo's use of experiments and close observation. William Harvey discovered the circulation of the blood in 1628. Robert Boyle made various discoveries in chemistry, most famously Boyle's law of the compressibility of gas in 1662. Isaac Newton discovered the principles of gravity and motion in 1687.

It is generally thought that the basic principles of science were finalised by Newton (see Unit 2, 'Scientific method and its application'), but there is much argument as to whether the Copernican Revolution (as many historians call the change from an Earth-centred to a Sun-centred system) was simply a development of medieval science, the result of technology, or a new revolutionary idea.

You could use Unit 10 ('Transport issues'), Unit 4 ('Energy'), Unit 11 ('Computers') or Unit 9 ('Medical developments') to answer questions on scientific progress, but the subject of gravitational motion is a good way of doing so.

The progress of science as seen in gravitational motion

Early scientists did not realise that there was a connection between the way objects fall to Earth and the motion of the stars and planets. Aristotle claimed that the heavenly bodies were divine and in eternal, unchanging motion. As far as objects on Earth are concerned, they had a natural tendency to move towards the Earth's centre. These ideas led to a theory of motion that a body moving at a constant speed must have a constant force acting on it directly (i.e. interaction at a distance was impossible).

These ideas seemed to fit the facts as they were known. Indeed, the heliocentric theory causes problems. Galileo was asked why bodies do not fly off the Earth if it is spinning on its axis and circling the Sun. He was also asked why an object dropped from a tower falls to the bottom of the tower when the Earth has moved between it being dropped and it landing. Galileo's answer was that bodies do not fly off the Earth because, in revolutions per minute, they are not travelling very fast. Objects dropped from a tower share the Earth's rotation with the tower and so drop at the base of the tower. In his experiments of dropping objects, Galileo discovered that the distance a falling object travels varies as the square of the time.

Johannes Kepler (1571–1630) discovered that the planets move in ellipses rather than circles. He saw a great problem with planetary motion and suggested that the Sun emitted a magnetic force, which pushed the planets around it.

It was Newton who realised that it is the same force that makes objects fall to the ground and that makes the planets move in elliptical orbits. His law of universal gravitation states that there is a force of attraction between any two bodies that is proportional to the inverse square of their separation and the product of their masses ($F = GmM/d^2$). This law explains why objects of differing weights fall to Earth at the same speed and why planets have elliptical orbits.

Newton's laws were accepted until Einstein proposed that the elliptical paths of the planets were not caused by the gravitational effects of the Sun, but because the presence of a gravitational field caused a curvature of space-time. In the general theory of relativity, Einstein explained why objects fall and how the whole universe operates. His theory is generally regarded as having been confirmed at the eclipse of 1919, when scientists could see that light travels in curves rather than straight lines, and by the red-shift effect in light (which is also evidence for the Big Bang). This evidence came after the theory, but Einstein's theory is based on the mathematics of Bernhard Riemann (1826–66) about geodesics (the straightest curve possible in a curved grid). Some scientists also think that increased accuracy in telescopes showed that Newton's law was inaccurate in calculating Mercury's orbit before Einstein formulated his theory.

DID YOU KNOW?

Light, rain and rainbows
Medieval scientists investigated the nature of light in a rainbow by simulating the conditions under which the rainbows occur. Hollow glass balls filled with water were substituted for raindrops and light was passed through them. Conclusions about the behaviour of light could then be drawn without the huge difficulty of waiting for a rainbow to appear.

Figure 1.1 'The wonder is not that mankind comprehends the world, but that the world is comprehensible' (Einstein)

Activities

1. What is your paradigm?

2. Use the Internet to discover the scientific principles involved in: the building of Stonehenge; Archimedes' law of levers; Archimedes and the displacement of water; a water mill; a windmill.

3. What do you understand by Einstein's quotation about the world being comprehensible?

4. Thomas Kuhn argued that scientific advance is by a series of revolutionary jumps interspersed by long periods of relatively slow development. Critically discuss this model of scientific progress in reference to gravitational motion.

EXAM QUESTION

Read the Sources A and B below and answer the following question.

The Victorians believed in 'material progress' (**Source A**); and the writer of the editorial (**Source B**) approves of genetic screening in that it 'uses progress'. In what sense is such progress a *fact*, and in what sense a *belief*.

(40 marks)

AQA B June 2003

Source A: Unwritten history

Victorian geologists found examples of rocks laid down in each of the great periods in the history of the Earth, and they gave native British names to two of the four grand divisions of time which they called 'eras'. Thus, there was a Cambrian period, which took its name from Cambria (Wales), lasting about 100 million years, and a shorter Devonian period, initially an age of ferns and fishes, which lasted for about 60 million years. There were also Ordovician and Silurian periods: these less homely labels derived from the names of 'ancient British tribes'.

The labels tell us more about the social and intellectual history of the nineteenth century than they do about the making of the Earth itself. While the physical making of the island has been achieved only through cosmic violence and a consequent total transformation of the environment, human history has been more peaceful and continuous. The very same Victorians who revolutionised geology and biology were proud of this relative absence of revolutions in English history, little imagining that some late twentieth-century social historians would argue

that England had suffered through their seldom having taken place.

It is no coincidence that the term prehistory was first used in England in 1851, the year the Great Exhibition was displayed in the Crystal Palace. If the products of all nations in the nineteenth century could be assembled in witness of material progress, would it not be possible to periodise* progress through the collection and display of the products of each of the different stages of man's past? Already, by 1851, stone, bronze and iron age

periodisation had made its way into England.

*periodise = divide the time into periods (with the implication that each period was an advance on the last)

Source: Asa Briggs, *A Social History of England* (Weidenfield & Nicholson/Book Club Associates, 1983)

Source B: Why Mr and Mrs Hashmi were right to choose life

The decision of the Human Fertility and Embryology Authority (HFEA) to allow a couple to select genetically their next baby was bound to raise concerns that advances in biotechnology are racing ahead of our ability to control the consequences. The couple at the centre of this case have a son who suffers from a potentially fatal disorder and whose best hope is a marrow transplant from a sibling, so the stakes of this decision are particularly high.

The HFEA's critics believe that it sanctions 'designer babies' and does not show respect for the sanctity of individual life. Certainly the authority's backing for Shahana and Raj Hashmi's plea for genetic screening raises fundamental questions about producing one human being to cure another's disease. But the parents' view is simple and compelling. The IVF treatment is available to help produce a baby whose tissue will match his or her elder brother's bone marrow. They require, as Mrs Hashmi puts it, 'a helping hand' from the HFEA.

Screening for genetic disorders has been permissible for some time. Those who oppose the treatment on grounds that it echoes destructive eugenics programmes have misplaced their concern. The use of such techniques to weed out genes that might result in a disability does not suggest that disabled people are 'defective'. It merely uses progress to prevent a malfunction of nature. They would not reject medical intervention to put right other things that go wrong with the body. Yet they ask that mankind pass up the chance to use scientific advances in biotechnology to prevent unnecessary suffering. The inconsistency is striking and would be cruel if it were allowed to impede a beneficial solution.

The HFEA already backed tissue-type screening in principle in December. This latest move is a logical advance. We can welcome that and still accept the need to maintain the distinction between these and more frivolous or dubious reasons why parents might want to opt for genetic pre-selection.

Source: The Independent on Sunday, *24 February 2002*

EXAMINER'S ADVICE

- This question is from Section B of A2 Unit 6 set in June 2003. It requires an answer in essay form, and is based typically on a comparison, or bringing together, of two sources. In this section you have a choice of one of two questions based on different sources. See page 1 for more information about this paper and also the end of Unit 2 for another example of a Section B question.

- Unit 6 is the synoptic paper, which means that it brings together different sorts of knowledge, ideas and skills from the whole subject. It is therefore the most demanding part of the examination and you can expect to find it hard, particularly in terms of the ideas under discussion. You have 1¾ hours for the whole test, but quite a lot of material to read through before you tackle the questions, and each question is worth 40 marks.

- Good planning supported by detailed study of the extracts is essential before you start to write your answer, so don't be afraid to spend at least 20 minutes planning your response. This will still leave around 35 minutes for writing, which is plenty of time, if you have worked out what you are going to say.

- The question itself is about the differences between what we can regard as *facts* and what are essentially matters of *belief*. In addition to the ideas about scientific progress in the unit you have just read, you should also look back over the discussion in the introduction about the nature of knowledge, as it will help to refresh your understanding of the key concepts in the question.

- You should also use ideas generated by the sources, but for higher marks try to think outside of the sources, in particular here about what we mean by *progress*. Can we regard all scientific discoveries as genuine *advances*? Think of different examples, for example in medicine, where you can confidently say that progress has been made. Is this sufficient to make it a *fact*? What about 'material items' such as electricity, automatic washing machines, refrigerators, etc? Think also of other examples where the case for progress is not so obvious. Consider the problems which particular discoveries throw up, as well as those they are designed to solve. Good examples might be the motor car or military weapons. Perhaps progress depends on how we choose to put those discoveries to use?

- This is a hard question, but the ideas are important ones, particularly at A2 level, so work hard to master them. When you have made your attempt, turn to page 248 for some possible arguments.

Scientific method and its application

Science is concerned with the phenomena of the universe, i.e. the physical things that happen in the universe. The methods used by scientists to explore the phenomena and come up with laws or theories to explain them are known as scientific method.

The scientific method

A seventeenth-century English scientist, Francis Bacon, worked out a formal method of scientific investigation based on studying empirical evidence ('empirical' means evidence that can be tested by the senses). This has been developed into the method that you probably use for GCSE science coursework.

All of science has to be *inductive* rather than *deductive* because it argues from a set of particular observations to a general law. However, what makes it scientific is that it is difficult to reject the conclusion without being irrational, and, more particularly, the experiments can always be repeated and will have the same conclusion (this is often called predictability – science can predict what will happen).

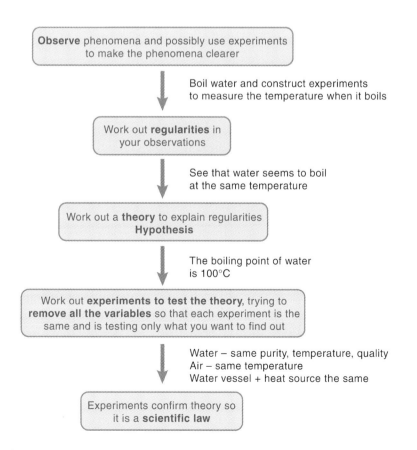

Observe phenomena and possibly use experiments to make the phenomena clearer

Boil water and construct experiments to measure the temperature when it boils

Work out **regularities** in your observations

See that water seems to boil at the same temperature

Work out a **theory** to explain regularities
Hypothesis

The boiling point of water is 100°C

Work out **experiments to test the theory**, trying to **remove all the variables** so that each experiment is the same and is testing only what you want to find out

Water – same purity, temperature, quality
Air – same temperature
Water vessel + heat source the same

Experiments confirm theory so it is a **scientific law**

Figure 2.1 The scientific method

Some philosophers of science follow Karl Popper and claim that the scientific method is based on *falsifying* rather than *verifying* ('verifying' – the use of scientific experiment to test whether a theory is true). They claim that science makes progress as scientists test theories or laws and find areas where they are false. Then they amend the law or theory to fit the new evidence (e.g. changing the air pressure and discovering that water does not always boil at 100°C and then devising the law that water boils at 100°C minus 1°C for every 300 m above sea level).

Using scientific method

The crucial points when trying to apply scientific method to any issue are to:

- Use evidence that can be tested by the senses.
- Work out a theory to explain the evidence.
- Work out tests of the theory (experiments) that reduce the number of variables to as few as possible.
- Decide whether the tests have given enough evidence to say that the theory is valid (true beyond reasonable doubt).

The application of scientific method – evolution

Some scientists would regard the most important theory in the biological sciences as evolutionary theory. Evolution means gradual change over the course of time and the theory is that life on Earth has evolved over 3–4 billion years, from very simple to very complex organisms, through modifications in each generation.

Observations

Naturalists such as Linnaeus (the first person to classify plants) and Lamarck had observed similarities between species in the eighteenth century. Linnaeus proposed that species could change, and Lamarck devised an evolutionary tree from tiny animals to human beings. Technological advances in canal and road building led to geological discoveries and fossils that seemed to show gradually changing life forms.

Charles Darwin, on his voyage to the Galápagos Islands on *HMS Beagle*, observed differences between species living on neighbouring islands and a similarity between living creatures and fossil remains in the same area.

The theory

In his *On the Origin of Species* (1859), Darwin proposed that life on Earth has evolved from the very simple forms of life seen in the earliest fossils to complex mammals such as humans through 'natural selection'. In each generation, more offspring are produced than can survive and some of the offspring have slight variations. The forces of nature (restricted food supply, disease, predators, etc.) destroy those less adapted to survive and those that do survive will pass on their successful variation to the next generation, so that over long periods of time, major changes will occur.

The evidence

Since Darwin's time, much testing of the fossil record has been possible. Discoveries in DNA have shown that the history of evolution is stored in the gene strands of DNA, and molecular biology is now able to trace some parts of the evolutionary process.

Conclusion

Scientists regard evolution in terms of organisms being related by common descent as a fact. There is so much evidence that it is irrational to doubt it. What is still regarded as theory is *why* evolution occurs.

The application of scientific method – plate tectonics

Some scientists would regard the most important theory in the Earth sciences as plate tectonics. This is a recent theory, which has been as revolutionary for Earth sciences as Copernicus was for astronomy and physics. It claims that all the geological processes of the Earth – mountains, oceans, volcanoes, earthquakes, etc. can be explained by the structure and behaviour of a small number of huge rigid plates, which form the outer part of the planet Earth (known as the lithosphere).

Observations

In 1911, Alfred Wegener claimed that observation of the early geological history of the Earth showed that there was once only one continent (which he named Pangaea). This was modified by du Toit in 1937 to the existence of two continents. Both these scientists had observed that the fossils in the pre-Cretaceous rock strata of Africa and South America (over 140 million years old) and the pre-Jurassic rocks of India, Australia, Madagascar and Africa (over 200 million years old) are so similar that they appear once to have been part of the same land mass. In the 1950s, it was observed that the magnetised remains in rocks indicate that the magnetic poles were at different places on the Earth at different periods in the Earth's history.

The theory

In the mid-1960s, the Canadian geologist Tuzo Wilson suggested that the regularities of the observations could be explained if the Earth's crust were made up of plates much thicker than the continents and the ocean floors. These plates cover the whole surface of the Earth, but where they meet each other, the nature of the plates either results in one plate going lower (creating oceans) or a collision (creating mountain ranges). Where two plates pass each other without subduction (one going lower) or collision, there is a fracture zone (for example, the San Andreas Fault in California). Wilson claimed that most of the Earth's seismic activity occurs along plate boundaries.

The evidence

Drilling of the ocean floors in the 1970s and 1980s confirmed that the ocean floors are less than 200 million years old, whereas the Earth itself is around 4.5 billion years old. Computer graphics have shown that at about 1000 m depth, the continents do match each other.

KEY TERMS

Core the innermost part of the Earth – the inner core is up to 1600 km around the centre of the Earth and is thought to be solid, while the outer core (1820 km thick) is liquid

DNA double-stranded nucleic acid, which contains all the information needed to build, control and maintain a living organism (discovered by Crick and Watson, 1953)

Gene pool the sum total of all genes and combinations of genes in organisms of the same species

Genome the genetic material of an organism

Igneous rocks rocks solidified from a molten state, e.g. from cooling magma

Mantle the section of the Earth's surface between the crust and the core

Magma the molten liquid of the outer core from which lava (which comes to the surface from volcanoes) is formed

Mendel an Austrian biologist who began genetics through studying peas

Neanderthal the nearest form of hominid to Homo sapiens, which seems to have lived on Earth alongside Homo sapiens

Scientific criteria things which can be tested by the senses and so can be researched by scientists

Scientific principles general laws in science which are based on experience and are used in scientific investigation, e.g. the Uncertainty Principle says that it is impossible to give accurate measurements of sub-atomic particles

Seismic connected with earthquakes and movements of the Earth

Isotopic dating has shown that the pre-Cambrian rocks in Africa and South America are the same in age and composition.

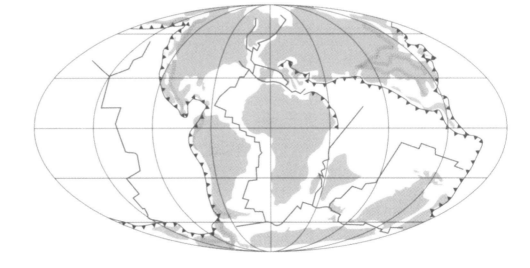

Figure 2.2 Continental distribution 80 million years ago

1. Look at the photo in Figure 2.3 and try to formulate a theory to explain the phenomena of people seeing UFOs.

2. Work out some experiments to test your theory and explain what would be needed for scientific proof of the existence of UFOs.

3. It has been claimed that left-handed people are more skilful at sports requiring hand–eye co-ordination than right-handed people. Explain how you would test this theory scientifically and how you would present your results.

Conclusion

Plate tectonics is still a theory rather than a fact because there are some pieces of evidence that do not fit the theory (e.g. the Rocky Mountains of North America cannot be explained by plate collision). However, the theory does seem to work and scientists are using the method suggested by Popper to adapt the theory to cover the exceptions.

Figure 2.3 Science fact or fiction?

Read the Sources A and B below and answer the following question.

It is suggested in **Source A** below that science is about finding 'the answers'. To what extent are writers, artists and musicians (**Source B**) looking for 'answers'?

(40 marks)

AQA B June 2004

Source A: The truth is relative

It was a striking claim. If the group of scientists who asserted that light has slowed down were right, it would have been a blow to one of the cornerstones of modern science. Ever since Einstein devised his special theory of relativity, scientists have held that the speed of light in a vacuum is an absolute constant. Now it seems his most famous equation, $E = mc^2$, may no longer hold true.

The fact that the constancy of the speed of light is now being challenged, and by astronomy, should come as no surprise. As ever, astronomy is at the frontier of science. Like the wild west, this frontier is a lawless place; its inhabitants hold no respect for rules – even ones laid down by Einstein. Armed with improved telescopes, they are now able to see further into the cosmos, and with greater detail, than ever before. It has given them a new confidence. In the past, when their observations didn't fit the theory, they were inclined to disbelieve their results. Now they are more likely to accept what they see, and challenge the theory. As early as 1999 some physicists realised that they could solve several of the outstanding problems in cosmology if they accepted that the speed of light has changed. If the new evidence proves correct, and light really has slowed down, it won't be a disaster; it may actually solve more problems than it raises.

On the other hand, if the varying speed of light remains unexplained, it will be in good company. There is much about the world that we still don't understand. Despite centuries of endeavour, science is still a long way from finding all the answers. Newton's laws describe how gravity behaves, but how it works is still a mystery. Darwin's theory of natural selection tells us how species evolved, but we have no idea how life itself started. When Crick and Watson unravelled DNA they revealed the genetic building-blocks of our brain, but the source of our free will is still an enigma. And, although physicists have traced back the history of the universe to a millisecond after the big bang, that is not the question on everyone's lips. 'Who cares about the half second after the big bang?' asked Fay Weldon. 'What about the half second before?'

Where we came from, who we are and where we are going are the fundamental questions that people want answered. They have been around for thousands of years. Science may eventually find the answers, but expect a lot more mistakes along the way.

Source: Martin Gorst, The Guardian, 17 August 2002

Source B: Introduction to music

Compared to the other arts, music does seem more self-absorbed, more self-referential. Words have an existence in everyday life; so do physical objects, shapes and colours. Words and physical phenomena give a way in to the analysis of literature and painting; there is here, on the whole, a level of reference to the 'real world' which is absent in music, where reference is much more 'internal' – from one theme to another, from a repetition to its precursor, from one note and the expectations it arouses to the next. I don't want to over-press this point, because it doesn't follow that words are used in the same way in literature (and shapes and colours in paintings) as in everyday life, or that there aren't systems of internal reference there too. Nevertheless, in everyday life, sound (at least non-spoken sound) is less important, less involved in achieving practical ends, than words and physical objects. Music has always been regarded as more of a luxury practice, having to do with magic, play, ritual or the realm of the aesthetic as well as – perhaps more than – with 'practical' functions. The religious and ritual associations which surround music in so-called simple, primitive societies have been very slow to disperse; indeed, they have still not entirely done so, as those who have felt the 'bewitching' effects of a Wagner music drama or the 'Dionysian'* involvement created at many rock concerts will testify. At the same time, the strongly collective nature of music making and listening has also been slow to disappear. The making, owning and enjoyment of books and paintings by individuals, in private, began long before similar developments in music. Even today, a high proportion of music making and listening is social activity. As a result, the pressure to communicate about music is at least as strong as the difficulties of doing so.

* Dionysian – abandoned, heady, intoxicating

Source: Richard Middleton, Introduction to Music *(The Open University Press, 2002)*

EXAMINER'S ADVICE
- This is another question from Section B of A2 Unit 6, this time set in June 2004. Like the previous one at the end of Unit 1 it requires an answer in essay form and is based on a comparison, or bringing together, of two sources. See page 1 for more information about this paper. As a synoptic question it brings together different sorts of knowledge, ideas and skills from the whole subject, and before you attempt it, it will help to refer also to Unit 25 'Creativity and innovation'.
- Good planning supported by detailed study of the extracts is essential before you start to write your answer, so don't be afraid to spend at least 20 minutes planning your answer. This will still leave around 35 minutes for writing, which is plenty of time if you have worked out what you are going to say.
- The first question to consider is what is meant by 'answers', or rather answers to 'what questions?'. Think about the role of science and the kinds of questions science sets out to answer and then those that science cannot answer. Consider also the role of the different arts and what they can tell us about ourselves, our existence, the human condition and so on. Not all forms or works of art set out to do this, of course, but you will need to think of some specific examples from both science and the arts to illustrate relevant points.
- Like other Unit 6 questions, this is a hard question, but the ideas are central to General Studies B, particularly at A2 level, so work hard to master them. When you have made your attempt, turn to page 248 for some possible ideas.

Religion and science

As a working generalisation, it could be argued that science asks the question, 'Given that there is a world, *how* do things within it work?' Religion tends to ask the question, '*Why* is there anything at all?'

The nature of science

The modern age has often been described by historians and other thinkers as 'the age of science'. The value of science is that it provides us with accurate information about the world, which has been established by the most reliable methods available. Scientists produce an *hypothesis* – a starting point for future experiments and systematic observations that either confirm or refute the original assumption and then enable the observer to formulate a theory. This theory will be based on *repeatability* – the fact that the experiment has been repeated endlessly and has produced the same result given identical conditions – and *predictability* – the extremely high probability that the same result will occur in the future.

Science is useful because it helps us to explain and formulate rules about the way the physical world works and to control, adapt and survive in it, for example by:

- Producing a theory to explain tides in sea and rivers.
- Designing a steel bridge that will successfully cope with any future loads.
- Discovering that cyanide is poisonous to human beings.

The nature of religion

'Religion' can be defined as 'a particular system of faith and worship, usually involving recognition of a superhuman controlling power, such as a personal god or gods entitled to obedience and worship'. Unlike science, which is based on the *empirical* view that real knowledge comes to us by experience (i.e. via the senses), religion tends to claim that its knowledge comes from three sources:

- *Natural theology.* This is the view (particularly strong in the Roman Catholic tradition) that by the use of human reason, you can argue from evidence within the world to the existence of God. An example is the design argument, which was very popular during the eighteenth and nineteenth centuries. The complexities of a human eye or a butterfly's wing suggest a designer in the same way that the complexities of the world as a whole suggest a divine designer, rather than randomness.

- *Revealed theology.* God has revealed knowledge about himself to human beings through special writings such as the Bible or the Qur'an, through special creeds passed on by the Church or other religious institutions, and through special people such as Jesus of Nazareth or the Prophet Muhammad.
- *Personal or mystical experience.* Human beings can have intensely personal experiences of the divine, which may drastically change their lives and their understanding of the world.

The relationship between science and religion

Generally speaking, in the medieval period in the Western world, it was assumed that all knowledge would lead to God, who had created the world and whose mighty acts were described in the Bible. Knowledge was based on reason, authority and tradition:

- *Reason.* In general, this meant things which could be worked out by argument and logic, although Thomas Aquinas, the thirteenth-century theologian, also included evidence from the real world.
- *Authority.* This meant the Church's spiritual authority headed by the Pope.
- *Tradition.* This meant what had always been believed and taught by the Church and what was contained in ancient writings, for example, Aristotle's view of the universe, which was accepted by the Church.

Development of science and the modern outlook

In the Middle Ages, no philosophers or theologians would have imagined that the conclusions of faith and reason could diverge. What you could find out for yourself – *reason* – and what you believed – *faith* – both came to the same conclusion. In addition, there was what God might reveal to you, which was to be accepted even if you did not understand it. However, after the cultural developments of the *Renaissance*, which started in the fifteenth century, the growth of scientific method transformed what we know and our views about how we acquire knowledge. There was a fundamental shift from a God-centred world towards a human-centered one. Humans became the measure of all things. Eventually, this led to a divergence between scientific knowledge and the traditional teaching of the Church.

Period of transition

The seventeenth, eighteenth and early nineteenth centuries could be described as a transitional period. Most early scientists never doubted that their scientific examination of the world would reveal evidence of design, law and order, which would reinforce their belief in God as creator. Many sixteenth and seventeenth century thinkers, such as *Galileo, Descartes* and *Isaac Newton,* combined their belief in scientific method with more traditional beliefs. When Newton could not account mathematically for the irregular orbits of some of the planets, for example, he attributed their paths to the work of God.

Examples of conflict between science and religion

The trial of Galileo

Galileo has been described as the first scientist in the modern sense. In 1610, after his own observations using a telescope, Galileo published *The Message of the Stars*, in which he argued that the Earth went round the Sun, rather than the other way round. This view was condemned by the Church on the grounds that it contradicted the 'revealed truth' of scripture and the official Church view, based on Aristotle. But in 1632, Galileo supported the earlier astronomer, Copernicus, who had also argued that the Sun was the centre of the universe round which the planets revolved. Galileo was put on trial in 1633 and forced to withdraw his views by the Pope because he supported Copernicus's theory as a scientific fact, not just as a hypothesis. Galileo challenged the authority of established religion because:

- He based knowledge on the evidence of his senses – a modern empirical view.
- He claimed that the universe can be explained in terms of mathematical principles and in terms of cause and effect (Galileo himself thought that God could be seen both in the 'book of nature' and in the 'book of scripture' – they were complementary, rather than in conflict).

Charles Darwin and evolution

In 1859, based on his long research, including five years spent on *HMS Beagle* as a naturalist, Darwin published *On the Origin of Species*, in which he put forward several radical theories:

- Different species have evolved from one common ancestry.
- *Natural selection.* Natural genetic mutation produces some characteristics that help some individuals to survive better than others and they pass on these favourable characteristics to future generations over a very long period of time. Less favourable characteristics cause some species to die out.
- Human beings have evolved from earlier species, such as apes.

Darwin's theory, despite its imperfections, makes a fundamental contribution to the scientific view of the world. But it was furiously opposed at the time by many traditional religious believers, supported by others and criticised by some contemporary scientists. Darwin challenged the traditional views that:

- The world was created in 4004 BCE.
- Each species had been created separately by God and was distinct.

- Human beings were specially created by God and were different from other animals.
- The Genesis creation myths were a true historical account of how the world started.

Is it possible to believe in science and religion in the twenty-first century?

Some modern thinkers have suggested that the contrast between scientific thinking and religious thinking is not as great as has been claimed, and, indeed, that science still leads to God.

It is not true that everything is certain in science. In physics, light is sometimes described as waves, sometimes as particles. At one stage, the Newtonian view of fixed space and time was regarded as scientific fact, but now Einstein's theory of relativity, which argues that space and time can be affected by gravity, holds sway. In quantum physics, the behaviour of sub-atomic particles can only be predicted with probability, rather than certainty. At this level, scientists need the same powers of imagination, creativity and the ability to trust their judgement, which characterises religious belief.

The philosopher, Ludwig Wittgenstein, argued that we need to understand the context in which language is used in order to discover its meaning. Scientific language and religious language serve different purposes, and both are equally valid in their own situation. Religion asks questions such as, 'Who am I?' or 'What is the meaning of life?' Like general scientific theories (such as relativity), these questions are looking for truths that affect our lives, and they can be discussed rationally, but they produce answers that cannot be observed by the senses. This implies that science and religion are ways of looking at life that should be seen as complementary to each other, rather than in conflict.

Some scientists argue that the evidence for the Big Bang and evolution is also evidence for the existence of God. The fact that if the Big Bang had been a micro-second earlier the universe would have imploded and a micro-second later it would have exploded so fast that everything would have disappeared, implies that God determined the moment of the Big Bang. Some scientists also argue for the anthropic principle (that at the moment of the Big Bang, the nature of matter, the size of the bang and the laws of science made it inevitable that humans would be created) as evidence of God using science to create humans. Other scientists claim that the scientific coincidences necessary for life on Earth (stars being made out of hydrogen and helium to produce carbon and supernovae being needed to spread the carbon to planets like Earth) are so great that it could not have happened by chance, and so God must have caused it.

Some religious philosophers argue that the way we live our lives (and especially the way in which scientists conduct science) is based on the principle that everything has an explanation. The search for explanations has worked well in science and if everything in the universe has an explanation, it seems reasonable to accept that the universe itself must have an explanation. The only being who could explain the universe would be God, therefore it is reasonable to believe that God exists.

Extraterrestrial life

Given the size of the universe (there are at least 100 billion stars in our home galaxy alone and perhaps 100 billion galaxies of much the same size scattered throughout deep space) few scientists believe that the Earth is the only home of life. But, until quite recently, the field of exobiology – the study of extraterrestrial life also known as astrobiology – was almost defunct. It could come up with some interesting speculations but that was about all.

The robot planetary explorers that swept through the solar system in the 1960s and 1970s found no trace of life, or even potential life-supporting environments. Exobiology's most adventurous experiment – when the 1976 Mars Viking Lander tried to find biological activity in the soil of Mars – yielded discouraging results. The Mars disappointment was a low point for the hopeful new science. With the exception of the Earth, the solar system appeared to be barren. As for life beyond the solar system, the colossal distances involved made it simply unreachable, and in any case, no one knew for sure if other stars had planets at all, far less living planets.

Since those bleak days, exobiology's prospects have brightened enormously. A whole succession of discoveries has vastly increased the probabilities that life exists elsewhere in the solar system – as well as our chances of actually finding it.

Some of these discoveries have come from recent space probes and careful astronomical observation. For example, in the last few years, scientists have found evidence for planets around more than 60 nearby stars. The Galileo spacecraft has found what is almost certainly a liquid salty ocean beneath the surface of Jupiter's moon Europa. Mars most likely once had liquid water flowing on its surface. Scientists now believe that much of it is still there, locked beneath the surface.

The most vital discoveries of exobiology, though, were made right here on Earth. Biologists have learned that life is much more robust that most scientists believed 30 years ago. Earth micro-organisms have been found thriving in astonishingly hostile environments. Deep beneath the oceans, for example, near the volcanic vents known as black smokers, some microbes grow and multiply at temperatures above 110 degrees, and according to some scientists, perhaps as high as 170 degrees. Others thrive in acid conditions that would strip the skin from a human, while others still make a comfortable living in hot rocks kilometres below the ground. Some even prefer cold to heat: Antarctic life-forms can manage very well in what amounts to a permanent deep-freeze.

The existence of these so-called extremophile organisms radically changed our view of what might be called 'the necessities of life'. Extremophiles live happily without sunshine, without moderate warmth, without organic molecules to feed off and with no need for photosynthesis – many digest raw minerals and fuel themselves with basic chemical reactions.

Many share another fascinating characteristic, too. The genetic code of these creatures suggests that they are not recent adaptations that have moved away from 'mainstream life' into awkward niches shunned by their competitors. Instead, in evolutionary terms they are among the oldest living things on Earth, probably among the very first to appear.

DID YOU KNOW?

Scientific thoughts
Copernicus (1473–1543), a Polish priest, published his main work on the movement of heavenly bodies in 1543. He argued that the Sun is at the centre of the universe and that the Earth revolves around it once a year.

The Heisenberg uncertainty principle argues that it is impossible to know for certain both the position and the momentum of an electron at the same time. This appears to attack the view that science can explain and predict the behaviour of material objects exactly.

Evidence for *evolution* is strongly suggested by the fact that 99 per cent of a chimpanzee's genetic material is the same as that of a human.

The implications for life elsewhere in the solar system are huge. We know now that all life needs is liquid water – even a little dampness will serve – and some kind of energy source. Exobiology is back in business.

Mars remains the best candidate for the breakthrough discovery of an extraterrestrial organism. In the early solar system four billion years ago, it may well have offered better prospects for life than the Earth. In 1998, NASA scientists found what may have been fossilised ancient Martian bacteria in a meteorite blasted from the planet's surface by a cosmic impact. The Mars rock drifted through space for millions of years before eventually crashing down in Antarctica.

Exobiology will be a major element in the Mars missions of the first half of the twenty-first century. ESA's Mars Express arrived in Martian orbit in December 2003. The Aurora Programme is looking at plans for a sample return mission and even a human visit. Some of Earth's Antarctic life-forms could probably live on Mars today. Perhaps below the Martian surface, the corresponding native organisms are just waiting to be discovered.

Figure 3.1 'Two things never fail to fill me with awe, the starry heavens above the Earth and the moral world within' (Immanuel Kant)

Europa, ten times more distant than Mars, is a more difficult proposition. But plans for Europa missions are on the drawing board, too. Exobiologists no longer restrict themselves to planetary environments. Comets, for example, are rich in organic material and certainly could be colonised by some kind of extremophile. Some theorists even think that life originated first in a cometary environment then reached Earth and, perhaps, other planets.

Religious implications

If extra-terrestrial life forms are found, this will be a challenge for traditional religions. The religions such a Judaism, Christianity and Islam will have to reconcile their traditional views that God made human beings in his own image so that we occupy a unique place in creation with the evidence that there may be untold millions of life-forms out there. Also, as space travel probes further into the cosmos it may well find more and more irrefutable evidence for the Big Bang theory. This will conflict directly with the creationist view that God created the universe in seven days.

Activities

1. Recently, a county school board in America banned the teaching of evolutionary theory in their school because it contradicted their Creationist views. How far do you think this action can be justified?

2. Is 'Where did the world come from?' a scientific or a religious question and why?

3

EXAM QUESTION

The source below suggests that much real power in the United States is in the hands of religious fundamentalists. Discuss the prospects for social and political change in these circumstances.

(40 marks)

AQA B June 2004

Creationism

The Judeo-Christian conception is still the most popular theory of human nature in the United States. According to recent polls, 76 per cent of Americans believe in the biblical account of creation, 79 per cent believe that the miracles in the Bible actually took place, 76 per cent believe in angels, the devil, and other immaterial souls, 67 per cent believe they will exist in some form after their death, and only 15 per cent believe that Darwin's theory of evolution is the best explanation for the origin of human life on Earth. Politicians on the right embrace the religious theory explicitly, and no mainstream politician would dare contradict it in public.

But the modern sciences of cosmology, geology, biology, and archaeology have made it impossible for a scientifically literate person to believe that the biblical story of creation actually took place. As a result, the Judeo-Christian theory of human nature is no longer explicitly avowed by most academics, journalists, social analysts, and other intellectually engaged people.

Source: Steven Pinker, The Blank Slate *(London: Book Club Associates, 2002)*

EXAMINER'S ADVICE

- This question is adapted from Section B of A2 Unit 6 set in June 2004. See page 1 for more information about the Unit 6 paper. As a synoptic question it brings together different sorts of knowledge, ideas and skills from the whole subject, and before you attempt it, you should refer also to Units 15 and 19 in this book on the themes of Social Change and Power and Control.
- The question is partly about the compatibility of scientific theories and religious belief and their ability to coexist side by side. Use the ideas in the two previous units to gather your arguments and compile points for discussion on this aspect of the question.
- Then consult Units 15 and 19 and try to identify what key factors determine where power and control lies in society and what can bring about social and political change. Think about the issues which influenced the Republican victory in the 2004 election in the USA and its implications in particular for the losing Democrats. Will it always stay like that and how powerful do you think the relationship between religious belief and political power is in any case?
- Like other Unit 6 questions this is a hard question, but the ideas are central to General Studies B, particularly at A2 level, so work hard to master them. When you have studied the relevant units and assembled your ideas, allow yourself 35 minutes for writing your answer and then turn to page 248 for some possible further ideas.

SCIENCE AND TECHNOLOGY

Energy

Energy is the capacity to do work. There are many forms of energy, such as *potential* (such as the string of a taut bow, which has the potential energy to fire an arrow); *kinetic* (the energy associated with movement, such as the movement of pistons in a car engine, which have the potential energy to move the car); *chemical* (the energy stored in food or fossil fuels); *gravitational* (the potential energy created when an object is raised above the Earth), etc.

In physics, *the law of conservation of energy* states that energy can neither be created nor lost, it can only be transferred or converted into another form. This can be seen in the process of creating electricity (see Figure 4.1). Another example of the conservation of energy is throwing a ball. When you throw a ball into the air, it rises according to the energy you have put into it. All the way up its trajectory, it is gaining gravitational potential energy. When all of your energy has been converted into gravitational potential energy, the ball begins to come down.

As far as humans are concerned, the conversion of energy into usable mechanical forms has been of huge importance. All animals convert the chemical energy of food

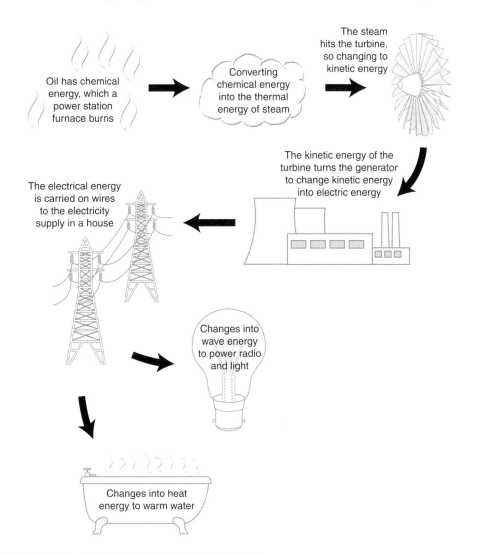

Oil has chemical energy, which a power station furnace burns

Converting chemical energy into the thermal energy of steam

The steam hits the turbine, so changing to kinetic energy

The kinetic energy of the turbine turns the generator to change kinetic energy into electric energy

The electrical energy is carried on wires to the electricity supply in a house

Changes into wave energy to power radio and light

Changes into heat energy to warm water

Figure 4.1 The creation of electricity: the law of conservation

into the kinetic energy of their bodies, but humans are the only animals who have managed to convert other forms of energy for their own uses, so being able to adapt their environment, rather than having to adapt themselves to their environment (for example, converting the heat energy of wood into the thermal energy of a fire enabled humans to live in cold climates).

Human energy conversion (the harnessing of energy)

As already stated, the first human conversion of energy was transforming wood and animal waste into fires so that the energy could be used for heating and cooking. By 5000 BCE, wood was changed into charcoal, whose greater heat was used for smelting metals. At first this process created bronze (a mixture of copper and tin, both of which occur naturally). Later, in about 1500 BCE, iron was produced from iron ore. This use of the energy of wood to make metals allowed humans to make tools and other implements necessary to produce other means of transforming energy. The first central heating systems were made by the Romans in about 100 BCE.

The first transfer of other energy into kinetic energy occurred in water mills, which first appeared in about 100 BCE as a means of grinding grain and olives. The Domesday Book of 1086 records a tidal mill operating at Dover (i.e. a water mill powered by the tides, rather than by a stream of water). Windmills first appeared in Iran in the seventh century. However, the great harnessing of energy did not come until the eighteenth and nineteenth centuries.

The inventions of Savery, Newcomen and Watt (see Unit 10, 'Transport issues') allowed the chemical energy of coal to change water into steam to produce the kinetic energy of a steam engine. This energy was used to drive machines (which allowed the creation of better metals, such as steel) and to revolutionise transport through the railways. In 1860, Lenoir of Belgium invented an internal combustion engine, which transformed coal into gas to move pistons. This discovery allowed Daimler to build the first petrol engine in 1883 for his motor car.

It was Faraday's discoveries in electricity, however, which led to the great changes of the twentieth century. Faraday invented an electric motor in 1821 and a transformer in 1831, from which all the inventions using electricity have been developed. So much of modern life depends on electricity that the major energy question of the twenty-first century is, 'What is the best way of transforming energy into electric energy ?'

Methods of transforming energy into electricity

Non-renewable methods
Fossil fuels such as coal and oil have chemical energy, which can be transformed into kinetic energy to drive turbines, which make electricity.

SCIENCE AND TECHNOLOGY

Good points

- Very cheap to build, fairly cheap to run and very efficient.
- Easy to build near to centres of population.

Bad points

- Fossil fuels cannot be renewed, so they will run out.
- Cause lots of pollution (especially acid rain and the greenhouse effect).

Nuclear fission bombards uranium with neutrons releasing *nuclear energy* to transform water into steam to drive turbines (pressurised water reactor) or using plutonium to create more atoms from the uranium and heating sodium to make steam (fast breeder reactor).

Good points

- Fairly cheap to build, very cheap to run.
- No pollution.
- Very efficient.

Bad points

- Produce radioactive waste, needing special storage for thousands of years.
- Danger of leaks with huge health risks (for example, Chernobyl).
- Fuels can be used for nuclear weapons.
- Reactors must be built near large water supplies for cooling, usually on the coast.
- Uranium and plutonium resources will eventually run out.

Natural gas (a fossil fuel produced in the same way as oil and gas) is now being used to fuel power stations.

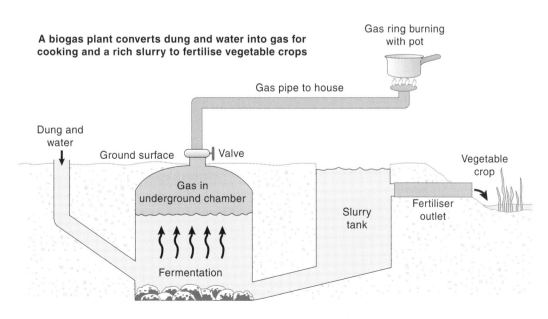

A biogas plant converts dung and water into gas for cooking and a rich slurry to fertilise vegetable crops

Figure 4.2 A biogas plant

Good points
- Cheap to build and run.
- Very efficient.
- Easy to build near centres of population.
- Much less pollution than other fossil fuels.

Bad points
- A fossil fuel, so it will eventually run out.
- Transport can cause problems, as the gas is highly explosive.

Semi-renewable methods

Geo-thermal energy (the heat from the rocks in the Earth's core) can be used to create steam to drive turbines. The first geothermal power stations used the steam from hot water springs and were not very efficient. Over the past 20 years, new methods of drilling have allowed a system where two deep holes are sunk to near the Earth's mantle, then water is sent down one hole and comes back up the other as steam to drive a turbine.

Good points
- Fairly cheap to build.
- Very cheap to run.
- No pollution.
- It will take a long time for the heat source to disappear.

Bad points
- Only creates small amounts of electricity.
- Production depends on special geological features, so there is a restricted number of places where they can be built.

Energy from waste is a recent innovation in the UK, where incinerators are changed into power stations to transform the energy of the waste into electricity, instead of just burning it. Some countries are experimenting with sewage power stations, which would be completely renewable and possibly more efficient.

Good points
- Cheap to build.
- Very cheap to run.
- Efficient.
- A good way of getting rid of waste.

Bad points
- They cause pollution (but not as much as oil and coal), but the pollution would be caused anyway in getting rid of the rubbish.
- The more recycling there is, the less fuel there will be.

Renewable methods

The most efficient renewable method is *hydroelectric power* (HEP), which converts the energy of flowing water into mechanical energy to drive turbines.

Good points
- Very cheap to run.
- Very efficient.
- Causes no pollution.
- Fuel will never run out.

Bad points
- Very expensive to build.
- Can only be built in certain areas, well away from cities.
- Long lines of pylons are required to transport the energy to civilisation.
- Huge areas of land have to be swamped in order to fuel the plant.

Wind generators are now widely used to transform wave energy of wind into electricity. Hawaii now has a wind station producing 1500 megawatts, equivalent to a fossil fuel power station.

Good points
- Fairly cheap to build.
- Very cheap to run.
- Cause no pollution.
- Energy source will never run out.

Bad points
- Not very efficient – each set of blades only produces a small amount of electricity.
- Have to be built in wide open spaces and are a very prominent feature in the landscape.

Solar energy can be directly transformed into electricity using silicon or gallium arsenide cells. Other methods involve storing the heat and using it not only to produce electricity, but also to power heating systems, etc.

Good points
- Very cheap to run.
- Causes no pollution.
- Energy source will never run out.

Bad points
- Expensive to build.
- Need to cover a large area to produce a reasonable amount of power.
- More suitable for hot, sunny countries.

The *energy of the sea* can be converted into electricity through either tide or wave power stations. The Rance river estuary in France has a *tidal power station*, which drives turbines by damming the tide. In Japan there is an oscillating water column, which converts the *energy of the waves* to create an air turbine that drives a generator.

Good points
- Very cheap to run.
- Causes no pollution.
- Energy source will never run out.

Bad points
- Very, very expensive to build.
- Not very efficient yet.
- Can only be built in certain areas.

Activities

1. Investigate how much of your daily life is dependent on electricity.

2. Think of an example other than the power station to illustrate the law of conservation of energy.

3. If you could begin electricity generation from scratch, which methods of generating electricity would you choose, and why?

4. Explain, with illustrations, why energy can only be converted, not created.

EXAM QUESTION

Explain the advantages and disadvantages of using wind farms to generate energy.

(12 marks)

AQA B January 2002

Tourism chiefs go full tilt at windmills

Councillors concerned about the visual impact of electricity-generating wind farms have blocked a building application by an environmental energy company EcoGen. On Wednesday, Port Talbot Borough Council voted overwhelmingly against an application for a farm which would sprawl across the Upper Afan valley – one of South Wales's most popular recreational areas.

The valley is referred to locally as 'little Switzerland': one of the key objections to the application was that tourism to the area could be affected.

Figure 4.3

Source: The Telegraph, *29 January 1994*

EXAMINER'S ADVICE

- This question is from A2 Unit 5 set in January 2002. It is one of five compulsory short essays, with each title taken from a different section of the specification and each worth 12 marks. Make sure that you attempt all five in the test, so as not to lose marks unnecessarily. See page 1 for more information about this paper. There are lots of Unit 5 questions scattered throughout this book. Even if you are not taking A2, these questions are similar to those set for AS Unit 1, so you should sensibly have a go at them.
- Note that the question asks for both advantages and disadvantages and the wording implies balanced 'objective' explanations for each – it does not ask solely for your opinions. You should also use the prompts in both the picture and the text, which point to the environmental and aesthetic implications of wind farm installations, as well as the economic effects on tourism.
- Research the topic using information from the unit you have just read (also Unit 5 and elsewhere if you wish). You should then write out your answer in no more than 15 minutes, which means perhaps no more than a page and a half of normal-sized handwriting and not too much elaboration of points. For 12 marks in this case you might aim for six arguments in support of wind power and six against.
- When you have completed your answer, turn to page 249 for some suggested key points.

Environmental issues

Environmental issues refer to the concerns raised by the way in which human beings have treated their surroundings and the long-term and possibly irreversible effects of such treatment. Most of these concerns are to do with two main interrelated areas:

- How we treat the natural world and its resources, for example, the use of fossil fuels, deforestation, acid rain and global warming.
- How we treat the animal world, for example, conservation, extinction and animal cruelty.

Modern ecologists have identified four important areas that are crucial to our understanding of the environment:

- *The ecosystem.* This refers to the way in which forms of life interact with each other, such as in food chains, which link different species and interlocking elements and chemical compounds (see Figure 5.1). This interconnection must be regarded as a system where a change in the delicate balance at one point can have

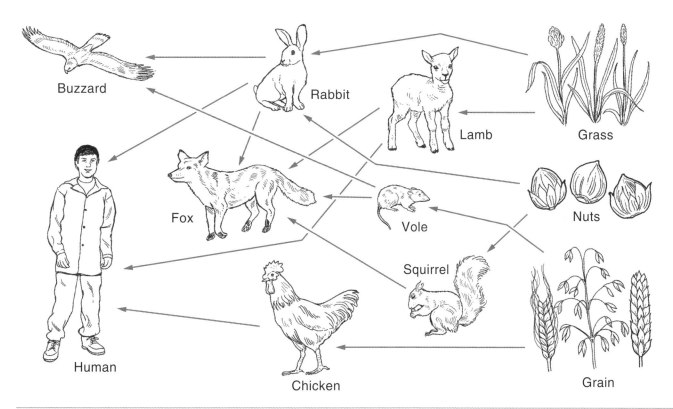

Figure 5.1 A food chain

far reaching effects in other parts of the system. For example, introducing rabbits to Australia, where there are no natural predators, led to them overrunning the continent and possibly led to the extinction of some native animals.

- *Growth.* The environment has a limited capacity. Modern scientists have recognised that there cannot be unlimited growth. Just as the animal population in its natural environment is limited by the availability of food, territory, mates and inter-species competition, so human beings must recognise that population, food consumption and pollution cannot increase indefinitely.

- *Ecological stability.* In the natural world, stability is maintained by a constant process of change and adjustment to continually changing conditions. Nature is never static. However, species with very small numbers of plants or animals are at much greater risk of extinction from disease, predators or changes in their food supply than species with large numbers.

- *The future.* Ecologists are concerned about the long-term effects of human intervention in nature. The natural environment needs continuity in order to flourish, so we need to consider what effect an activity carried out for short-term gain, such as chopping down trees for timber without an adequate system of replanting, may have on future generations. In relation to the age of the world as a whole, human beings have only been around for a few seconds, but the irreversible damage inflicted on the environment during that time has been immense.

Biological diversity

Diversity refers to the fact that the natural world contains at least 1.5 million different species. However, this figure only includes those that have been discovered so far. It is estimated that there may be between 5 million and 40 million more, including 500,000 plants and untold numbers of insect species. This diversity is essential for our own survival and that of the ecosystem as a whole for the following reasons:

- The more species there are, each with its own physical characteristics, the more chance there is of resistance to natural disasters.
- Half of all our medical cures, such as morphine and quinine, come from plants. Loss of species means a loss of important natural curative substances.
- Food and natural materials used as a basis for manufacturing are based on a wide range of natural species. Extinction means a loss of important food sources.
- The complex relationships within the whole ecosystem means that the loss of one plant, for example, can mean the possible extinction of a considerable number of other animals and insects.

Attitudes to the environment

Traditionally, Christianity has based its attitudes to the environment on the Creation myths in Genesis, Chapters 1–2. This suggests that the Earth was created by God for a purpose and that human beings, because they are superior to animals, have a responsibility or 'stewardship' over nature. However, this attitude was later modified by the idea that it is an individual's duty to work hard and make profits. The idea that nature is there to serve human need has led to its exploitation. This was further reinforced by the ideas of mathematicians and philosophers such as Sir Isaac Newton and René Descartes. Newton's mathematical laws explaining the way in which the physical world operated, led to a *mechanistic* view of nature as consisting of impersonal masses and forces operating according to deterministic laws. Descartes argued that animals are machines without minds or feelings. Also, the Industrial Revolution encouraged the view that the natural environment was merely an inexhaustible source of raw materials. The development of capitalism also led to the view that the need for private profit justified the damage to the environment caused by industrial technology. However, Charles Darwin's work on *evolution* emphasised:

- The way in which all natural living things, including human beings, are related to each other.
- The fact that nature is not static but constantly changing to survive.

Important environmental issues

Population

The population of the world is now six billion. It is estimated that it will grow by one billion every 11 years. This population explosion has mainly taken place in underdeveloped countries and continents and it has raised the following interrelated problems for the environment.

- *Pressure on land.* As more and more people try to live off the land, it becomes exhausted. Land that is overfarmed becomes desert. Two thousand years ago, large areas of North Africa supplied the Roman Empire with wheat. Much of this once fertile land is now desert, particularly in the Sahel region of West Africa. Poverty prevents the use of more 'eco-friendly' farming methods, such as the use of fertilisers, which might help to replenish the soil.
- *Deforestation.* This problem has various causes, of which population is one. During the past 30 years, huge areas of rain forest in South America and elsewhere in the world have been chopped down. This has taken place for a variety of reasons, including the need for firewood as a fuel by poor people, for timber, for paper making, to clear the land for agriculture and to get at valuable mineral deposits. This deforestation has led to desertification through the loss of topsoil, the loss of habitat for a large number of species, resulting in their actual or near extinction, and the loss of oxygen produced by jungle vegetation, which has contributed to global warming.
- *Urbanisation.* By 2030, it is estimated that 60 per cent of the world's population will live in urban areas. In poor areas, this leads to a drastic decline in local wildlife

and cultivable land and a large increase in environmental damage caused by sewage, industrial waste, transport systems and other forms of pollution.

Acid rain

This important example of pollution is mainly caused by the chemicals released by smoke from fossil-fuelled power stations, such as sulphuric and nitric acid, which change rainwater from pH5/6 to pH3, making it more acidic. In Sweden, which receives most of Britain's acid rain, some lakes and forests have been completely destroyed by the fall-out.

Ozone layer

The ozoneosphere is a region in the upper atmosphere, between 10 km and 50 km altitude, where there is much more ozone (O_3) than at lower levels. The presence of the ozone layer blocks all solar radiation of wavelengths less than 290 namometres from reaching the Earth's surface. If this did not happen, most living things would die. Ozone is formed by the reaction of short-wave ultraviolet radiation from the Sun on oxygen, but it is also destroyed by chlorofluorocarbons (CFC gases in aerosols) and nitrogen oxides (found in car and plane exhaust gases). The ozone layer is gradually being depleted, leading to an increase in the incidence of skin cancer in fair-skinned people. CFC gases have been banned by developed countries, but it is expensive for developing countries to stop using them.

Animal issues

Humans relate to animals in the following ways:

- as companions and working partners (for example, guidedogs and sheepdogs)
- as zoo animals for observation, research, conservation and enjoyment
- as food – worldwide, people eat about 140,000,000 tons of meat every year
- for medical or product research – over 200 million animals are used annually
- for hunting – animals are hunted for food, fashion, fun or for profit.

Recently, animal rights has become a widely discussed issue. It is no longer generally accepted that animals can be killed indiscriminately for pleasure or for profit. Poaching elephants for ivory or rhinoceroses and tigers for their horns and bones is now illegal in most countries. Causing animals pain for either medical or cosmetic purposes is now regarded by many as an infringement of basic animal rights. Many methods of animal rearing for food are now regarded as cruel (for example, factory farming and battery hens).

Global warming

The Arctic is warming rapidly, with the loss of polar ice projected to accelerate global warming as well as contributing to the sea level rising and flooding, according to a comprehensive four-year scientific study of the region conducted by an international team of 300 scientists that was released in 2004.

According to the scientists' most conservative estimates, about half of the summer sea ice in the Arctic is projected to melt along with a significant portion of the

Greenland Ice Sheet, as the region warms an additional 7°F–13°F by 2100. Rising sea levels are already observed and are predicted to accelerate as warming continues, according to the final report of the Arctic Climate Impact Assessment (ACIA).

The study confirms that the warming is human-caused, through heat-trapping emissions from the burning of fossil fuels. The United States is the largest world contributor of those emissions, yet has failed to enact limits.

The report comes out at a time of increasing pressure on the Bush administration to enact US emissions reductions. In November 2004, the Queen privately pressured Tony Blair to press the US on global warming policy, and she opened a 'climate change summit' of senior government officials from the UK and Germany to discuss the problem. Russian president Vladimir Putin signed the Kyoto Protocol, thus bringing the accord into effect worldwide.

'President Bush needs to change his approach to global warming in light of the damage already being seen in the Arctic,' said Dr. Daniel Lashof, Science Director of the NRDC Climate Center. 'It is now clear we have to cut the pollution that causes global warming to prevent dangerous changes in the climate. The purely voluntary approach taken in the President's first term will leave the nation and the world in great danger from the threat of global warming.'

The assessment was commissioned by the Arctic Council, a ministerial inter-governmental forum comprised of eight nations, including the United States, and six Indigenous Peoples organisations; and the International Arctic Science Committee, an international scientific organisation appointed by eighteen national academies of science.

'The impacts of global warming are apparent now in the Arctic,' said Robert Corell, chair of the ACIA. 'The Arctic is experiencing some of the most rapid and severe impacts on Earth. The impacts of global warming on the region and the globe are projected to increase substantially in the years to come.'

Additional findings include:

- In Alaska, western Canada, and eastern Russia, average winter temperatures have increased as much as 4°F–7°F in the past 50 years, and are projected to rise 7°F–14°F over the next 100 years.
- Polar sea ice during the summer is projected to decline by 50 per cent by the end of this century with some models showing near-complete disappearance of summer sea ice. This is very likely to have devastating consequences for polar bears, ice-living seals, and local people for whom these animals are a primary food source. At the same time, the reduced extent of sea ice is likely to increase marine access to some of the region's resources.
- Warming over Greenland will lead to substantial melting of the Greenland Ice Sheet, contributing to global sea-level rise at an increasing rate. Greenland's ice sheets contain enough water to eventually raise sea level by about 23 feet.
- In the United States, low-lying coastal states like Florida and Louisiana are particularly susceptible to rising sea levels.
- Should the Arctic Ocean become ice-free in summer, it is likely that polar bears and some seal species would be driven to extinction.

KEY TERMS

Air pollution the release of harmful chemicals into the atmosphere by industrial processes, traffic emissions and incinerators, etc.

Biodegradable a substance that can be converted to simpler compounds by bacteria (most plastics are not biodegradable)

CFCs chlorofluorocarbons are manmade gases used in aerosols, refrigeration and air-conditioning, which are responsible for the increasing hole in the ozone layer

Composition of pure air 78 per cent nitrogen, 21 per cent oxygen, 1 per cent noble gases, 0.03 per cent carbon dioxide

Eutrophication an overgrowth of aquatic plants caused by an excess of nitrates coming into rivers from fertilisers, which causes a depletion of oxygen, which kills fish

Population explosion the huge increase in the world's population, mainly occurring in developing countries

Radiation the lethal fall-out produced by the use of nuclear power and weapons, with the highest potential to do long-lasting damage

Thermal pollution releases of warm water from power stations and factories – has the same effect as eutrophication

- Arctic climate changes present serious challenges to the health and food security of some indigenous peoples, challenging the survival of some cultures.
- Over the next 100 years, global warming is expected to accelerate, contributing to major physical, ecological, social, and economic changes, and the assessment has documented that many of these changes have already begun.

The assessment's projections are based on a moderate estimate of future emissions of carbon dioxide and other greenhouse gases, and incorporate results from five major global climate models used by the Inter-governmental Panel on Climate Change.

Conclusion

There has been a general realisation that the natural world is not a limitless, endlessly renewable resource. Human beings must learn to manage the environment so that the right of other species to life is protected and the damage caused by human pollution and activities is drastically reduced. Recent international ecological conferences have tried to draw up conservation plans, such as reducing emissions of harmful gases and the rate of deforestation. However, some countries have tended to put their short-term financial interests first. The agreements made at the 1992 UN Conference on the Environment and Development in Rio (East Summit) had still not been implemented by the end of the millennium.

Figure 5.2 Melting ice caps in the Arctic

EXAM QUESTION

5

We know that we shall probably exhaust available oil supplies in this century; and we know what effect the burning of oil has on the global climate – yet we go on using it as if there were no tomorrow.

Discuss what this behaviour tells us about our values.

You might consider the following in your answer:

- other contributors to global warming
- the practicality of a switch to renewable energy sources
- the political implications of a retreat from oil
- what new knowledge might change our behaviour.

(30 marks)

AQA B May 2002

EXAMINER'S ADVICE

- This essay question is from AS Unit 2 set in May 2002 and is the second of two extended pieces of writing you have to do in this test. The first is compulsory and based on a passage, but for this question you have a choice of two topics. See page 1 for more details on this paper.
- The question asks for a discussion about our values in relation to oil consumption. It is asking for an explanation, a justification if you like, of why we use oil in the ways and to the extent we do. Perhaps we use it because oil is the most available, usable, cheap and efficient of the fossil fuels we have at the moment. It would not be sufficient to say that our values and way of life are rubbish, even though you may feel we are risking disaster with current rates of consumption. How should we begin to address the implication of this? The highest marks will go to those answers that have a good grasp of the science and technology involved and of the practical realities of the economic and political situation. You are given some prompts in the question and you should use these to develop your answer.
- For 30 marks you should expect to write a full essay of at least two pages, and in the exam proper you will have about 30–35 minutes to complete the task.
- When you have written your answer, turn to page 249 for some suggested arguments. For another type of test involving environmental issues go to the end of Unit 13.

Genetic engineering

Genetic engineering refers to the techniques and consequences associated with the technology of altering the information carried by genes. Genes are the basic building blocks of life and they contain all the information required to enable cells to replicate themselves.

Human genetic engineering

Genetic diseases affect large numbers of people. Defective inherited genes can cause mental retardation, physical deformity or early death. Some diseases can be detected by prenatal tests, while others, such as *Huntington's disease* (which causes paralysis, mental deterioration and death in middle life) can be detected in early adulthood, before the symptoms have actually appeared. This process is called *genetic screening*. Various techniques have been developed to try to alter the genetic structure that gives rise to such diseases.

Somatic-cell therapy

This technique is based on the fact that, although, in theory, every cell in a human body carries all the information needed to grow that whole human body, it can block off the information not needed for its specialised function in a particular part of the body. This *somatic* or body cell can reproduce itself exactly and then divide. Somatic-cell change involves replacing faulty cells where the genes do not work properly with cells containing genes which do, although these new cells will themselves need renewal.

For example, with the disease of cystic fibrosis (CF), faulty CF genes, which failed to control the passage of salt and water in and out of the body's cells in the lungs, were replaced with normal ones successfully.

The next stage of research is to develop a reliable technique that would enable self-renewing genes to be introduced so that the body will start manufacturing normal genes for itself.

Experiments have also been tried with muscular dystrophy, Tay-Sachs disease and sickle-cell anaemia, which involved the implant of white blood cells armed with a gene for a toxin that destroys tumour tissue.

Germ-line therapy

Somatic-cell therapy cannot be passed on from one generation to another by sexual reproduction because the cells involved are not connected to the *gametes* or reproductive cells. In germ-line therapy, new DNA is introduced in order to *recombine* with DNA in the reproductive cells. This results in the possibility of changing the genetic profile of a child of parents who carry a genetically based disease. Once the new gene is recombined, it can be reproduced over many generations. The advantage of this type of therapy is that inaccessible brain cells or widely distributed tissue cells could be corrected in a fertilised egg. In experiments on animals, a generation of 'super mice' was developed, which grew to be 50 per cent larger than its parents, as well as a mouse that was designed to develop cancer for use in drug tests.

Cloning

A clone can be defined as 'an individual organism that was grown from a single body cell of its parent and that is genetically identical to it' (*Encyclopaedia Britannica*).

Gene cloning can be used for all sorts of purposes. *Plasmids* (small rings of DNA) are inserted into a bacterium to produce a specified protein, so that an endless supply of copies will then be created. Such cloning is being used to produce insulin and hepatitis B vaccine, among other proteins.

Even more controversial is cloning a complete animal. The first cloned animals were frogs, created when frog DNA was transplanted into a frog egg whose own genetic material had been removed. The cells began to divide to form an embryo and then a frog, which was identical to the DNA inserted into the egg.

The first successful clone of an adult animal was carried out by a team of scientists at the Roselin Institute in Edinburgh. The nucleus of a cell from the mammary gland of an adult sheep was implanted into the embryo of another sheep's unfertilised egg, from which the nucleus had been removed. An electric current was passed through and the egg began to divide, so becoming an embryo, which was implanted into the uterus of another sheep. The lamb – Dolly – was a clone of the sheep whose mammary gland was used.

The practical implications of cloning are financially good, for example, there would be an unending supply of top-quality livestock. However, there are obviously ethical issues involved in cloning.

The Human Genome Project

Begun formally in 1990, the Human Genome Project was a 13-year effort co-ordinated by the US Department of Energy and the National Institutes of Health. The project originally was planned to last 15 years, but rapid technological advances accelerated the completion date to 2003. Project goals were to:

- Map the entire genetic blueprint, approximately 20,000–25,000 genes in human DNA.
- Determine the sequences of the 3 billion chemical base pairs that make up human DNA.
- Store this information in databases.
- Improve tools for data analysis.
- Transfer related technologies to the private sector.
- Address the ethical, legal, and social issues (ELSI) that may arise from the project.

To help achieve these goals, researchers also studied the genetic makeup of several non-human organisms. These include the common human gut bacterium – Escherichia coli – the fruit fly, and the laboratory mouse.

A unique aspect of the US Human Genome Project is that it was the first large scientific undertaking to address potential ELSI implications arising from project data. Another important feature of the project was the US federal government's long-standing dedication to the transfer of technology to the private sector. By licensing technologies to private companies and awarding grants for innovative research, the project catalysed the multibillion-dollar US biotechnology industry and fostered the development of new medical applications.

What is a genome and why is it important?

A genome is the complete make up of DNA in an organism, including its genes. Genes carry information for making all the proteins required by all organisms. These proteins determine, among other things, how the organism looks, how well its body metabolises food or fights infection, and sometimes even how it behaves.

DNA is made up of four similar chemicals (called bases and abbreviated A, T, C, and G) that are repeated millions or billions of times throughout a genome. The human genome, for example, has three billion pairs of bases.

The particular order of As, Ts, Cs, and Gs is extremely important. The order underlies all of life's diversity, even dictating whether an organism is human or another species such as yeast, rice, or fruit fly, all of which have their own genomes and are themselves the focus of genome projects. Because all organisms are related through similarities in DNA sequences, insights gained from non-human genomes often lead to new knowledge about human biology.

What is gene therapy?

Genes, which are carried on chromosomes, are the basic physical and functional units of heredity. Genes are specific sequences of bases that encode instructions on how to make proteins. Although genes get a lot of attention, it's the proteins that perform most life functions and even make up the majority of cellular structures. When genes are altered so that the encoded proteins are unable to carry out their normal functions, genetic disorders can result. Gene therapy is a technique for correcting defective genes responsible for disease development.

How does gene therapy work?

In most gene-therapy studies, a 'normal' gene is inserted into the genome to replace an 'abnormal', disease-causing gene. A carrier molecule (called a vector) must be used to deliver the therapeutic gene to the patient's target cells. Currently, the most common vector is a virus that has been genetically altered to carry normal human DNA. Viruses have evolved a way of delivering their genes to human cells. Scientists have tried to take advantage of this capability and manipulate the virus genome to remove disease-causing genes and insert therapeutic genes.

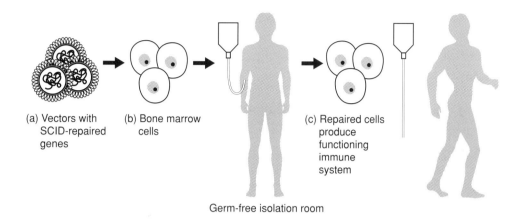

(a) Vectors with SCID-repaired genes

(b) Bone marrow cells

(c) Repaired cells produce functioning immune system

Germ-free isolation room

Figure 6.1 The process of gene therapy (Source: *FDA Consumer Magazine*, August 2000)

Target cells, such as the patient's liver or lung cells, are infected with the viral vector. The vector then unloads its genetic material containing the therapeutic human gene into the target cell. The generation of a functional protein product from the therapeutic gene restores the target cell to a normal state. See Figure 6.1 showing this process.

Some of the different types of viruses used as gene-therapy vectors are:

- Retroviruses – a class of viruses that can create double-stranded DNA copies of their RNA genomes. These copies can be integrated into the chromosomes of host cells. Human immunodeficiency virus (HIV) is a retrovirus.
- Adenoviruses – a class of viruses with double-stranded DNA genomes that cause respiratory, intestinal, and eye infections in humans. The virus that causes the common cold is an adenovirus.
- Adeno-associated viruses – a class of small, single-stranded DNA viruses that can insert their genetic material at a specific site on chromosome 19.
- Herpes simplex viruses – a class of double-stranded DNA viruses that infect a particular cell type, neurons. Herpes simplex virus type 1 is a common human pathogen that causes cold sores.

Besides virus-mediated gene-delivery systems, there are several non-viral options for gene delivery. The simplest method is the direct introduction of therapeutic DNA into target cells. This approach is limited in its application because it can be used only with certain tissues and requires large amounts of DNA.

Another non-viral approach involves the creation of an artificial lipid sphere with an aqueous core. This liposome, which carries the therapeutic DNA, is capable of passing the DNA through the target cell's membrane.

Therapeutic DNA can also get inside target cells by chemically linking the DNA to a molecule that will bind to special cell receptors. Once bound to these receptors, the therapeutic DNA constructs are engulfed by the cell membrane and passed into the interior of the target cell. This delivery system tends to be less effective than other options.

Researchers also are experimenting with introducing a 47th (artificial human) chromosome into target cells. This chromosome would exist autonomously alongside the standard 46 – not affecting their workings or causing any mutations. It would be a large vector capable of carrying substantial amounts of genetic code, and scientists anticipate that, because of its construction and autonomy, the body's immune systems would not attack it. A problem with this potential method is the difficulty in delivering such a large molecule to the nucleus of a target cell.

What is the current status of gene therapy research?

The US Food and Drug Administration (FDA) has not yet approved any human gene-therapy product for sale. Current gene therapy is experimental and has not proven very successful in clinical trials. Little progress has been made since the first gene-therapy clinical trial began in 1990. In 1999, gene therapy suffered a major setback with the death of 18-year-old Jesse Gelsinger. Jesse was participating in a gene-therapy trial for Ornithine Transcarboxylase Deficiency (OTCD). He died from multiple organ failures four days after starting the treatment. His death is believed to have been triggered by a severe immune response to the adenovirus carrier.

Another major blow came in January 2003, when the FDA placed a temporary halt on all gene-therapy trials using retroviral vectors in blood stem cells. FDA took this action after it learned that a second child treated in a French gene-therapy trial had developed a leukaemia-like condition. Both this child and another who had developed a similar condition in August 2002 had been successfully treated by gene therapy for X-linked Severe Combined Immunodeficiency Disease (X-SCID), also known as 'bubble baby syndrome'.

FDA's Biological Response Modifiers Advisory Committee (BRMAC) met at the end of February 2003 to discuss possible measures that could allow a number of retroviral gene-therapy trials for treatment of life-threatening diseases to proceed with appropriate safeguards. FDA has yet to make a decision based on the discussions and advice of the BRMAC meeting.

What factors have kept gene therapy from becoming an effective treatment for genetic disease?

- *Short-lived nature of gene therapy.* Before gene therapy can become a permanent cure for any condition, the therapeutic DNA introduced into target cells must remain functional and the cells containing the therapeutic DNA must be long-lived and stable. Problems with integrating therapeutic DNA into the genome and

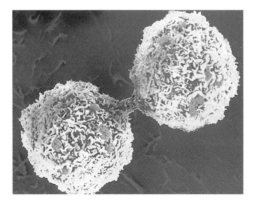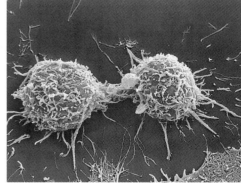

Figure 6.2 Dividing cells. Left: healthy liver cells; right: cervical cancer cells.

SCIENCE AND TECHNOLOGY

the rapidly dividing nature of many cells prevent gene therapy from achieving any long-term benefits. Patients will have to undergo multiple rounds of gene therapy.

- *Immune response.* Any time a foreign object is introduced into human tissues, the immune system is designed to attack the invader. The risk of stimulating the immune system in a way that reduces gene-therapy effectiveness is always a potential risk. Furthermore, the immune system's enhanced response to invaders it has seen before makes it difficult for gene therapy to be repeated in patients.
- *Problems with viral vectors.* Viruses, while the carrier of choice in most gene-therapy studies, present a variety of potential problems to the patient – toxicity, immune and inflammatory responses, and gene control and targeting issues. In addition, there is always the fear that the viral vector, once inside the patient, may recover its ability to cause disease.
- *Multigene disorders.* Conditions or disorders that arise from mutations in a single gene are the best candidates for gene therapy. Unfortunately, some of the most commonly occurring disorders, such as heart disease, high blood pressure, Alzheimer's disease, arthritis, and diabetes, are caused by the combined effects of variations in many genes. Multi-gene disorders such as these would be especially difficult to treat effectively using gene therapy.

Important issues raised by genetic engineering

- Germ-line therapy cannot be recalled. Recombinant DNA becomes a living part of the host body and its successors.
- Like natural DNA, it becomes liable to random mutation, so that its future behaviour could be dangerously unpredictable.
- Genes tend to interact in their effects. There is no way of knowing how the introduction of one gene may affect all the others.
- If insurance companies or employers got hold of the results of someone's genetic screening, they might use the information to discriminate against them in terms of insuring or employing them.
- The ability to identify the sex of or possible genetic abnormalities in a fetus means that some parents might opt for abortion in order to fulfil their expectations of a perfect child.
- In the past, *eugenic programmes* aimed at improving society have involved the selection of certain favoured human physical or mental characteristics and the deliberate destruction of those considered to be inferior. The possibility of genetic manipulation may increase this danger.
- Genetic research is very expensive and tends to be carried out by large multinational medical corporations who will 'own' the results of their research. This will give them very powerful monopolies.
- The cost of genetic treatment may result in a two-tier society, consisting of those whose parents could afford to 'improve' their offspring and those who may well be regarded as inferior.

DID YOU KNOW?

Genetics
One human cell may contain up to 100,000 genes. Most of the pioneering work in genetics was done by an Austrian monk called Gregor Mendel (1809–84), who did thousands of experiments with pea plants to work out how characteristics were transmitted from one generation to another. In 1953, in Cambridge, Francis Crick and James Watson discovered the double helix shape and the chemical bases of DNA, for which they received the Nobel Prize.

KEY TERMS

Amniocentesis prenatal screening of a foetus to look for genetic abnormalities

DNA deoxyribonucleic acid, the chemical inside molecules that contains genes

Chromosomes lengths of DNA containing genes, which can make proteins

Mutation damage to part of a genetic code which, if occurring in gametes, may result in new physical characteristics (e.g. an albino squirrel)

Somatic-cell change altering the behaviour of non-reproductive cells by the introduction of new genetic material

Other ethical and religious issues

- Some critics have argued that all human genetic engineering is 'tampering with nature' – it is a violation of the principle that 'nature knows best'.
- Another religious view is that there is a permanent, universal '*natural law*', which reflects divine intentions and that genetic engineering is against what God intended.
- Other concerns have been expressed about the economic implications. Rich countries, which can afford both genetic research itself and the results of that research, will benefit the most. This will increase the gap between wealthy and poor countries.

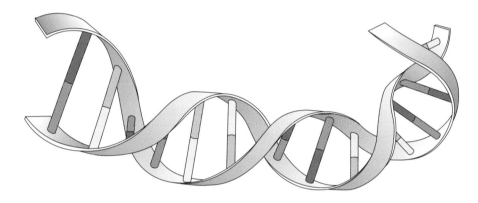

Figure 6.3 The structure of DNA

> Some of the more frightening social and moral implications of the new biotechnology involve the sort of knowledge it would generate and what we might do with such knowledge.

Source: M. Talbot, 'The Stuff of Life Itself', General Studies Review, September 2000

Why might the knowledge that we have of genetic engineering be frightening?

(12 marks)

AQA B June 2003

EXAMINER'S ADVICE

- This question is from A2 Unit 5 set in June 2003. It is one of five compulsory short essays, with each title taken from a different section of the specification and each worth 12 marks. See page 1 for more information about this paper.
- With these short essay questions you are always given some prompts and you should use them to help structure your answer. Here, the clues are in the phrases 'social and moral implications', 'sort of knowledge it would generate' and 'what we might do with such knowledge', i.e. the uses to which it might be put.
- Remember also that this is a science/technology essay, so you will get good marks for showing that you are aware of and understand the scientific aspects of the topic, without being too technical.
- Although the question asks why genetic engineering might 'be frightening', you are entitled in General Studies to challenge the question (or any assumptions behind the way it is asked), so part of your answer could well be to question the notion that it is frightening, particularly if you disagree.
- For 12 marks you might aim for 12 arguments, either for or against the proposition. Dealing with both possibilities would give your answer a rounded and balanced quality, which would also add to the marks you could gain. As before, once you have researched the topic, write out your answer in no more than 15 minutes.
- When you have completed your answer, turn to page 249 for some possible arguments.

7 Agriculture and food production

Introduction

Throughout history, human beings have tried to find new ways to produce more and better food. Our ancestors learned by trial and error how to breed and domesticate a wide range of animals, how to develop improved varieties, and found ways of processing and preserving raw foods. Successful experiments by plant breeders also led to the introduction of more disease-resistant and higher yielding crops. For example, the average wheat yield in the UK in 1900 was two tonnes per hectare. Now it is eight tonnes per hectare.

The crucial problems facing world agriculture are:

- Whether the increased use of bio-technology – the *gene revolution* – will be sufficient to feed and sustain a world population which will grow by two billion over the next 30 years.
- Whether the disadvantages associated with the use of pesticides, fertilisers, genetically modified crops, etc. arc outweighed by the benefits resulting from increased production.

Hunger

One in five of the population in developing countries suffers from *malnutrition*. This is 30 per cent of the total world population. Hunger is both a violation of human dignity and an obstacle to social, political and economic progress. Apart from the purely physical issues related to the production of food, there is also a political dimension. International law recognises that everyone has the fundamental right to be free from hunger and thirst. National governments have a duty to do everything possible to make sure that people have the physical and economic access to enough safe and nutritious food to lead healthy and active lives.

Violations of the right to food include blocking access on the grounds of race, sex, language, age, religion or political belief. In societies where civil and political rights are recognised, there is far less likely to be famine than in countries run by dictators and/or extreme religious or political factions. In Africa, for example, millions of people have died from starvation and related diseases caused by the deliberate destruction and neglect of crops and harvest and the diversion of large amounts of monetary aid into the pockets of corrupt political leaders and government officials.

In Rwanda, during the civil war, three out of four farmers were forced off their land and the harvest was halved. Similarly, in Afghanistan as the result of prolonged armed conflict, 700 square miles of arable land were sown with landmines which continue to kill or injure 300 people a month.

Major problems facing agricultural development

- The last World Food Summit set a target of reducing world hunger by half by 2015. Apart from the diseases which malnutrition leads to, such as anaemia, vitamin deficiency, stunted growth, blindness and shortened life expectancy, those suffering can rarely work to normal capacity because of chronic lethargy.
- Other problems include natural occurrences such as floods, drought, locusts, the AIDS epidemic, over-fishing and the misuse of land in order to make quick profits as seen in deforestation.
- In order to guarantee access to the results of agricultural development for all who need it worldwide, the world trading system would have to be restructured so that the rich developed countries no longer had the power to control prices, dictate to less developed countries what they should grow, exploit cheap labour and/or adopt restrictive practices towards foreign goods.

Significant developments in agriculture

The challenge facing world agriculture in the twenty-first century is to develop programmes which are sustainable and which will achieve the following objectives:

- Increase yields.
- Reduce costs.
- Protect the environment.
- Improve the reliability of food delivery.
- Improve the material welfare of those engaged in farming.
- Reach international agreement on such issues as the use of dangerous chemicals.

Biotechnology

The Food and Agriculture Organisation, a United Nations Agency concerned with the development of all aspects of agriculture and food production, has argued that there are controversial areas such as the use of genetically modified crops and transgenic experiments involving the cloning and organ transfer of animals. But in other areas such as vaccination, the development of high-yield, salt-water-resistant and disease-resistant crops and breeding programmes, biotechnology has already produced significant benefits.

Genetic modification (usually referred to as GM)

Genes control the traits that are passed from generation to generation, for example, the colour of a flower's petals or a child's eyes. A plant can have up to 50,000 genes.

In many cases, scientists can now identify the individual gene that governs a desired trait, extract it, copy it and insert the copy into another organism. That organism (and its offspring) will then have that trait. This process is known as *genetic modification* and enables desirable traits to be transferred between different species of micro-organisms, plants or animals which normally could not breed with each other.

DID YOU KNOW?

Approximately 850 million people worldwide are malnourished. Children are the most visible victims of malnutrition. Malnutrition plays a role in at least half of the 10.9 million child deaths each year.

Vitamin A deficiency can cause night blindness and reduces the body's resistance to disease. In children, vitamin A deficiency can also cause growth retardation. Between 100 million and 140 million children are vitamin A deficient. An estimated 250,000 to 500,000 vitamin A-deficient children become blind every year, half of them dying within 12 months of losing their sight.

The world produces enough food to feed everyone. World agriculture produces 17 percent more calories per person today than it did 30 years go, despite a 70 percent population increase. This is enough to provide everyone in the world with at least 2,720 kilocalories (kcal) per person per day. The principal problem is that many people in the world do not have sufficient land to grow, or income to purchase, enough food.

Figure 7.1 Greenpeace activists set up a mock corn-on-the-cob field in front of Berlin's parliament building in 2003 to protest against genetically modified corn

Bio-technology any technological application that uses biological systems, living organisms or derivatives thereof, to make or modify products or processes for specific use. For example, the use of genetic engineering techniques to clone sheep or to produce higher yielding crops through genetic modification

FAO Food and Agriculture Organisation the United Nations Agency which is particularly concerned with the improvement of food production worldwide through the funding of research into crop disease, irrigation systems, and more efficient use of land

Sustainability the idea that agricultural development and practice has to consider the effects of its actions so that the environment is not damaged. It means that cultivation of land, for example, has to avoid soil erosion through over-intensive farming or toxic damage caused by chemicals. It is about long-term food production in harmony with the environment

Although the insertion of new genes into the cells of a crop plant is relatively straightforward, there is an enormous amount of work involved in identifying, isolating and characterising the gene, and years of trials are necessary to develop commercial varieties. Even so, it is much quicker than the traditional method of trial and error.

Genetic modification is a major advance in biotechnology. It is seen by some as offering great benefit to agriculture and food production. Others, however, see it as potentially very dangerous with the possibility of catastrophic consequences. For example, the accidental transference of the herbicide-resistant trait developed in a variety of wheat to a nearby actual weed, could result in a plant that could not be controlled.

Organic farming

An alternative approach is *organic farming* which claims that its methods tend to support and preserve those parts of the environment which intensive farming methods tend to damage. Organic farming emphasises environmental protection, animal welfare and the use of sustainable resources. The amount of land now converted to organic farming in the UK has increased significantly during the last 20 years.

Organic farming is a system which excludes the use of artificial fertiliser and most pesticides and growth regulators. It relies on crop rotation, the use of recycled organic material in the form of animal and green manures and the natural resistance which healthy plants have to predators. A small number of naturally occurring pesticides and simple chemical ones are permitted in some circumstances. The disadvantage of organic farming is that it requires more land to produce a given amount of food than intensive farming does using a full range of fertilisers, etc.

At the present time, 50 per cent of the organic crops consumed in the UK are home grown.

Those in favour of organic farming argue that it does the least harm to the environment, enhances animal welfare and produces healthier more natural tasting products. However, current research has not yet shown any significant difference in terms of nutritional value or food safety.

Sustainability

One crucial issue facing world agriculture is the problem of producing food in such a way that non-renewable natural resources are not depleted beyond recovery. The irreversible damage to local flora and fauna caused by contamination from powerful chemical fertilisers and pesticides is one example. Deforestation caused by ruthless timber extraction without replanting is another.

Activities

1. 'Many people talk about the poor, very few actually talk to them' (Mother Teresa). Discuss the meaning of this statement with your fellow students. What actions could be taken to avoid this criticism in future?

2. 'Charity begins at home.' What arguments could be used to support or refute this point of view?

3. Research the work of one major charitable organisation and describe in detail one recent project with which it has been involved.

4. Identify one major world problem and organise a committee with the aim of making some practical contribution towards helping some of its victims.

EXAM QUESTIONS

Look carefully at the tables below. Table 1 shows the contribution of agriculture to the regional economy in 2001. Table 2 shows the area of land converted to organic farming from 1995–2000.

Having studied the tables, answer all of the questions which follow.

Table 1 Agriculture's contribution to the regional economy (UK, 2001)

	Total contribution to the area (£ millions)	Agriculture's percentage contribution	Workforce in agriculture (thousands)	Total workforce in employment (thousands)
United Kingdom	6535	0.8	556	27,662
England	4860	0.7	372	24,488
Wales	362	1.1	56	1076
Scotland	848	1.2	70	1367
Northern Ireland	465	2.6	58	731
English Regions				
North East	140	0.5	12	1076
North West	430	0.5	40	3171
Yorkshire and Humberside	687	1.1	40	2300
East Midlands	675	1.2	43	1921
West Midlands	565	0.8	46	2555
East of England	979	1.1	54	2518
South East and London	632	0.2	57	8583
South West	753	1.2	80	2364

Source: adapted from MAFF (Ministry of Agriculture, Food and Fisheries)

Table 2 Area of land converted to organic farming (thousand hectares)

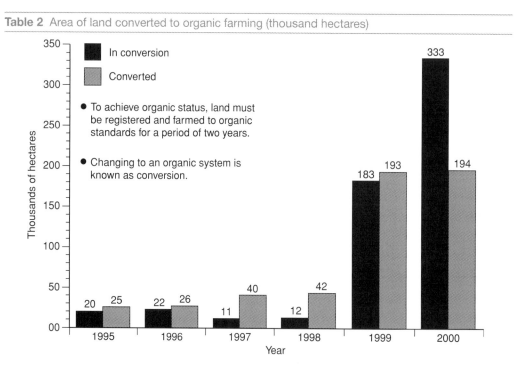

Source: MAFF (Ministry of Agriculture, Food and Fisheries), 2001

(a) (i) Using Table 1 calculate the percentage of the UK workforce employed in agriculture.

(2 marks)

(ii) Work out the mean of the contribution (£ millions) from the North East, North West, East Midlands and West Midlands.

(2 marks)

(b) Table 1 includes information about the agricultural workforce in the English Regions. Give reasons for the differences.

(4 marks)

(c) Give reasons why the data in Table 2 might be of limited value.

(4 marks)

(d) Using Table 2 and your own knowledge give reasons for the rise in area of land converted to organic farming.

(8 marks)

(e) 'Smaller farms will fail in the present economic climate.' How far is this a valid assertion?

(10 marks)

Total: 30 marks

AQA B May 2004

EXAMINER'S ADVICE

- This set of questions is from AS Unit 3 set in May 2004 and is the second of two exercises in data analysis. From 2005 onwards there will be one exercise and one set of questions only, to complete for a total of 60 marks. The questions here, however, are typical of those in the new test, except that they do not require you to construct a graph. See page 1 for more details about this paper. There are other examples of questions from this paper at the end of Units 10, 13 and 26.

- The first two questions require calculations. If you have any doubts about how to do these, consult pages 93 and 96 in Unit 13 on Mathematical applications. Always show your working, as one mark is given for this if you have used the right process but made a mistake in the final figure.

- For Question (b) you need to study the different rows and columns in Table 1 in relation to each other. Look at the proportions and totals and, using a combination of deduction and your knowledge, make comparisons between the different regions of the UK and their farming populations.

- In Question (c) you have to consider the limitations in the information contained in Table 2. How much does it actually tell you about the growth of organic farming in relation to farming as a whole? What more do you need to know before you can get a genuinely useful picture?

- Questions (d) and (e) are worth eight and ten marks respectively (60 per cent of the total) and require more extended responses and some of your own knowledge about the growing demand for organic food and issues of farm size, economies of scale in production, the quality and marketing of produce and so on.

- You should allow approximately 45 minutes to complete these questions. Make sure you leave enough time to do justice to the last two. When you have finished, turn to page 250 for the answer notes.

Human and animal behaviour

Psychology is the science of the mind. The human mind is the most complex machine on Earth. It is the source of all thought and behaviour. Even if we were to split open the skull of a willing volunteer and have a look inside, we would only see the gloopy grey matter of the brain. We cannot see someone thinking. Nor can we observe their emotions, or memories, or perceptions and dreams.

So how do psychologists go about studying the mind? In fact, psychologists adopt a similar approach to scientists in other fields. Nuclear physicists interested in the structure of atoms cannot observe protons, electrons and neutrons directly. Instead, they predict how these elements should behave and devise experiments to confirm or refute their expectations.

Although we cannot observe the mind directly, everything we do, think, feel and say is determined by the functioning of the mind. So psychologists take human behaviour as the raw data for testing their theories about how the mind works. Since the German psychologist Wilhelm Wundt (1832–1920) opened the first experimental psychology lab in Leipzig in 1879, we have learned an enormous amount about the relationship between brain, mind and behaviour.

Psychology and other disciplines

Psychology lies at the intersection of many other different disciplines, including biology, medicine, linguistics, philosophy, anthropology, sociology, and artificial intelligence (AI). For example, *neuropsychology* is allied with biology, since the aim is to map different areas of the brain and explain how each underpins different brain functions like memory or language. Other branches of psychology are more closely connected with medicine. *Health psychologists* help people manage disease and pain. Similarly, *clinical psychologists* help alleviate the suffering caused by mental disorders.

A good example of the link between psychology and other disciplines is the notion of freedom. You can discuss this from the political, sociological, physiological, etc. points of view and they are all equally valid. Any attempt to explain why humans think and behave in the way that they do will inevitably be linked to one or another branch of psychology. These include *behavioural psychology*, *cognitive psychology*, *social psychology*, *biological psychology* and *psychodynamic psychology*.

What all these different approaches to psychology have in common is a desire to explain the behaviour of individuals based on the workings of the mind. And in every area, psychologists apply scientific methodology. They formulate theories, test hypotheses through observation and experiment, and analyse the findings with statistical techniques that help them identify important findings.

The psychology of memory

Why do we have different ways of remembering things? Memory underpins every thought we have and everything we have learned, from how we walk and talk, through to recognising our favourite movie stars in a magazine.

Memory is at the heart of cognitive psychology, the branch of psychology that deals with mental processes and their effects on human behaviour. Most of us take memory for granted until the point when it fails and we forget something.

Psychologists talk about different kinds of memory: *sensory memory, working memory* and *long-term memory*. When we have to remember a new phone number without the help of pen and paper, we are using our working memory. When it comes to words, we can only keep fresh as many words as we can say in about two minutes. People who speak very quickly tend to have a high working memory capacity because they can pack more words into those two minutes than slow talkers.

Even information in working memory will fade unless it is transferred to the permanent store known as long-term memory. But once it is there, we cannot always get it out. We have all had trouble recalling someone's name or the answer to an easy quiz question.

Psychologists have found that new memories can interfere with old ones, making us believe that something happened when it never actually did. This finding is of great importance in criminal prosecutions, when witnesses try to recall events of critical importance. It also has implications for cases of recovered memories, where adults who previously thought they had had a normal childhood begin to recall traumatic events such as sexual abuse.

Developmental psychology

Researchers in developmental psychology are interested in processes of change. They want to know how babies learn and grow to become mature adults with a sophisticated knowledge of the world. Newborn infants appear to be the most helpless of all mammalian offspring, but it has been discovered that they come into the world already equipped with abilities that provide the springboard for future growth. Babies do maths: adding and subtracting. For example, even four-month-old babies seem capable of rudimentary counting. Of course, they cannot count out loud, because infants do not speak their first words until they are about one year old. But psychologists can gain an insight into what babies know by presenting them with impossible events, a bit like magic tricks or illusions. If babies show surprise, we can be fairly sure that their expectations have been violated. And their expectations are based on what they know about the world.

The psychology of animal behaviour

In the past century, animal behaviourists have discovered a great deal about what makes animals behave in the way that they do.

Animals carry out behaviours in response to situations that they come across in their environment. There are all sorts of ways in which an animal can organise a response when faced with a particular situation. Some require no 'thought' at all, while others are extremely complex and only open to a few species.

Reaction to stimuli

The simplest behaviour is one in which a single factor, known as a stimulus, is perceived in some way (seen or heard or smelt or tasted or felt) and an automatic behaviour is triggered in response.

Hard-wiring

There are a whole host of reactions like this, and they are called innate or hard-wired behaviours. The circuits are laid down before birth, and cannot be controlled in any conscious way. Some animal behaviours that appear to require a lot of thought are actually innate behaviours. For example, Egyptian vultures use stones to break open eggs. At first glance this looks like an example of an animal that has learnt to use a tool – one of the cleverest things that animals do. But vulture chicks hatched in isolation do the same behaviour from a young age – the behaviour is innate. When Egyptian vultures see an egg, they respond automatically by throwing stones at it, and there's no 'thought' involved.

Habituation-poking and sea slugs

A slightly cleverer version of this hard-wired system is one in which the response can be switched off if there's no advantage in doing it. This is called habituation, and it was first demonstrated in the simple sea slug.

Sea slugs have floppy, vulnerable gills that they retract with the slightest touch. But if they are poked repeatedly, and nothing bad happens, they switch off the retraction behaviour because it's a waste of energy.

Learning and Pavlov's dogs

A breakthrough happened when our understanding of memory evolved. In essence, memory is the ability of a nervous system to grow new connections. This means that an individual animal could learn from their experiences by adjusting or adding to its hard-wiring.

The simplest learning is when animals swap one stimulus for another. A Russian researcher, Ivan Pavlov, did a famous experiment with a dog in which the dog came to associate the ringing of a bell with the arrival of food. In the end, the sound of the bell alone was enough to bring about a behavioural response – the dog began drooling. Though Pavlov didn't know it at the time, he had encouraged new connections to grow in the dog's brain that linked perception of the bell with the production of saliva.

It sounds hideous, but this sort of learning happens all the time in the wild. It makes sense for an animal to be able to learn new cues within the environment that tend to lead to food.

Figure 8.1 Pavlov and his staff demonstrating their behavioural response work

Trial and error learning

This involves trying out different patterns of behaviour until a successful one, i.e. one that brings a reward, is discovered and adopted. This process lies at the heart of all animal training. The animal learns to behave in a way that will win it a reward. It looks like 'thinking', but really it's just learning to respond in a suitable way. There's a popular technique called *clicker training* in which the animal performs trained behaviours in order to hear the sound of a 'click'. These animals have been previously trained to associate the click sound with a reward, just as Pavlov's dog thought that the bell meant food, so they'll do anything for a 'click'.

Problem-solving

This is a step up from trial and error learning. Here, when faced with a situation, an animal tries out various responses that it's done before in its head. This involves firing off various nerve cell networks in the brain without doing the behaviour itself, and using a sophisticated brain 'tool-kit' to predict the outcomes of their actions. Running these 'what-ifs' is extremely clever and relies on a detailed understanding of the real world.

It is argued that animals of several species are capable of solving a range of problems that involve abstract reasoning. In 1914, Wilhelm Kohler carried out some experiments with nine chimpanzees. Their pen contained a variety of objects, including boxes, poles, and sticks, with which the primates could experiment. Kohler constructed a variety of problems for the chimps, each of which involved obtaining food that was not directly accessible. In the simplest task, food was put on the other side of a barrier. Dogs and cats in previous experiments had faced the barrier in order to reach the food, rather than moving away from the goal to circumvent the barrier. The chimps, however, presented with an apparently analogous situation, set off immediately on the circuitous route to the food. Kohler concluded that chimpanzees were capable not only of problem solving with training, but also of *insight* – grasping the solution to a new problem without help.

Insight

To use insight an animal must be in a situation it has never encountered before and be able to try out responses they've never done before in their heads before coming up with the solution. In this way, they've solved a problem without referring to any of their memories. It's a sort 'penny drops' type of thinking. Using a lifetime of memories, the animal can draw upon the results of the behaviours it has used before.

Behaviourism

Burrhus Frederic Skinner (1904–90) was an American psychologist and author. He conducted pioneering work on experimental psychology and advocated behaviourism, which seeks to understand behaviour entirely in terms of physiological responses to external stimuli. He also wrote a number of controversial works in which he proposed the widespread use of psychological behaviour modification techniques (primarily operant conditioning) in order to improve society and increase human happiness.

His research suggested that punishment was an ineffective way of controlling behaviour, leading generally to short-term behaviour change, but resulting mostly in the subject attempting to avoid the punishing stimulus instead of avoiding the stimulus that brought about being punished. A simple example of this is the failure of prison to eliminate criminal behaviour. If prison (as a punishing stimulus) were effective at altering behaviour, there would be no criminality, since the risk of imprisonment for criminal conduct is well established. However, individuals still commit offences, but attempt to avoid discovery and therefore punishment. The punishing stimulus does not stop criminal behaviour. The criminal simply becomes more sophisticated at avoiding the punishment.

Biological psychology

This works on the principle that, ultimately, human behaviour depends on physiological activity, i.e. what the body does.

Neurophysiology is a branch of biological psychology which is particularly concerned with the role of the brain in behaviour, thinking and feeling. It investigates such activities as sleeping and dreaming and it would assume that any unusual characteristics in these functions are caused by chemical changes in the brain.

Sleep

For many years, sleep researchers have known as absolute fact that sleep loss is associated with progressive impairment of alertness. On the other hand, we have had to say that we do not know the vital biological function or functions of sleep.

Sleep homeostasis

When we need continually to maintain a constant level or flow of something in our bodies, it is called *homeostatic*. An example of such a process is the regulation of body temperature to maintain it close to 98.6 degrees Fahrenheit. When our prior nocturnal sleep time has been reduced, our tendency to fall asleep the next day increases, and we tend to sleep more deeply the next night. When we obtain substantial 'extra' sleep, we are less likely to fall asleep or become drowsy on the next day, and we may not sleep as deeply the next night. The obvious purpose of this homeostatic process is to ensure that each of us will obtain a certain amount of sleep as a daily average.

Sleep need

Each of us needs a certain amount of sleep which, if obtained on a daily basis, will maintain our homeostatic equilibrium. When we have lost a great deal of sleep and are feeling very sleepy and extremely miserable, it may seem that we would become extremely ill and even die if the sleep deprivation continued. In addition, the homeostatic regulation of a process ensures that a vital function is strongly protected, for example, fluid intake and food intake. We are not absolutely certain that sleep is vitally necessary, but the intense desire to sleep after only a night or two without sleep, points in that direction.

Long-term sleep deprivation studies have been carried out mainly in human beings and rodents, primarily laboratory rats. In the case of rats, total sleep deprivation is fatal in 16–20 days without exception. At this point, the direct cause of death in the rodents appears to be huge numbers of live bacteria in the blood stream and body tissues.

The function of sleep

The question of whether sleep is vitally necessary for humans would be relatively easy to answer if there were an easy, non-stressful method to maintain very prolonged wakefulness. However, the increasing strength of the sleep drive and the increasing difficulty of preventing sleep make prolonged sleep-deprivation studies in humans very difficult. After a few days without sleep, methods that are considered dangerous and unethical would be required.

So, what does sleep do for us? It might not be vitally necessary, but sleep is certainly helpful to human existence. Human beings evolved as a day active species and are highly dependent upon vision to interact with their environment and are pitifully helpless in the dark. Accordingly, one huge advantage of the homeostatic drive to sleep is to force the human species to seek a safe place in which to sleep during the nocturnal hours. Not only are human beings drawn towards day activity by their highly developed visual senses, but also the timing mechanisms of the circadian system have evolved such that the biological clock promotes wakefulness and activity during the daylight hours. Another huge adaptive advantage of sleeping every night is the substantial reduction in energy expenditure. If human beings were fully active 24 hours a day, they would need many more calories and their food requirement would be perhaps 50 per cent higher, creating a vulnerability to food shortages.

Behaviourism approach to psychology which emphasises scientific method, is primarily concerned with observable human behaviour rather than internal emotion, and which believes that virtually all human behaviour is learnt through either positive or negative experiences referred to as 'conditioning'

Dreams seem to be a way for the subconscious mind to sort out and process all the input and problems that are encountered in waking life. According to Freud, dreams are the result of subconscious thoughts and desires. Other psychologists consider dreams to be random 'noise' in the neurons without special meaning

MRI (Magnetic Resonance Imaging) process which produces a detailed image of sections of the brain. This can be used by neuropsychologists to establish whether a particular illness is caused by some physical damage to the brain itself

Psychodynamism type of psychology which argues that our present feelings and behaviour are heavily influenced by previous events, particularly unpleasant ones. Many of these pressures are deeply rooted in our subconscious so that we are completely unaware of them. Sigmund Freud (1856–1939) is most famously associated with this approach

Psychology the science of mind and behaviour

Sublimation according to Freud, this is the transformation of unwanted impulses into something less harmful – a defence mechanism. For example, many sports and games are sublimations of aggressive urges

Territorial instinct a defensive response which occurs when one animal invades the space of another of the same species (including humans), e.g. sticklebacks turn red and puff out their chest

There have been several reports of studies of individuals who appeared to need very small amounts of sleep, as little as one hour in some cases. It is not clear, however, if these individuals were fully alert in the daytime. Presumably they were normally alert, but tests to demonstrate this were not undertaken.

The restorative function of sleep

Some evolutionary psychologists have argued that sleep is necessary to fully restore some physiological functions. Certain vital chemicals essential for cell growth, the production of hormones and neuro-transmitting cells vital for internal brain communications can only develop during sleep.

Aggression

Aggression is the intentional harming of another who is trying to avoid the harm. The study of aggression is considered an important one in psychology as it deals with a major social problem. In 1980, one out of every 180 Americans was a victim of a violent crime – murder, robbery, rape or assault. Furthermore, while the incidence of some crimes has dropped in recent years, violent crime hasn't by the same amount. In the USA, the number of murders doubled over the ten years from 1970–80, but has declined slowly over the 20 years from 1980–2000.

What are the origins of aggression?

Ethological approach – Konrad Lorenz

This approach suggests that humans are the most dangerous of animals, not only in terms of danger to other species but also to their own species. This is because we have not evolved any mechanisms that inhibit intra-species aggression. Other animals have lengthy rituals during fights – baring teeth, making loud noises, and adopting aggressive postures – and often these alone will prevent a fight with one animal backing off. If a fight starts then a submissive posture will often signal the end of the fight and the stronger animal will let the loser live. There is also lots of ritualised fighting where animals go through the motions but avoid any serious injury, this is good for the survival of the species.

Humans, however, are relatively weak and harmless when it comes to fighting. We have no fangs, claws, venom, etc. with which to kill an opponent. As a result, we have not developed ritualised aggression inhibiting mechanisms to ensure the survival of the species. However, our superior intelligence has led us to be able to overcome our weakness. An old weak lion with bad teeth can not kill a healthy strong rival, but an old weak man can kill a strong fit young man – all he needs is gun. For this reason, man is considered a very dangerous animal.

Furthermore, it is suggested that humanity's social evolution has led to a situation where an individual's aggression builds up and is not released through everyday activity. We no longer have to hunt for food, etc. and so have to expend very little energy just staying alive, warm and dry. In addition, Lorenz suggests that there are far more things in society to be unhappy about, and that we have far more time to think about them. This means that we build up aggression that can be released in physical activity – physical activity that we are not undertaking. This is the theory of catharsis, and it suggests that if people undergo physical activity they can reduce their levels of aggression and therefore reduce the likelihood of aggressing toward others. However, the research in this area has produced mixed findings.

Why do people aggress?

Frustration always leads to aggression. Aggression is always a product of frustration. This hypothesis assumes that the relationship between these two is basically a result of innate predispositions, and that aggression will follow more or less automatically from feelings of frustration. It is proposed that frustration is anything that blocks your goals, or interferes with goal-orientated behaviours.

Survival of the species

It was not until the 1930s that a serious attempt to conduct research on animal behaviour from evolutionary and selectionist perspectives was begun. Konrad Lorenz (1903–89) grew up on his family's estate near Vienna with dogs, cats, chickens, ducks, and geese. In this setting, his observations of animal behaviour led to the founding of the field of *ethology,* defined as 'the comparative study of behaviour', which applies to the behaviour of animals and humans all those questions asked and methodologies used as a matter of course in all other branches of biology since Charles Darwin's time.

By extending Darwin's theory of natural selection to behaviour, Lorenz posited a genetic basis for specific behaviours that was subject to the same principles of cumulative blind variation and selection that underlie the adapted complexity of biological structures. In the case of the greylag goose, goslings that maintained close contact with the first large moving object they saw (usually the mother goose) would be in a better position to enjoy her protection and nurture. Consequently, they would be more likely to survive and to have offspring that would similarly show behavioural imprinting. Those goslings that lacked this behavioural characteristic would be less likely to survive to maturity and reproduce. In much the same way that we understand how a tree frog can become so well-camouflaged over evolutionary time through the elimination by predators of those individuals who are less well-camouflaged, we can also understand how instinctive behaviour can be shaped through the elimination of individuals whose behaviours are less fit to their environment.

Activities

1. Investigate the views of B. F. Skinner, the behavioural psychologist. Explain why you think he called one of his books *Beyond Freedom and Dignity.* Why do some people regard his views as rather sinister?

2. In small groups, make a list of significant positive and negative experiences which you may have had. Keeping the views of Sigmund Freud in mind, discuss how far you think that those experiences may have affected your current behaviour, feelings and attitudes?

3. Should employers be allowed to give prospective employers sophisticated psychological tests? Are these a useful tool or an invasion of privacy? Discuss.

Now show us a man who can run 100m in 6 seconds!

Since performances first began to be chronicled by the International Amateur Athletics Federation in 1913, men's and women's bests have continued to rise, but in recent times the curve has flattened considerably. Most experts expect it to flatten still more as advances in nutrition, equipment and training go no further.

'I think all of the statistical analysis and the science points towards improvements in world records getting smaller and smaller', says Dr Joe Doust, Head of the School of Sport and Exercise and Leisure at Roehampton University of Surrey. Indeed so small will improvements in events such as the 100 metres become, Doust believes, that we may be forced in future to measure performances in thousandths of seconds, rather than hundredths.

Dr Robert Schultz, a statistician at the University of British Columbia, goes even further. He has extrapolated last century's world and Olympic records in order to predict the ultimate 'ceiling' in different events. He

suggests that a time of 9.51 seconds will never be bettered in the 100 metres (Maurice Greene's current record stands at 9.79 seconds), nobody will be able to beat 33.97 seconds in the 400 metres (almost 10 seconds faster than Michael Johnson's current record), and a marathon will never be run in under two hours and 43 seconds (five minutes faster than Khalid Khannouchi's current world best).

'People said years ago that records had been set that would never be broken and they've been made to look absurd', says Ron Maughan, Professor of Human Physiology at Aberdeen University medical school. 'It's very difficult to envisage a situation where somebody runs 100 metres in three seconds, but are you brave enough to say the limit's nine point five? Nine point four? Nine? I'm not. It's probably going to take a long time, but it's not inconceivable.'

According to Maughan, in other words, there will always be room for improvement, especially when the number of people around the world who

take part in organised sport is such a small fraction of the total population. 'Somewhere in Ethiopia or Morocco or China or Siberia there's a guy who can break the world record in every event', he says. 'It just so happens that either he or she is not interested in sport or they don't have the facilities or they have to struggle to survive and don't have the opportunity. But when we increase the opportunity, we attract more people at the extremes of the gene pool. So I think we will see records continuing to be broken.'

Peter Radford, Professor of Sports Science at Brunel University, agrees that as sport's net is cast ever wider, potential record-breakers will inevitably be discovered. 'In the early days you were looking at an elite few countries that had an economic status to allow people time off from work, upper-middle-class people by and large, basically Europeans, who were setting what they called world records, but without the rest of the world', he says. 'Now we've got very many more populations

taking part who have unusual and peculiar talents. Over the years the performances will keep on increasing as we draw more diverse groups in.'

Radford also believes that the great improvements in performances seen since records first began at the beginning of the last century paint a false picture and that there has really been a very slow increase in performance over a very long period of time. Hc says there is evidence that highly paid professional athletes in the eighteenth century were running 20 and 30 mile races in times equivalent to a two hour, ten minute marathon.

'This is the age before the internal combustion engine, before electricity, when men and women led very physical lives, so why should we believe they were wimps?' he says. 'What happened was that when the amateur athletic age came, middle-class young men at Oxford and Cambridge treated sport as an afternoon's diversion and their performances were abysmal. We tend to see these huge improvements from that.'

Source: Tim Hulse, Independent on Sunday, *1 October 2000*

The passage is an extract from an article in which the point is made that three *Olympic* records were broken in Sydney in 2000, but no *world* records were broken. Read the passage then complete the task below.

Imagine a debate whose motion is:

Sport ought not to be about breaking records.

Using the source and your own ideas, write a speech in which **either** you defend this motion **or** you oppose it.

(40 marks)

AQA B January 2002

EXAMINER'S ADVICE

- This question is from AS Unit 2 set in January 2002 and is the first of two extended pieces of writing you have to do in this test. Here you have to write a speech, using the article as a source and a basic prompt for ideas. In other Unit 2 tests for this question you might be asked to produce a report, a newspaper article, a dialogue or another type of writing generally different from an essay. The second question on this paper is a more conventional essay. See page 41 for an example of the latter and check out page 1 for an overview of the test as a whole.

- You either have to defend the motion or oppose it, as if you were taking part in a debate. You should try to imagine yourself standing up in front of an audience and delivering your ideas orally. The ideas you employ will be those you would use in an essay, but speeches tend to be more personal and use perhaps more lively and colloquial language. You can capture a flavour of this through the beginning and end. Remember that you are trying to persuade the audience to your point of view and think about how you would actually say the words. Perhaps use some rhetorical questions to address points directly to them.

- Obviously there are some ideas and information you can use from the source, but you will also gain good marks for introducing ideas and debating points of your own. If you opt to defend the motion you need to consider the wider value and benefits of sport for all. Not all sports or sporting competitions lend themselves to records anyway. Think also about including some of the negative aspects of record-breaking in sport, for example drugs and other forms of cheating. If you are opposing the motion, you should concentrate on the achievement aspects of sport. Records don't have to be *world* records – they can be personal to an individual to help them improve, for example.

- There are 40 marks for this part of the test. Once you have read the article and sorted out your main points in a plan, you should write out your answer in no more than 30 minutes. See page 251 for some possible arguments from the mark scheme.

Medical developments

The application of scientific method and technology to the problems of the human body has led to enormous advances in the capacity of medicine to deal with life-threatening diseases, both in terms of prevention and cure. Many once fatal or dangerous conditions can now be treated successfully. Diseases such as smallpox have been eradicated in most of the world. Tuberculosis and diphtheria, for example, no longer kill enormous numbers of people, particularly children, in many developed countries. National health systems, which utilise *vaccination programmes*, have led to continuing improvements in public health so that diseases such as rickets, measles, poliomyletis and whooping cough no longer represent the same threat to the quality of life or to life itself. Other important medical advances, often interrelated, have been made in such areas as

- genetics
- embryo and reproductive technology
- immunology
- neurology and scanning techniques
- surgery and transplants, including cosmetic surgery
- life extension
- obesity.

Genetics (see Unit 6 'Genetic engineering')

Arguably, genetic research was the most spectacular and far-reaching area of medical development in the twentieth century. Genetic screening, which examines human beings for malfunctioning or defective genes, could soon be as commonplace as blood tests and could become linked to procedures that can replace or repair genetic damage. The successful completion of the *Human Genome Project*, which was set up to map all the genes in the human body, has not only enabled the identification of differences in genetic make-up in different ethnic populations, but will also help to identify possible causes of various diseases and conditions. *Germ-line gene therapy* will enable genetic changes to be made to those cells that transmit information from one generation to another, thus enabling permanent changes to be made. Diseases already identified as having genetic components include asthma, leukaemia, sickle-cell anaemia, Huntington's disease, diabetes and cancer.

Developments in genetic technology have also led to the possibility of *cloning*. (See also Unit 35 'Ethical issues'.) This involves the exact duplication of one human being's genetic code in order to reproduce an identical person. In 1998, the Human Genetics Advisory Committee argued that cloning in order to produce 'spare parts' such as kidneys or livers should be allowed but that the cloning of complete human beings should be banned. One of the advantages of cloning human tissues is that they would not be rejected by the human being from whom they were originally cloned.

Embryo and reproductive technology

Medical advances in this area now mean that infertility no longer automatically leads to childlessness. There are now 13 different ways to have a baby other than through sexual intercourse, including:

- *In vitro fertilisation.* This was first developed in the 1960s by the British gynaecologist Patrick Steptoe and involves the removal of an egg from a woman's womb, which is then fertilised by the husband's sperm in a test tube or culture dish. The process has partly depended on the ability to remove eggs successfully from the womb, to store them at freezing temperatures and to re-implant them.
- *Surrogacy.* Infertile couples now have the possibility of genetically related children through surrogacy. This involves the implantation of an embryo into the womb of a woman who is not genetically related but who will carry the embryo until the child is born and then return it to the real parents. Embryos can also be created in the test tube for research purposes but may only be used for up to 14 days after fertilisation.
- *Fertility drugs.* These have been developed as an aid to overcoming infertility and to increase the chance of a woman conceiving. They often involve '*superovulation*', which results in the production of more ripe eggs than would normally be produced. This can lead to the problem of multiple births, which may damage rather than enhance the possibility of survival of embryos.

Immunology

Immunology is 'the study of resistance to disease in humans and animals'. Great developments took place in this field in the second half of the twentieth century, particularly after the discovery that the body's immune system is based on the activities of various types of white blood cells, found in blood, lymph vessels and tissue fluids. The main centres of activity are the *thymus, spleen* and *lymph nodes*. An immune response is triggered when the body detects the presence of a foreign body. By 1900, medical technology had already identified serum defence and developed vaccinations and antitoxins against such killer diseases as cholera, rabies, bubonic plague and typhoid. Important work on blood cells was done by *Karl Landsteiner* (1868–1943), whose experiments led to the possibility of blood transfusions. Further immunological research has led to a greater understanding of why transplanted organs are rejected by the host body and this has saved thousands of lives. In the 1970s, *molecular biology, cell biology* and *immunochemistry* have shared spectacular interconnected results, in particular, a greater understanding of the way cancers and human immuno-deficiency (HIV) develop, although there are as yet, no certain cures.

Figure 9.1 AIDS viruses on the surface of a T-lymphocyte cell

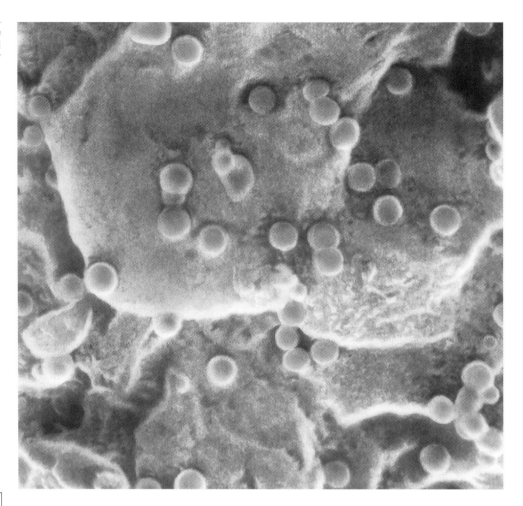

Neurology and scanning techniques

Following on the work of several seminal researchers in the late nineteenth century, particularly in relation to the minute electrical charges produced by certain functions of the brain, scanning techniques have been developed that have helped us to understand how the brain works. Specific 'brain waves', produced by impulses emanating from the cerebral cortex and reflecting states of consciousness, external stimuli and 'mental' operations, can be used to diagnose malfunctions such as epilepsy. Further work on these brain waves has helped with the diagnosis of psychiatric disorders, migraine and blood pressure, as well as contributing to sleep research. Recent developments in scanning technology have helped scientists to build up a far more accurate picture of the central nervous system and the damage done to it by strokes or Alzheimer's disease. Neuroscientists such as the Nobel prize-winning *Gerald Edelman* have developed sophisticated maps to show how flexible and adaptable the brain actually is. To a certain extent, some parts of the brain can take over functions damaged elsewhere. This research has also led to a greatly increased ability to diagnose and cure a wide range of psychiatric and personality problems.

SCIENCE AND TECHNOLOGY

Surgery and transplants

Advances in surgery have been driven partly by the need to treat dreadful wounds received during wartime. Up until the Second World War, many surgeons believed that a wide range of medical conditions could be cured by the 'knife', including tumours, tuberculosis, throat cancer, hernias, etc. However, it took a long time before many of these operations developed a high success rate, based on improved sterilisation and increased understanding of how internal organs and cell growth actually work. Enormous strides have been made in heart surgery. In 1931, Werner Fossman, injected a radio-opaque substance via a catheter into his heart, thereby allowing the first heart X-ray to take place. This was followed by the technique of forcing a tiny balloon through a constricted artery in order to clear it and allowing the heart to function properly. By 1939, surgeons were able to suture and repair damage to the walls of the heart without a strong risk of infection. The development of the heart-lung machine, which takes over the functions of these organs, has led to the replacement of blocked arteries leading to the heart and the use of artificial valves and pacemakers.

Transplants

In modern times, the emphasis in surgery has changed from *excision* – cutting and removal – to *replacement* and *plastic surgery*. This can include:

- cosmetic surgery
- removal of skin tumours, cleft palates and cleft lips
- skin grafts to repair burn damage and scars – these techniques were significantly improved by *Archibald McIndoe*, who developed reconstructive and plastic surgery in response to the horrific burns suffered by young Air Force pilots in the Second World War.

Organ transplants involving the replacement of lungs, liver or spleen and particularly kidneys have drastically increased success rates because of:

- a greater understanding of how immune reactions work
- the recognition that the tissue types of the organ being transplanted have to be matched exactly with those of the recipient
- the development of immunosuppressive drugs such as cortisone and cyclosporine.

Life extension: science fact or science fiction?

Recent discoveries in genetics have lead to an increased interest in *gerontology* – the science of aging. Some scientists have argued for the existence of genes which are responsible for how long we live. Theoretically, it may be possible to manipulate these genes so that human life could be extended to a lifespan of 150 years.

Scientists studying certain worms and fruit flies have found several genes that seem to control how long these creatures live. By making a change in just one of these genes, they have almost doubled the average lifespan of both fruit flies and one type of worm. Others looking at longevity have shown that one particular gene, already

KEY TERMS

Acquired immuno-deficiency syndrome (AIDS) a usually fatal breakdown in the body's immune system caused by a virus which destroys white blood cells

Angioplasty a surgical technique that clears a blocked artery by inserting a tiny balloon in order to clear away obstructions

Antibodies protein molecules produced to combat microbial infection and provide immunity

Electrocardiograph a machine that records the minute electrical currents produced by the heart

Immunisation the artificial creation of immunity to disease by vaccination

shown to control how fast yeast cells age, may do the same thing in mice. This gene is also present in humans.

Genes alone, however, are only a part of the reason that some people live a long time. How people live, their lifestyle, may be more important. For example, does someone smoke? Do they exercise? Are they under a lot of stress? What do they eat? Some scientists think what people eat and how much they eat can lead to a longer life. Caloric restriction is one area of research on aging. A calorie-restricted diet has 30 to 40 per cent fewer calories than a normal diet, but it has all the needed nutrients. This diet seems to extend the life of almost every animal type in which it is studied. It has worked in protozoa (very small, one-celled organisms), fruit flies, mice, and rats. However, scientists are not sure why this works.

The chemical approach

Antioxidants are natural substances in foods. It may be possible to strengthen the way in which they help to protect the body from the accumulative effects of stress, smoking, strong sunlight and heart disease, for example. Other scientists have argued, however, that there is no 'magic pill' and no real evidence that any of the chemicals tested really work. Some of the more common dietary supplements include ginkgo biloba, ginseng, saw palmetto, echinacea, and St. John's wort. Although there may be a lot of hype about these supplements, we don't have scientifically proven facts about their effects. However, dietary supplements are widely available. Each year, people spend billions on these vitamins, minerals, herbs, and hormones. They are hoping for more energy, stronger muscles, better memory, protection from disease, and maybe even a longer life.

Conclusion

Many of these recent developments in medicine have saved thousands of lives and made the lives of the chronically ill or disabled far more bearable. However, the technology involved is hugely expensive. National Health Service hospitals with limited resources have to make 'life and death' decisions such as who should have access to a kidney dialysis machine, or whether such scarce resources be 'wasted' on the old. The desperate shortage of organs such as hearts and livers means that difficult decisions have to be made about who should have them. Progress in medicine brings with it complex ethical issues.

EXAM QUESTION

How far do the benefits of medical advances offering life-saving treatments outweigh the drawbacks?

(12 marks)

AQA B January 2002

EXAMINER'S ADVICE

- This question is from AS Unit 1 set in January 2002. From 2005 onwards there will be four short essays like this for you to answer from a choice of six, with each title taken from the five different areas of the specification. Note also that they will be worth 15 marks each, instead of 12. It is absolutely essential to give equal time and attention to each of your four answers, so as not to lose vital marks. See page 1 for more information about this paper. There are other examples of this type of question at the end of Units 18, 23, 28 and 35.

- The question asks you to discuss benefits and drawbacks and the wording 'how far … outweigh' implies a largely positive but balanced consideration of pros and cons and coming to a conclusion. In General Studies you can argue whatever case you want, but you must support it with evidence.

- Research the topic using information from the unit you have just read, and from elsewhere if you wish. You should then write out your answer in no more than 15–20 minutes, which means perhaps a page and a half of normal-sized handwriting and not too much elaboration of points. For 15 marks in this case you might aim for a range of benefits and drawbacks, considering such issues as finding cures and improved treatments through medical research, the cost of treatment, low success rates, 'keeping patients alive', poor future quality of life, and so on.

- When you have written your answer, turn to page 251 for some further possible points.

Transport issues

The history of transport

As transport until the nineteenth century was dependent on the horse, it is sometimes argued that the key event in transport was the domestication of the horse, which occurred sometime around 1500 BCE. However, others would argue that the greatest influence was the invention of boats, enabling goods to be carried along rivers and across seas. The earliest boat discovered so far is a pine canoe dating from around 7000 BCE and found in Holland. Nevertheless, all modern forms of land transport rely on the invention of the wheel which was probably invented between 4000 and 3000 BCE. The wheel enabled carts, chariots and carriages to be built which allowed one horse to carry several people and considerably more goods.

Steam

A huge advance in transport came with the invention of the steam engine. The first steam engine was built by Savery in 1698, followed by Newcomen's 1712 engine – the first proper steam engine using a piston. However, it was not until James Watt introduced a condenser and gears that it became possible to use a steam engine for transport. Several steam locomotives were designed at the beginning of the nineteenth century, and George Stephenson's *Locomotion* hauled the first public passenger railway between Stockton and Darlington in 1825. So began 'the Railway Age', and between 1825 and 1914, railways were built across all countries and continents, revolutionising not only transport, but also the development of suburbs and communications (newspapers and the telegraph).

Cars

The invention of the internal combustion engine (Karl Benz, 1885) and Henry Ford's mass production methods (Model T Ford, 1908) made cars the most popular form of transport. The car puts the individual in charge of their transport. The popularity of the car led to the need for a modern road system. The first motorways were built in Germany before the Second World War (autobahns), and from the beginning of the M1 in 1959, Britain developed an interconnected motorway system completed by the London Orbital Motorway (M25).

Planes

The first flying machine of the Wright Brothers (1903) had little effect on ordinary people's lives. However, after the First World War, the USA used aircraft for mail routes, and after the Second World War, the development of jet airliners (Comet, 1959, Jumbo Jet – Boeing 747 – 1969, Concorde, 1969) made flying faster, more comfortable and cheaper. Travel between continents, which had taken days or weeks on ships, now takes hours.

Space travel

Space travel began when the Russian Yuri Gagarin made an orbit of the Earth in 1957. By 1969, space travel had developed rapidly enough for the Americans

Armstrong, Aldrin and Collins to land *Apollo 11* on the Moon. Although space travel has been mainly used for exploration (for example, of Mars), research (for example, the Hubble Telescope) and satellite communications, it is beginning to be used for tourism as the Russian space centre now sells flights into space.

Science or technology?

There is often argument as to whether the advances in transport have been made by science or technology. Cayley worked out the three basic principles of flight (lift, thrust and control) in 1804, but it was another 100 years before the technology was developed to make aircraft.

Frank Whittle patented his theory of the jet engine in 1930, but it was 1939 before the German firm *Heinkel* built the first jet plane. The whole theory of electricity was discovered before Faraday invented the first electric motor (1821), but it was 1879 before an electric motor big enough to drive a vehicle was invented (Siemens' electric train).

However, the development of the steam engine seems to have been more affected by changes in technology, such as better iron and steel making and the needs of industry. Savery, Newcomen, Watt and Stephenson were all engineers with little knowledge of science. Even so, they must have developed theories, of the power of steam, for example, in order to think of a steam engine.

It appears that science and technology have always been intertwined, with some scientific discoveries requiring developments in technology (for example, particle accelerators to make discoveries in atomic physics) and some developments in technology requiring scientific theories (for example, space travel and the Earth's gravitational pull).

Transport issues

Public or private?

Public transport refers to the types of vehicle which can transport a large number of people with one means of propulsion (railways, buses, trams, ferries, planes for which tickets can be bought) whereas private transport is transport which is owned by an individual for their own use (for example, cars, private jets and yachts).

In the 1980s, the Conservative Government privatised the public transport system. Local bus services, which had been run by councils, were opened to competition with different companies competing with each other on the same routes. Councils were allowed to pay subsidies to private bus firms for routes which were not profitable. British Rail (which had run all rail services) was abolished and RailTrack (a private company) took over the tracks while the services were divided into franchises to compete with each other wherever possible (for example, WAGN and GNER on the London to Peterborough route). A major argument surrounding transport today is whether this privatisation has worked, i.e. should public transport be privately or publicly run?

Arguments in favour of privatisation	Arguments against privatisation
1. Competition is the best way of ensuring efficiency and there can only be competition if there are private transport companies. 2. Since the privatisation of the railways, there has been a great increase in the number of passengers travelling by rail. 3. Theoretically, the financial cost of maintaining and developing the railways has been taken from the government. 4. Competing private bus companies should provide more services, so making buses more attractive to travellers. 5. Private companies will be trying to get more passengers, and be run more efficiently, so they will offer cheaper fares.	1. The countries with the most efficient public transport systems (e.g. Japan and Switzerland) are publicly owned. 2. On railways, dividing ownership of the tracks from ownership of the trains will lead to conflict and inefficiency (e.g. if there is a delay caused by the track, the rail company claims compensation from the track authority). Any competition is going to be artificial unless there are separate tracks. 3. Competition among bus services has almost died out as large companies like Stagecoach have divided up the routes among themselves rather than competing. 4. The government is now paying more in public transport subsidies than it did before privatisation. In 2004, 45 per cent of the costs of the railways were provided by the government.

Cars or buses and trains?

Traffic congestion has been a problem for cities at least since Roman times. In the first century BCE, Julius Caesar banned wheeled traffic from Rome during daylight hours. In several European cities parking restrictions and one-way streets were introduced in the seventeenth century to deal with the congestion. The arrival of railways as a faster means of transport reduced congestion, but the age of the car has led to massive problems.

In the UK there are now around 30 million vehicles on the roads. On occasions the centres of cities experience gridlock (a traffic jam affecting a number of intersecting roads so that nothing can move). A small accident on the busiest motorways sometimes causes traffic queues of up to 25 miles.

Several solutions have been proposed:

- Banning cars from city centres, or charging for access to city centres (this seems to be working in Central London, but requires an expansion of public transport).
- Making petrol and car tax so high that people give up their cars (this also requires a big expansion of cheap public transport, otherwise people will just pay the extra to keep their cars).
- Making bus lanes to give rapid transit for public transport (intersections, however, are a major problem as it is impossible to keep buses and cars separate).
- Forcing freight onto the railways and waterways, as in much of Europe (however, rundown rail and waterway systems means there are insufficient facilities to expand).

SCIENCE AND TECHNOLOGY

- Introducing computerisation from a traffic control centre (automatic vehicle-control system) where a vehicle is checked into a control station, gives its destination and is put into a traffic lane with its spacing to the vehicle ahead controlled by an on-board computer (it is estimated that this could increase traffic flow from the current maximum of 2000 vehicles an hour to at least 10,000 vehicles an hour).
- Encouraging people on to public transport with schemes such as 'park and ride' and 'save as you travel' where the bus or train company allocates a portion of the ticket cost to a savings account for the traveller so that the more public transport is used, the greater the saving.

All of these measures (especially the expansion of public transport) will require a large Government investment (which could be funded by using increased car taxes). The Government published a transport White Paper in 2004 requiring local authorities to produce five-year plans to make it easier to walk or cycle than to drive and to integrate buses and rail in their area. It also set out the ways in which the Government would take a more direct role in the running of the railways.

Air travel arguments

There has been a massive increase in air travel since 1990, partly due to the rise of low-cost airlines like EasyJet and Ryan Air. More than 200 million people take low-cost European flights from the UK every year. Forecasts are for a doubling of air travel by 2015. In 2003, 131 million passengers used UK airports. This could rise to 400 million by 2020, the equivalent of four new Heathrows. However, this is now being contested because:

Figure 10.1 One horsepower will move 150 kg by road, 450 kg by rail and 3600 kg by canal

Astrolabe an instrument that can measure the height of the Sun and stars to aid navigation

Dynamo a device for making electricity by using magnetism

Green tourism tourism which uses the least polluting forms of transport, e.g. trains or boats instead of planes, public transport or bikes rather than cars

Electric telegraph a system of sending messages over long distances by making and breaking electric connections. It was developed on the railways and by 1880, there were trans-oceanic wires allowing immediate contact between countries using Morse code

Horsepower the standard unit of power representing 550 foot–pounds force per second or 746 watts

Integrated transport system a system of transport where everything fits together, e.g. the buses system connects with the trains and trains to different places connect with each other

Science theories of how the universe works, e.g. how a liquid forms a gas

Technology engineering and mechanics, which may involve the application of science, e.g. a gas turbine to make electricity

Transformer a device for increasing the strength of an electric current

- Aircraft cause massive amounts of pollution as kerosene emits more greenhouse gases than petrol. It is estimated that airlines are responsible for 3.5 per cent of man-made pollution.
- Over 300,000 people suffer noise pollution from living near Heathrow.
- Motorists pay taxes on their fuel to pay for the damage they cause, aircraft do not (airlines pay about 18p a litre for fuel, compared with 80–90p a litre by motorists).

Some transport experts believe that short haul flights should be banned as trains are as quick and cause much less pollution. They also believe that there should be no car parks at airports to force passengers to use public transport (much of the congestion on the M4 and M25 is caused by passengers travelling to and from Heathrow and Gatwick).

Pollution and new methods of propulsion

Almost all land and air transport use fossil fuels (mainly oil) which cause pollution and are likely to run out. This has led to the development of new forms of propulsion:

- Car manufacturers have tackled pollution by fitting catalysers, using unleaded petrol, improving fuel consumption and recycling steel, plastic, batteries, etc. Some cars are now made of 75 per cent recycled materials and it is estimated that it would take 50 small cars produced in 2000 to cause the same pollution as one small car produced in 1976. Car manufacturers are aiming to reduce the total tonnage of pollution caused by cars by 75 per cent in the year 2010 compared with 1992.
- Some firms are now producing cars powered by the hydrogen from water. Ford and BP are working together on hydrogen-powered vehicles. Hydrogen is most likely to be the fuel of the future. It holds the possibility of ending the dependency on oil in the long term, and of producing cars with totally green exhausts. A hydrogen-powered car emits nothing but droplets of pure water. Ford is part of a gigantic global research effort into hydrogen cars. But no one will buy such machines until they know they can get the fuel. So BP is building a series of hydrogen filling stations. Ford and BP are responding to a US-government initiative to put hydrogen cars and vans on the road and get people to drive and refuel them in everyday conditions.
- Rolls-Royce is making marine gas turbine engines which are more fuel efficient and emit much less SO_2 and NO_2 than diesel marine engines (SO_2 and NO_2 from ships are linked with acidification of soils and sea and freshwater systems).
- The *Firebird* is a new type of helicopter which uses hydrogen peroxide to produce superheated steam to give the upward thrust using jets on each end of the rotors rather than having a conventional engine.
- The European Space Agency is developing a new type of rocket propulsion known as solar-electric propulsion which converts sunlight into electricity via solar panels and uses it to electrically charge heavy gas atoms which propel the spacecraft at very high velocity. These are also known as ion engines and have successfully lifted the *Artemis* satellite into orbit.

Safety

Death and serious injury from road accidents has gone down from 80,132 in 1985 to 44,255 in 1998, despite an increase in road traffic from 22,152,000 in 1987 to 27,538,000 in 1998.

There are many reasons for this, most of which have come from science and technology:

- The use of cameras, radar and videos has led to a greater adherence to speed limits.
- The building of more roads with carriageways separated by a crash barrier.
- The use of 'soft' signs and lamp-posts and guard rails around objects such as bridge piers.
- Improved car safety features such as seat belts, collapsible steering column, air bags, side impact bars, improved brakes and tyres.
- The breathalyser to reduce 'drink' driving.
- MOT tests for older cars to keep unsafe vehicles off the road.

More improvements to safety could come from onboard computers, which could reduce speeds, warn drivers of approaching hazards, stop drivers from falling asleep, etc.

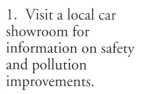

Activities

1. Visit a local car showroom for information on safety and pollution improvements.

2. What scientific methods would you use to test a new fuel that is claimed to be pollution-free?

10

EXAM QUESTIONS

Look carefully at the two tables below. They give information relating to problems which commuters face on a daily basis. Table 1 shows the percentage of trains more than five minutes late, whilst Table 2 shows the percentage of passengers in excess of capacity during the morning and evening rush hours.

Having studied the tables, answer all of the questions which follow.

Table 1 Trains more than five minutes late

Operators serving London area	September 1999 (percentage)	September 1998 (percentage)
Chiltern	6.6	12.8
Connex South Central	9.8	8.5
Connex South East	10.9	6.3
Gatwick Express	13.6	13.6
Great Eastern	6.1	6.7
LTS Rail	8.4	4.3
Silverlink	10.6	11.4
South West Trains	9.8	11.0
Thames Trains	7.9	11.4
Thameslink	11.0	6.0
WAGN	7.4	4.6

Table 2 Passengers in excess of capacity during the morning and evening rush hours

Operators serving London area	Autumn 1998, percentage (passenger totals in brackets)	Autumn 1997, percentage (passenger totals in brackets)
Chiltern	0.5 (12,005)	2.0 (12,693)
Connex South Central	2.9 (122,705)	4.8 (118,575)
Connex South East	1.8 (214,731)	3.0 (214,548)
Great Eastern	2.7 (91,816)	3.3 (91,042)
LTS Rail	0.6 (49,408)	1.4 (44,405)
Silverlink	2.7 (30,812)	1.9 (30,913)
South West Trains	3.9 (137,954)	3.8 (129,218)
Thames Trains	2.6 (18,481)	2.1 (17,312)
Thameslink	7.1 (52,181)	4.4 (48,691)
WAGN	1.2 (84,125)	0.6 (81,269)

Source: all statistics from the Shadow Strategic Rail Authority

SCIENCE AND TECHNOLOGY

(a) (i) Construct and label a bar graph showing the change in percentage of trains more than 5 minutes late from September 1998 to September 1999 for each operator.

(4 marks)

(ii) What conclusions can be drawn from the figures?

(4 marks)

(b) Why might the figures in Table 1 give cause for concern?

(4 marks)

(c) Why might the information in Table 2 be of limited value?

(8 marks)

(d) 'The problems demonstrated in these charts show that we need more roads.' Using the tables below and your own knowledge, how far do you agree with this assertion?

(10 marks)

Total: 30 marks

AQA B January 2001

EXAMINER'S ADVICE

- This set of questions is from AS Unit 3 set in January 2001 and is the first of two exercises in data analysis in this test. From 2005 onwards, the two exercises will be merged into one, but these questions are still typical of those that will be set. See page 1 for more details about this paper. There are other examples of this kind of question at the end of Units 7, 13 and 26.
- The first question here requires a bar graph. Make sure that the bars show the **percentage change** in each case and not just the figures shown. Your graph will also need to allow for positive and negative changes, i.e. improvement or deterioration in the percentage of trains late. If you have any doubts about how to do this task consult page 96 in Unit 13 on Mathematical applications.
- For Question (a)(ii) you should try to identify some trends (or lack of them) in the data and for four marks you should try to come up with four clear and different points.
- Similarly for Question (b) you should aim to make four clear and different points. It might help to

think about broader issues affecting London transport and government transport policy.
- In Question (c) you have to consider the limitations in the information contained in Table 2. This is a common theme in data–response questions. How much does it actually tell you about the trends and issues for London commuters and train operators? What more do you need to know before you can get a genuinely useful picture? You need quite a good range of points for eight marks.
- Question (d) is worth the most marks, so you should spend at least ten minutes on it. It is a broad question and it will help to focus on the particular transport problems of London or any other large city. Is building more roads possible/sensible and would it help? You are free to give your own view.
- You should allow approximately 40 minutes in total to complete these questions. Make sure you leave enough time to do justice to the last two. When you have finished, turn to page 251 for some answer notes.

11 Computers

A computer is an electronic machine that can store and perform calculations and process data at very high speeds. Computers require programmes (a sequence of operations) by which the computer can process the data to produce the intended outcome. For example, if a manufacturer wants a business to be able to input all its billing data so that the computer can output individual bills, the programmer has to work out every step of the process and write each step into a command performable by the computer. Since their invention, computers have revolutionised many aspects of life and now affect everyone.

The history of computers

It is generally accepted that Charles Babbage designed the prototype computer in 1834. It was a machine that could both perform and store the results of calculations. However, it was too complicated to build. Howard Aitkin of Harvard University succeeded in building on Babbage's idea, with a combination of the technology of IBM and Harvard, producing the *Automated Sequence Control Calculator* in 1944. The first electronic digital computer, the *Electronic Numerical Integrator and Calculator*, was built at the University of Pennsylvania in 1946. Although it was progammable and could store problems, it occupied 1500 square feet of floor space and could only process one programme or problem at a time.

It was the invention of the *transistor* (a miniature device to amplify electronic signals) and the *printed electronic circuit* (replacing the copper wires used for carrying the electric current with a small board) that allowed the building of the first computer, the *Manchester Mark I*. The first computer to be sold commercially was the *Ferranti Mark I* in 1951. In 1958, Texas Instruments produced integrated circuits on a silicon chip. The major breakthrough in computing came in 1969 when Hoff of the USA developed the *microprocessor* by placing all the circuits that do the work of a computer onto a single silicon chip. The era from 1970 to 1999 is often referred to as the Microprocessor Revolution, similar in impact to the Industrial Revolution of 1750–1850.

Early computers were huge, but the invention of the microprocessor allowed the development of much smaller computers and the first personal computers (PCs) that could be used in homes. The first PC was the *Altair*, marketed in 1975, which never achieved great success because it came in kit form and had to be assembled at home. The first successful PC was the *Apple II*, which was small enough and cheap enough to be used in small businesses, schools, offices and homes. In 1981, IBM introduced their PC, which was no faster than the Apple, but used the Microsoft Corporation's operating system MS-DOS, which became the industry standard so that any competitors had to market their equipment as 'IBM compatible'.

During the 1980s and 1990s, operating systems and microprocessors developed to give greater speed and memory, but the next big development was the CD-ROM, which allowed computers to use digital sound and video images, so becoming 'multimedia'. However, the most important computer development of the 1990s was the *World Wide Web* (WWW) and the connected *Internet*. The Web was released to the public in 1992 and by 1999 there were millions of users worldwide.

Types of computer

Although most people are likely only to use PCs, there are many different types of computer. The largest are called *supercomputers*, which are mainly used in scientific research, such as the particle laboratory in Geneva, and are designed for shared use. Next are the *mainframe computers*, which are also designed for several users and are often used as a central repository for a mass of data that is accessed through a network by PCs or workstations. Next is the *minicomputer*, which can be used to power a small network, or can be used by scientific researchers – again, it is for multiple use. Slightly less powerful than the minicomputer is the *workstation*, which is used in scientific research, engineering and business. Personal computers come in four types. The largest PCs are not portable and are known as *desktop computers*. Large portable PCs, which fit on your knee, are called *laptops*, whereas book-size ones are called *notebook computers*. The smallest pocket-sized computers are called *palm-sized computers*.

Computer networks are collections of computers (or terminals equipped with microprocessors such as supermarket tills) interconnected by telephone lines or other high speed communication links to exchange data or process information. The network can be a national one (such as those connecting shops with credit card centres), or a local one (known as a LAN – local area network) restricted to an area or an organisation or even to a building. Networks connected by telephone lines require a *modem* (modulator/demodulator) to convert the digital impulses from the computer into the analogue impulses required for telephone lines. Broadband networks either upgrade phone lines or use fibre optic cables for fast data transmission.

Uses of computers

Computers began as an aid to scientific research and to the defence industry, but are now used in every area of business and life. In industry, computers are used for flexible manufacturing systems (FMS) and computer-integrated manufacturing (CIM).

CIM begins with the design of a new product, and this can be done much more efficiently using CAD (computer-aided design) than it could by hand. The designer creates a drawing of the product (as a draughtsman would), then stores the drawing and uses various pieces of software to test the effects of heat, pressure, etc. on the new product. The results of these tests can then be incorporated into the design and detailed drawings drawn by the computer, so that the production team can make a prototype, which has already undergone many tests and adjustments without the time and expense of making products.

After the design, computers are used to formulate the best method of manufacture (computer-aided manufacturing, CAM). If there is a continuous manufacturing process, computers can be used to control the whole process. A computer will measure the important process variables such as temperature, flow rate and pressure. Then it works out the best manufacturing strategy and operates the devices (switches, valves, furnaces, etc.) in the manufacturing process to achieve the strategy. Finally, the computer produces management reports on production performance, product quality, etc. If there is no continuous process, the computer will plan the processes required for the most efficient production of the product.

Computers will then be involved in the business system: ordering raw materials and organising stock control, customer orders, employee payroll, customer service, etc. All this use of the computer is aimed at achieving the optimum product and profit for the company. Most companies use computers to operate a 'just in time' stock control system that saves considerable money on stock holding.

FMS is based on machine tools being linked together by a *material handling system* controlled by a computer. The computer system works out which machine should be doing what and organises the materials for them. This should result in the system being able to operate at maximum performance – whether a machine breaks down, there is a shortfall of supplies or whatever – but it requires the firm to invest in machine tools that can be computer controlled.

Banks are able to use their own networks to reduce the need for cash being moved around the country. The bank computerisation that affects most workers in the country is the BACS system, which enables firms to pay wages into individual workers' accounts without cash being used.

Networking has also made it possible for businesses to encourage their employees to work from home using a PC connected to a network. This saves the company a considerable amount of money in providing the office space for that worker.

The Internet

The Internet is a network connecting many computer networks based on a system called *transmission control protocol/Internet protocol*. It was established in 1983 to enable academics at universities around the world to share research with each other. The original uses of the Internet were electronic mail (e-mail letters sent immediately to another computer anywhere in the world) and newsboards or bulletin boards giving information. However, the development of the World Wide Web in 1989 by Tim Berners-Lee and colleagues at CERN, a European scientific laboratory researching the nature of matter in Geneva, transformed the Internet.

The Web converts documents into hypertext and then stores them so that they can be accessed through a word in the text. It also allows hypermedia documents (documents featuring images, sounds and moving pictures) to be accessed. The Web was made available to the public as part of the Internet in January 1992, and since then many companies have set up *Internet service providers* (ISPs) to allow individuals and businesses to use the Internet and the World Wide Web. The main ones are AOL (America On Line) and Microsoft Network. Obviously, the fees for using the Internet are mainly determined by the company owning the connecting cables. In the UK this is mainly BT, though some cable telephone/television companies are installing Internet cables, for example NTL. Companies like Yahoo and Google provide search engines which act as topic/index locators.

So many Internet businesses have been established, that in 1999 it was possible for a man isolated in a room with access only to the Internet, to be able to obtain all the food, drink, clothes, furniture, etc. he needed simply by clicking his mouse button. Most firms now have a website to advertise their business or to enable orders to be made by e-mail. Many Internet companies have been established to provide special Internet services. For example, it emerged in January 2000 that there is an Internet company that will provide addresses of people who have ex-directory telephone numbers (some unknown person used this service to discover Jill Dando's address). The Internet also allows small companies to advertise worldwide for a very small cost – some such companies, such as specialist cheese manufacturers, are finding their sales rocketing.

Many Internet companies have been established to provide special Internet services such as chat lines, research and entertainment. Interactive multi-media sites mean that films, computer games, television, music and radio can be accessed by an individual at a PC. MP3 enables Internet users to download music from the Internet onto MP3 players (the iPod being the most popular brand of these). This is revolutionising the media industry (it is thought to be the reason behind the merger between AOL and Time Warner, in January 2000, which created the world's largest company). AOL's Internet connections can now use all the films, cartoons, television programmes, music and magazine articles of Warner Brothers. It also has access to television stations to advertise itself, and use new technology to allow Internet access through cable and digital television. Digital television and radio makes it possible for the viewer/listener to take control through interactive links.

The Internet's major revolution has been *freedom of information*. It is impossible to censor the Internet as there is so much going on that no one would know where to start. Even in 1995, when the number of Internet subscribers was only about 25 million, the volume of information exchanged on 'the Net' was enough to fill 30 million books of 700 pages each!

The future

The phenomenal changes during the last ten years mean that no one can tell what will happen in the future.

Some, such as the science fiction novelist William Gibson who invented the term, believe that *cyberspace* will arrive. This means an artificial environment created by computers. People will work and be entertained via their PC.

Others believe that work patterns will be changed by networking and that the Internet will take over a lot of shopping. However, people will still be required to process orders made via the Internet, to deliver goods ordered by the Internet, to produce the goods ordered by the Internet, to make the music and television programmes downloaded from the Internet, and so on. There is already some evidence

---

KEY TERMS

Algorithm a set of rules used for calculation or problem solving

Analogue using signals or information represented by a continuously variable quantity, such as spatial position or voltage (the US form is analog)

Bit a unit of information expressed as a choice between two possibilities (also called a binary digit)

Byte a group of eight bits operated as a unit

Clients programmes that request documents from a server as users ask for them

Database a structured set of information held in a computer, which can be accessed in different ways, e.g. a list of customers and suppliers

Desk-top publishing using a desk-top PC's word-processing, images, charts, tables, etc. together

Digital using signals or information represented by digits (regarded as more efficient than analogue)

Floppy disk a disk that can be put into a computer to store information outside the computer

Hard copy a printout on paper

Hard disk the part of the computer that stores information

Hardware computers and peripheral machines like printers

Megabyte a million bytes (technically 1024 kilobytes)

Memory how much data can be stored by a computer

Server computers or programs that store and transmit data to other computers on the network

Software programs and systems that are put into a computer

Figure 11.1 A leading Wall Street analyst expects 100 million Windows users to own iPods by 2008

Activities

1. Ask a computing teacher how companies make money from the Internet.

2. Look in the business pages of a quality newspaper to see what is happening to computer companies.

3. Make a list of how your life is affected by computers, and what effects you think computers will have on your life over the next ten years.

that people do not want to work at home. Part of the value of work is the social element, meeting different people, forming friendships, gossiping, etc. and people do not want to give these up. Also many people find it difficult to work at home – there are distractions such as the family, and temptations such as daytime television!

There are also other problems. The very freedom of information on the Net means that parents can only exercise control by being in the room all the time their children are online. The much publicised cases of paedophile Internet stalking have led some parents to decide that the safest way to bring up children is to have no Internet connection. Some people are worried that they have to give credit card or bank details to shop on the Internet and that their details can be hacked into. This fear has been increased by the reaction of some banks to *phishing* (criminals using online bank accounts and pretending to be the bank to get confidential details from customers so they can use the account) – they have refused to reimburse customers losing money through giving out their details.

However, whatever individual complaints might be, there is no doubt that computers will continue to play a greater and greater part in industry and business, and so in everyone's lives.

11

Read the source below and answer the question which follows.

Urgent need to save digital heritage

The digital age may only just have dawned, but last night a group of eminent institutions issued a warning that large swaths of the nation's digital heritage risk being lost for ever without urgent action to preserve them.

While the average website or e-mail would hardly qualify to be described as vital cultural artefacts, electronic information and communications are now so vital to every aspect of daily life that future generations could find an enormous 'black hole in Britain's collective memory' if important digital material is allowed to disappear, according to the Digital Preservation Coalition.

At risk is everything from government records, which would previously have been published on paper but which now exist only in electronic form, to scientific data, computer games and personal websites, representatives of the coalition – made up of 17 British libraries, museums, archiving organisations and academic bodies – told a meeting at the House of Commons.

The task of archiving even a small slice of important digital material is massive. While books hundreds of years old can still be read, electronic material from just a few years ago may already have been lost because it was only available briefly online or was preserved in an obsolete form. The ephemeral*, do-it-yourself nature of the Internet also poses a huge challenge. Internet users may feel deluged by the vast amounts of information available online, with thousands of new pages appearing every day, the vast majority of it of little general interest.

'A lot of people think the web is just porn and music downloads,' Helen Shenton, head of collections care at the British Library, told *The Guardian*. 'Much of it certainly is, but there is also a lot of important stuff, ephemeral* publications, for example, which would have been published on paper before but now only exist as a web page.' As the legal repository for every book published by a UK imprint, the British Library receives about 150,000 paper publications a year to archive. But it believes that thousands of digital publications are being lost. Since January 2001, when it launched a voluntary repository for electronic material, it has received only about 3000 items.

Loyd Grossman, broadcaster and chairman of the Campaign for Museums, contrasted the experience of e-mail with that of the telegram. While the first telegram was preserved and has now been digitised, the first e-mail, sent 31 years ago, has been lost. Mr Grossman said: 'Sometimes the significance of key developments in new technologies may take several years to be recognised. The implications for our intellectual and cultural record and their preservation are profound.'

* ephemeral = short-lived, fleeting, impermanent

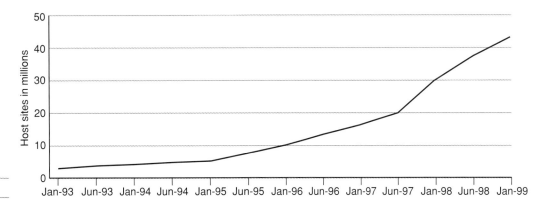

Figure 11.2

Source: from 'Corporate intelligence on retailing', The Guardian, August 1999

Source: adapted from Stuart Millar, The Guardian, 28 February 2002

'Information is not knowledge. If future generations are unable to access such ephemeral* material as

- government records
- scientific data
- computer games
- personal websites

of the present day, then they will have lost nothing of value'. How far do you share this view?

(40 marks)

AQA B June 2003

EXAMINER'S ADVICE

- This question is from Section A of A2 Unit 6 set in June 2003. It is the compulsory question in this paper, based on a single source, and requires an answer in essay form. The second question (Section B) is also an essay but is based typically on a comparison, or bringing together, of two sources and you have a choice of two questions. See page 1 for more information about this paper and the end of Unit 31 for another example of a Section A question. There are examples of Section B questions at the end of Units 1 and 2.
- Remember that Unit 6 is the synoptic paper, which means that it brings together different sorts of knowledge, ideas and skills from the whole subject. It is therefore the most demanding part of the examination and you can expect to find it hard, particularly in terms of the ideas under discussion. You have 1¾ hours for the whole test, but quite a lot of material to read through before you tackle the questions, and each question is worth 40 marks.
- Good planning supported by detailed study of the extracts is essential before you start to write your answer, so don't be afraid to spend at least 20 minutes planning your answer. This will still leave around 35 minutes for writing, which is plenty of time, if you have worked out what you are going to say.
- Also make sure that you use the prompts in the question. The question is structured in part to give you some ideas, but also to make you address the ideas being tested. For example, in response to the first sentence, you need to think about the difference between information and knowledge. The question invites you to explore this to show that you understand the point.
- Use the four examples given as bullet points. They are examples of sources of information but they are quite different from each other in terms of their interest and value to future generations. Or are they, if what you are seeking is knowledge about previous generations? Can you think of other examples? To some extent the question is about historical knowledge and the process by which this is gained or lost, and the source is about what should be preserved for future generations, and how, in the context of what is often called 'the *knowledge* explosion'.
- Finally, 'how far do you share this view…' (like 'to what extent…') does not mean that you have to come down on one side or the other. You are entitled, if you wish, to consider pros and cons in a balanced discussion of both possibilities. In this kind of context, this is most likely the best way of getting the most out of the question.
- When you have made your attempt, turn to page 252 for some possible arguments.

The relationship between science and culture

Printing

One of the most important impacts of technology on culture has been printing. Printing enabled the rise of literature (especially novels) and such developments as newspapers. It can be argued that printing was the major development of the second millennium, as it allowed ideas and information to spread rapidly. When books had to be written by hand, it was easy to prevent information from spreading, but it was almost impossible after the invention of the printing press. The Reformation could not have happened without printing, and it is possible that the scientific revolution would not have occurred either.

Music

Science has had some major effects on music, not only in such things as the invention of the piano (around the middle of the eighteenth century), but also such things as amplifiers, electronic instruments, synthesisers, etc. Perhaps the major effect was the invention of the gramophone. This was the musical equivalent of printing. Prior to the record, people could only hear live performances where audiences would be measured in thousands at most – after the record, audiences were measured in millions. Of course, the music industry has also been affected by the invention of radio, television and video – what effect has the invention of video had on the promotion of popular music?

Theatre, opera and ballet

Theatre, opera and the ballet have all been affected by scientific advances in construction, lighting and design, which enable a much wider range of staging and special effects (the special effects that science has given to the cinema, for example *Star Wars* and the Bond films have been adapted for use in theatres). It was thought that the scientific inventions of film and television would kill off live theatre, but this has not been the case. In fact, just as television has improved and popularised film (investigate how many great British films have been produced by Channel 4 television), so both television and film encourage people to go to the theatre. (How many TV soap stars appear in Christmas pantos at the theatre?) All theatres and live music shows now use computers, especially to control the lighting and other special effects.

Art

Art has always been affected by science. It was the discovery of oil paints that led to the great revolution in painting in the fifteenth century. The invention of photography led to changes in painting in the nineteenth century as people became

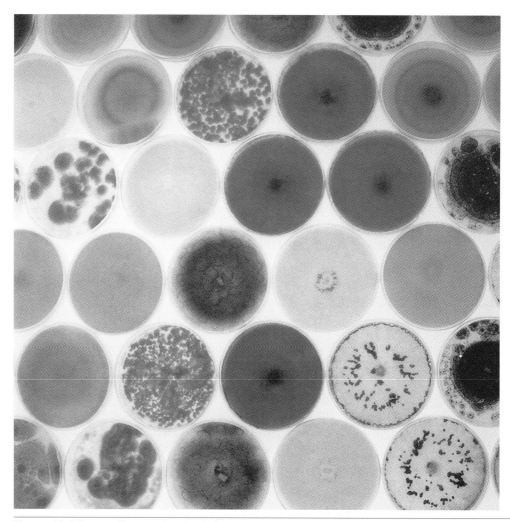

Figure 12.1 Sapros (Source: *Birkbeck College Magazine*, June 1999)

less interested in portrait painting so that Impressionism could develop. Sculpture has been affected by new tools and, particularly over the past 50 years, by welding and discoveries in metallurgy. Computers enable designs and graphics to be developed by artists in different ways. Artists have now much more chance of a commercial career through such things as cartoon films and computer games.

The impact of science on religion is dealt with in Unit 3 and should be included in any essay on the impact of science on culture.

The impact of science on society

Science has had tremendous effects on society. The units in this book on transport, energy and information technology should be used for any examination questions. The changes made to society by the inventions of railways, steam ships, cars and planes are not confined to having holidays abroad. Newspapers, the growth of suburbs where workers can live away from their factories, the possibility of all types of goods being transported round the world (until the growth of air freight, such fruits as strawberries could only be eaten in June and July) are all the product of scientific advances. The inventions of electricity, telephones, radio, television, film, records have revolutionised the ways in which humans can communicate. They have also revolutionised society. Entertainments that would have only been available to the very rich are now available in everyone's living room.

When combined with the effects of computers and the development of the Internet and e-mail, science has changed society from small communities in small nation states into what is now called 'the global village'. This term means many things:

- That what happens in one area of the world is immediately known elsewhere in the world, that finance and commerce are so worldwide that everyone is interdependent (see Unit 28 'Economic theories').
- That the same things can be bought anywhere in the world (for example, McDonalds).
- That there is a similar culture and set of values throughout the world.
- That work can take place anywhere in the world (for example, British firms having their call centres in India).
- That people can holiday anywhere in the world, so that there can no longer be communities unaware of other types of people.

There are those who argue that there is no such thing as a global village as there are so many differences between societies. However, one of the best indicators of how science has led to the world becoming a global village was the way in which the millennium was celebrated around the world, especially in countries such as Japan and Pakistan, where the indigenous culture has a different dating system. The effects of the scientific revolutions in transport and communications have been that all societies are now using the western dating systems, as such things as the Internet require common dating and time zones. For this reason the AD and BC letters (identifying the system as Christian) are being replaced by CE (Common Era) and BCE (Before the Common Era), so that the system can be used by anyone whatever their religion or culture.

Perhaps the greatest effect that science has had on society has been the way in which science has replaced religion or the government as the basic authority behind society. The fact that science is now the source of authority has also required the advance of democracy. Science requires that everyone has to have equality of opportunity, as ability and truth are the only criteria for someone's ideas to be accepted. Science can only thrive in a free society where thinkers can exchange ideas.

Some historians claim that science was the cause of the fall of the Soviet Union in the Cold War. The communist countries and NATO countries never actually fought each other, but kept developing more and more advanced weapons so that there was mutually assured destruction, resulting in the Star Wars programme (weapons in space which could block an opponent's missiles). This bankrupted the Soviet Union, leading to the collapse of communism.

KEY TERMS

Ampère (André) a French scientist who discovered the connection between electricity and magnetism

Babbage (Charles) English mathematician who invented the first, very basic, computer

Baird (John Logie) Scottish inventor of television

Bell (Alexander) Scottish-American inventor of the telephone

Benz (Karl) German inventor of the first petrol-driven car

Biro (Joseph) Hungarian inventor of the ballpoint pen

Crick (Francis) and Watson (James) English and American scientists who discovered the double helix structure of DNA

Daguerre (Louis) French inventor of photography

Edison (Charles) American inventor of the record player and the light bulb

Hertz (Heinrich) German scientist who discovered radio waves

Gutenberg (Johannes) German inventor of the printing press

van Leeuwenhoek (Antonie) Dutch inventor of the microscope

Linnaeus (Carl) Swedish scientist who developed the system for classifying plants

Lippershey (Hans) Dutch inventor of the telescope

Lumière brothers (Auguste and Louis) French inventors of the motion-picture camera (cinematographe)

Marconi (Gugliemo) Italian inventor of the radio

Nobel (Alfred) Swedish scientist who discovered dynamite and established Nobel prizes

Nuclear weapons weapons based on nuclear fission or fusion whose tremendous energy can cause massive destruction

Nuclear deterrent the idea that if a country has nuclear weapons, it will deter any other country from attacking them because of the horrendous consequences

Activities

1. Choose an area of culture in which you are interested (e.g. pop music) and investigate how far it has been affected by science and technology.

2. Investigate your own life (home, school, entertainment) to see what effects science and technology have on you.

3. Choose an area of design (e.g. a new car) and assess how far culture has had an effect on the science and technology involved.

4. Evaluate the scientific, economic, political and moral arguments that could be used to argue for and against a greater privatisation of the National Health Service.

The impact of culture and society on science

In the same way that science has had great effects on culture and society, so society and culture have had effects on science.

There are thinkers who argue that without the Reformation, modern science would not have been able to develop. Galileo was silenced by the Inquisition, but in countries such as England, Holland, Scotland and the Protestant German states his ideas were able to flourish. Indeed, Descartes moved to Holland so that he could have the freedom to publish his ideas. There is also a great connection between the rise of capitalism and the rise of science. Capitalism led to industrialisation and the two together encouraged scientists as new inventions were going to lead to greater profits for the capitalists. Capitalism also requires freedom (scholars such as Weber and Tawney have argued for a connection between Protestantism and the rise of capitalism) and so capitalist societies had the necessary freedom of thought for the rise of science. Science has often been funded by capitalism, either through research carried out in industry or through university research funded by capitalism. You need to ask such questions as whether some scientific advances, such as genetically modified crops or cloning, would have been developed if capitalism was not offering great profits to the scientists.

Perhaps the other great effect of culture and society on science is that some scientific advances have been halted or altered because society's values are opposed to the changes. For example, the generally accepted ethic is that life is sacred (even atheists accept that human life should be treated as a gift, even though not a gift from God). Consequently, scientific attempts to clone humans or to develop brain transplants have been stopped by society's culture. Clearly, there has always been a tension between society's culture and values and the free advance of science. Synoptic questions may focus on whether there should be any limits put on science by culture and society (all the information in Units 5, 10, 24 and 25 is relevant here). It might also be a good idea to use some of the arguments for and against censorship (Unit 27) to apply to science as well as the arts.

Read the following passage and complete the tasks which follow.

The £20 phone cover that cost £1 to make

Even the most up-to-date mobile phone is no longer enough for today's trendy young people. Not content with ring tones and musical gimmicks, teenagers are turning to different covers to stamp their personalities on their phones – at a staggering cost of £300 million last year alone, when 60 million covers were sold in Britain.

Although the designs, which include big sellers such as Harry Potter, Manchester United and Robbie Williams, may retail at £20, most cost barely £1 to make, shipped in by the million from cheap-labour countries such as Taiwan or China. Phone companies are reluctant to discuss figures, but there is no doubt the craze has brought a welcome boost to the mobile phone market, which had reached saturation point. A

Carphone Warehouse spokesperson said the covers were a new way of exploiting the market. '70 per cent of the market now has mobile phones, so accessories are an important new area,' she said.

Some of the covers come in contoured textiles, resembling the feel of a basketball or football. Mobile jewellery featuring sparkly, stick-on patterns is also popular among youngsters, who change their phone's look as often as they buy new clothes. The most expensive covers, featuring celebrities, films or big brands like Coca Cola, include licensing fees, adding between 10 and 14 per cent to manufacturing costs.

One mobile industry analyst said: 'If covers featuring the latest blockbuster film can become best-sellers, it shows

people are buying them as a fashion trend. The value of the market suggests youngsters are buying several a year to keep up with their peers. The range of designs is virtually limitless. This is a business that can only grow.' A Consumer Association spokesperson said youngsters used 'pester-power' to force their parents into buying goods for them. 'Children are fairly vulnerable to aggressive marketing,' he said.

The Walt Disney Corporation, however, refused to license mobile phone

covers featuring their characters, fearing a backlash if scientists' worries about the health effects of mobile phones on children proved to be true.

Recent years have seen a big increase in street-crime. Much of this is accounted for by the snatching of mobile phones. As fashion accessories they are a must-have for many young people – often schoolchildren – a small minority of whom, unable to afford to buy one, are tempted into stealing. Mobiles are easily snatched, hidden and customised.

Harry Potter phone cover estimated costs

Manufacturing costs	£3.00
Licensing cost of design	£0.30
Profit to supplier	£5.70
VAT at 17.5 per cent	£3.50
Profit to retailer	£7.49
Retail price	**£19.99**

Source: adapted from The Mail on Sunday, *6 January 2002*

Imagine you work for the Consumers' Association. Write a report for the general public, divided into the three following sections, that analyses

(i) the nature of the problem outlined in the article
(15 marks)

(ii) which parties you consider to be responsible for the problem and why
(15 marks)

(iii) what measures might be taken in the short and long term to resolve the problem.
(20 marks)

A further ten marks will be awarded for communicating in a concise and logical way in a form appropriate to report writing.
(10 marks)

Total: 60 marks

AQA B June 2003

EXAMINER'S ADVICE

- This is a complete set of questions from A2 Unit 4 set in June 2003. The unit is called Conflict-Resolution and the exercise is one of analysing the nature and source of a problem and proposing a solution. For more details on this paper check out page 1. Another example is given at the end of Unit 15.

- The prime question requirement is to write a report for Consumers' Association readers about the problem, with three main components as indicated. Use language, style and structure which is appropriate to report writing, i.e. title, headings, listed points, recommendations. The content and style should be committed to the interests of consumers, but also factual, objective and realistic.

- In problem solving, the subject matter is less important than the ability to see various sides of a question and the ability to grasp how problems might be resolved in a realistic and effective way. Always seek to make a distinction between facts and opinions. Study the details of the problem to identify its nature and source. Look for causes and behaviour which contribute to them. This part of the question requires the ability to summarise points carefully and accurately.

- In the final part, avoid the temptation to go for 'easy solutions', for example you are dealing with international corporations and market forces, so you can't just ban mobile phone covers. Think of the different groups involved: manufacturers, marketing and advertising companies, retailers, parents, children themselves, government, schools, and the part that each might play in contributing to a better solution.

- Don't be afraid to emphasise the difficulties of conflict resolution. Most problems are more difficult than they seem. Compromise is not always easy to reach and may not satisfy the parties concerned. There is merit in recognising this and showing why some problems are difficult to resolve. You will also be able to gain AO4 marks (see introduction) by showing that you recognise the limitations of knowledge and its applications. Nevertheless, the challenge is to come up with proposals here that address the problem but are also realistic.

- You have one hour in which to complete this paper, which includes the time taken to study the passage and questions. Note the distribution of marks for the four components. Slightly more marks are given to the solution. Once again a useful guideline might be: the number of marks for a question = the number of minutes to spend on it.

- When you have made your attempt, some suggested answer notes are given on page 253.

The application of maths

Much of the Maths in General Studies is also the Maths you need for Key Skills Level 3 Numeracy, and based on what you learnt for GCSE. This unit gives you some of the basic techniques you will need. It would be a good idea to practise some GCSE Higher Maths papers to brush up your knowledge and skills.

Mean, median, mode and range

The following were the scores in a golf tournament: 72, 86, 67, 94, 76, 82, 76, 69, 74, 76.

You find the *mean (average)* for the golf scores by adding together all the figures and dividing by the number of figures. This is 770 divided by 10 (the number of scores), giving a mean of 77. If you are given a table of statistics that gives the frequency of classes, you find the mid-value of each class (by halving it) and multiply by the frequency, add all those results together and divide by the number in the sample (see Table 13.1).

You find the *median* by putting the numbers into order of size, dividing the number of figures by 2 (essentially the middle value) and the median is the middle number. The golf scores put into order of size are: 67, 69, 72, 74, 76, 76, 76, 82, 86, 94. The fifth number is the middle number, so the median is 76.

The *mode* is the figure that occurs most frequently. In the golf scores, 76 occurs three times, but all the others only occur once, so the mode is 76. Sometimes a question will ask for the modal group rather than the mode, but it means the same.

The *range* is the difference between the lowest number and the highest number. In the golf scores, the highest number is 94, the lowest is 67, so the range is 27. Often you will need to find the interquartile range on a cumulative frequency graph (a graph where the frequencies of a statistics are added together as you go along). You do this by dividing the frequencies by 4 and plotting one-quarter and three-quarters. The interquartile range is the range between these.

There are some ideas you need to know about when interpreting these concepts. The bigger the range (especially the interquartile range), the more unreliable the mean is likely to be. If the range is large, the median is likely to be a more reliable figure than the mean. If the range is small, the mean is the most reliable figure. Interpreting statistics also requires you to think about who is using the figures and what they want them for, for example a shoe manufacturer will be more interested in the mode of shoe sizes than the mean (they will need to gear their production of shoes to the popularity of sizes).

Example

The table overleaf illustrates the distance between home and the town centre of a group of 75 students and shows how to work out the mean distance.

Table 13.1 Mean distance between home and town centre for a group of 75 students (km)

Distance in km (d)	No of students (frequency, f)	Mid-interval value (MIV)	f × MIV
1 km or less	6	0.5	3.0
$1 < d \leq 2$	7	1.5	10.5
$2 < d \leq 3$	15	2.5	37.5
$3 < d \leq 4$	18	3.5	63.0
$4 < d \leq 5$	10	4.5	45.0
$5 < d \leq 6$	10	5.5	55.0
$6 < d \leq 7$	7	6.5	45.5
$7 < d \leq 8$	2	7.5	15.0
Total	75		274.5

Mean = 274.5 (mid-interval value frequency added together) ÷ 75 (total no. in sample) = 3.66 km.

Example

The graph below illustrates how to draw a cumulative frequency graph and calculate the interquartile range using the figures from example 1.

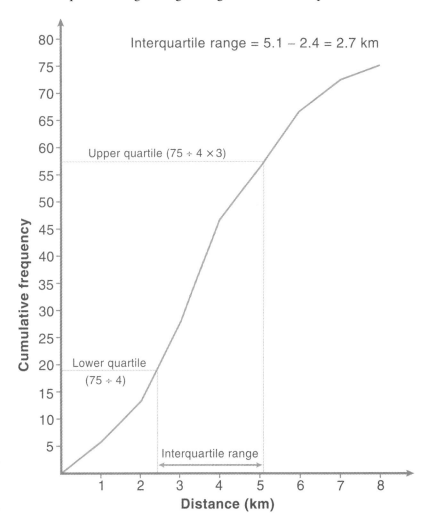

Interquartile range = 5.1 − 2.4 = 2.7 km

Upper quartile (75 ÷ 4 × 3)

Lower quartile (75 ÷ 4)

Interquartile range

Cumulative frequency

Distance (km)

Figure 13.1 Cumulative frequency and calculation of the interquartile range

Scatter graphs

A scatter graph is a graph that simply records a set of results without putting them into classes or groups. If you can draw a line of best fit through the results, there is a correlation in the results. The *line of best fit* is a straight line that is closest to the majority of points on the graph. If the line of best fit goes up, there is a *positive correlation* (if one variable rises, the other does as well). If the line of fit goes down, there is a *negative correlation* (if one variable goes up, the other will go down). If you cannot draw a line of best fit, there is no correlation.

Lines of best fit can be used to predict what will happen on the other variable (see the example below).

Example

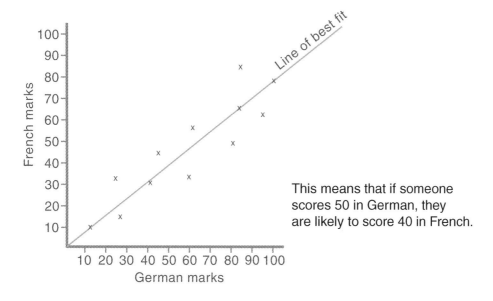

This means that if someone scores 50 in German, they are likely to score 40 in French.

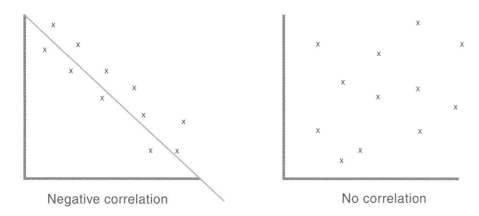

Figure 13.2 Lines of best fit

Calculating percentages

1 You are likely to be asked what percentage is represented by one of the figures in the tables. To do this, you work out the total number, then apply the formula:

$$\frac{(\text{figure you need} \times 100)}{\text{total number}}$$

For example, the percentage of golfers scoring 76 is: $\frac{3 \times 100}{10} = 30\%$

2 You may be asked to find a percentage difference. To do this, you work out the difference, multiply by 100 and divide by the original amount.

For example, a shopkeeper buys soap powder at £10 for five packets and sells it for £2.75 per packet. What is his percentage profit?

$$1000 \div 5 = 200 \text{ pence (the amount he pays for one packet)},$$
$$275 - 200 = 75 \text{ (the profit per packet)} \times 100 \div 200 = 37.5\%.$$

3 You may be asked to remove part of a percentage. To do this, you add the percentage you have to remove to 100, divide by the total and multiply by 100.

For example, if a computer costs £1175 including 17.5% VAT, what would be its price without VAT?

$$100 + 17.5 = 117.5; 1175 \div 117.5 \times 100 = £1000.$$

4 You may be asked to find an original amount when a percentage has been taken off. To do this, you subtract that percentage from 100, divide the current amount by your answer and multiply by 100.

For example, a Playstation costs £76 in a 20% off sale. What was its price before the sale?

$$100 - 20 = 80; 76 \div 80 \times 100 = £95.$$

5 You may be asked to work out compound interest. To do this, you add 100 to the annual interest, divide by 100 and store this in the memory of your calculator, then multiply by the capital (amount invested). You then keep multiplying by the stored number for the number of years of interest.

For example, what would £5000 be worth after 5 years if invested at compound interest of 6.5% per annum?

This is what you do on your calculator:

$$100 + 6.5 \div 100 \text{ STO M+} \times 5000 \times \text{RCL M+}$$
$$\times \text{RCL M+} \times \text{RCL M+} \times \text{RCL M+} = £6850.43.$$

If you are asked for the amount of interest, you simply subtract the amount invested from your calculator answer.

6 If you are asked to calculate depreciation, it is a very similar calculation to compound interest. You subtract the percentage depreciation from 100 and divide the answer by 100, store this in the memory, multiply by the initial value, then multiply by the stored number for every year of depreciation.

For example, if a car bought for £15,000 depreciates at 10% a year, what will its value be after five years?

This is what you do on your calculator:

$$100 - 10 \div 100 \text{ STO M+} \times 15\,000 \times \text{RCL M+} \times \text{RCL M+}$$
$$\times \text{RCL M+} \times \text{RCL M+} = £8857.35$$

Calculating probability

Any probability can be written as a decimal between 0 and 1 where 0 is impossible and 1 is certain. You work out the probability by dividing the chance by the total.

For example, the probability of throwing a six when you throw a die is 1 in 6 (there are six numbers and only one six); $1 \div 6 = 0.17$ probability.

When you have two possible outcomes you multiply the relevant outcomes to find the probability.

For example, Rebecca has a 2 in 3 chance of winning the darts competition and a 3 in 4 chance of winning the dominoes competition. What is the probability of her winning both competitions?

$$2 \div 3 \times 3 \div 4 = 0.5.$$

What is the probability that Rebecca will win only one of the competitions? She has a 2 in 3 chance of winning the darts and a 1 in 4 chance of not winning the dominoes; she has a 3 in 4 chance of winning the dominoes and a 1 in 3 chance of not winning the darts. So what are her chances of only winning one event?

What you put into your calculator:

$$(2 \div 3 \times 1 \div 4) + (3 \div 4 \times 1 \div 3) = 0.4167.$$

Calculating volumes

The basic formula for calculating volume is height × length × width. However, prisms cause problems because the volume is the area of the cross-section multiplied by the length.

The *volume of a cylindrical prism* is worked out by multiplying the area of the circle at the end of the cylinder by the height of the cylinder:

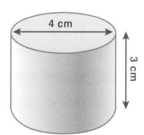

Volume = 2×2 (radius squared) $\times \pi \times 3 = 37.699$ cm^3 (cubic centimetres).

This means that, if you are given the volume and radius, you can work out the depth. For example, how deep is the water in a cylinder of diameter 4 cm if there is 37.699 ml of water in the cylinder?

$$37.699 \div (2 \times 2 \times \pi) = 3 \text{ cm, so the depth is 3 cm}$$
$$(1 \text{ ml} = 1 \text{ cm}^3 \text{ and } 1000 \text{ cm}^3 = 1 \text{ litre}).$$

The *volume of a triangular prism* is worked out by finding the area of the cross-section triangle and multiplying by the length.

Volume = 10 × 8 (half the base of the triangle multiplied by the height to get the area of the triangle) × 30 (the length) = 2400 cm³.

Mass is the weight of an object, *density* is the weight per item of length.

$$Mass = \text{volume density}$$
$$Density = \text{mass volume}$$
$$Volume = \text{mass density}$$

Conversions

Imperial measures	Metric measures
1 lb = 454 g	1 kg = 2.2 lbs
1 ton = 1 tonne	1 tonne = 1 ton
1 inch = 2.5 cm	1 cm = 0.4 inches
1 foot = 30 cm	1 metre = 1.1 yards
1 yard = 0.9 m	1 km = 0.625 miles
1 mile = 1.6 km	1 litre = 1.75 pints
1 pint = 0.5625 litres	1 litre = 0.22 gallons
1 gallon = 4.5 litres	

To convert imperial to metric:

- If you are given the imperial chart, multiply the imperial by the metric. For example, how many litres are there in 3 pints of beer? Answer: 1.6875 litres (3 × 0.5625).
- If you are given the metric chart divide the imperial measure by the imperial equivalent. For example, how many metres are there in 3 yards? Answer: 2.73 (3 ÷ 1.1).

To convert metric to imperial:

- If you are given the imperial chart, divide the metric by the metric equivalent. For example, how many pints are there in 3 litres? Answer: 5.33 (3 ÷ 0.5625).
- If you are given the metric chart, multiply the metric by the imperial. For example, how many yards are there in 3 metres? Answer: 3.3 (3 × 1.1).

The same processes can be used in converting currencies.

Exchange rate: £1 = 1.9358 dollars, 1.4464 euros, 198.36 yen

Using the above exchange rate:

How many pounds would you get for 30 dollars? Answer: 30 ÷ 1.9358 = £15.50

How many euros would you get for £30? Answer: 30 × 1.4464 = 43.39 euros

How many dollars would you get for 500 yen? Answer: convert the yen into pounds (500 ÷ 198.36), then convert the answer into dollars (2.52 × 1.9358) = 4.88 dollars

Ratio

Ratios are best thought of as fractions – the ratios are the numerators and the numbers added together are the denominators.

For example, Jamie, Sunita and Alice are in a lottery syndicate. Jamie buys 3 tickets, Sunita buys 2 tickets and Alice buys 5 tickets. If they win £100,000, how much will each receive? Answer: Jamie will receive 3 ÷ 10, Sunita 2 ÷ 10, Alice 5 ÷ 10, so dividing by the denominator and multiplying by the numerator gives £30,000 for Jamie, £20,000 for Sunita and £50,000 for Alice.

If the question asks for one ratio in terms of another, then you use the ratio given and divide by it, then multiply by the ratio you need.

For example, concrete is made by mixing sand, gravel and cement in the ratio 2:3:1. If I use 20 cubic metres of sand, how much gravel will I need? Answer: 20 ÷ 2 = 10, 10 × 3 = 30 cubic metres of gravel

Scale

Scale is the same as ratio. It is used to make drawings or maps of large things. To make a scale drawing, you have to work out a ratio based on the same measurements. This means that you have to change metres and kilometres into cms. There are 100 cm in 1 metre and 100,000 cm in 1 kilometre.

To work out how many cm there are in the drawing by looking at the real, you make the real into cm and then divide by the largest ratio.

For example, on a scale of 1:50,000 1 km is 2 cm (100,000 divided by 50,000 = 2).

To work out the real from the drawing, multiply the cm by the larger ration and then divide by 100 to change to metres or 100,000 to change to kilometres.

Cubics an equation where the highest power is 3. You solve a cubic equation by drawing a graph and finding the values of x from where the line crosses the x-axis (there are three answers)

Exponential change growth at regular intervals, which can be calculated in the same way as compound interest

Gradient how far a line goes up in ratio to how far it goes along. To find the gradient, you divide up by along. A downward gradient will be a negative number

Histogram a bar chart with the width of the columns in proportion to the size of the group, the vertical axis based on frequency density (frequency divided by the class interval) so that the area of the column represents the frequency

Networks often called critical path analysis, requiring you to work out which activities are connected and which activities depend on a previous activity and then link them together into a network

13 The application of maths

Activities

1. In a sale, a shop reduced all its prices by 15%.
   (a) Find the new price of an article that originally cost £55.00.
   (b) Find the original price of an article whose reduced price is £102.
   (c) In the week before the sale, the average number of customers per day was 250. During the sale, this number increased to 370. What was the percentage increase?

2. The ages of the members of a sports club were: less than 10 years, 2; 11–20 years, 16; 21–30 years, 30; 31–40 years, 16; 41–50 years, 10; over 50 years, 6.
   (a) Draw a cumulative frequency graph and use it to find the median and interquartile range.
   (b) State the modal group and estimate the mean.

For example, how far is it from Sydney to Perth? Answer:
The distance on the map is 16.5 cm, the scale is 1:20,000,000
20,000,000 divided by 100,000 = 200 therefore 1 cm = 200 km.
$200 \times 16.5 = 3300$
So the distance from Sydney to Perth is 3300 km.

Bearings

Bearings are based on 360 degrees in a circle.

North is	000
East is	090
South is	180
West is	270

You always write bearings as three numbers, so if the number is less than 100, you use 0 or 00 at the beginning. Whenever you work out the bearing, you make sure you are facing North.

For example, you are standing on the end of a pier when you spot a boat on a bearing of 123 degrees, your friend is standing 6 kilometres due South of you and sees the boat on a bearing of 065 degrees. Draw an accurate scale drawing showing this information.

Answer:

- Choose an appropriate scale of 1 cm per kilometre.
- Draw a vertical 6 cm line labelling the top, self, and the bottom, friend (due South of you).
- Use your protractor to measure 123 degrees from the top point and draw a line along that measurement.
- Use your protractor to measure 65 degrees from the bottom point and draw a line along that measurement.
- Label the point where the two lines cross, boat.

Inequalities

Inequalities are based on the signs:

>	greater than
<	less than
>=	equal to or more than
<=	equal to or less than

Therefore:
$-5 > x < 0$ means that x is -1 or -2 or -3 or -4
$3 >= x <= 5$ means that x is 3, or 4, or 5

If you are asked to solve an inequality, you treat it as a normal algebra equation until you write your answer.

For example, solve the inequality $15x - 2 \leq 11x + 14$.
Answer: $15x - 11x = 14 + 2$, $4x = 16$, $x = 4$
So x is equal to or less than 4.

Networks (critical path analysis)

This is a way of diagramming a process (such as manufacturing a product or organising an event) so that you can work out things such as the shortest time it will take for the product to reach the shops (critical path). It is based on nodes (a stage in the process), prerequisites (what has to happen before a node is reached) and activities (paths between the nodes).

For example, a firm wants to start manufacturing MP3 players. This will involve the following activities as shown in Figure 13.3:

A   order components
B   components delivered
C   manufacture sets
D   set up testing procedures
E   test sets
F   pack sets
G   deliver sets.

If each activity after A takes two days, what is the soonest that the MP3 players can be in the shops? Answer: Ten days (setting up testing procedures is off the critical path)

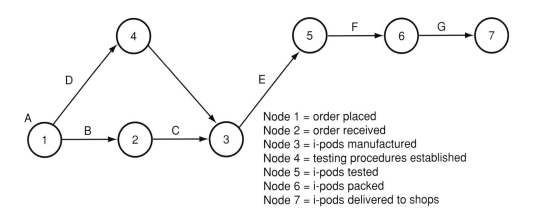

Node 1 = order placed
Node 2 = order received
Node 3 = i-pods manufactured
Node 4 = testing procedures established
Node 5 = i-pods tested
Node 6 = i-pods packed
Node 7 = i-pods delivered to shops

Figure 13.3 The critical path of the manufacture of MP3 players

EXAM QUESTIONS

Look carefully at Tables 1 and 2 below. Table 1 shows the percentage of households by size. Table 2 shows the 1991 Census results on housing in Camden, London.

Having studied the tables answer all of the questions which follow.

Table 1 Percentage of households by size, UK 1961–2000

	1961	1971	1981	1991	2000
One person	14	18	22	27	29
Two people	30	32	32	34	35
Three people	23	19	17	16	16
Four people	18	17	18	16	14
Five people	8	8	7	5	4
Six or more people	7	6	4	2	2

Source: Social Trends 2002

Table 2 Housing in Camden, 1991

		Census 1991	Projection for 2006	Projection for 2011
Residents	Persons	170,440	199,000	204,800
Gender	Males	80,190	94,900	96,800
	Females	90,250	104,100	108,000
Age Groups	0–15	27,400	31,100	32,000
	16–59	109,400	138,900	141,500
	60+	33,640	29,000	31,300
Households	Residents	162,000	190,300	195,700
	Households	80,150	95,000	99,000
	Occupied dwellings	160,000	190,000	198,700
	Average household size	2.00	2.00	1.98
	Owner occupied	27,100		
	Local authority	27,200		
	Other rented	25,900		
	Households + car	35,400		

Source: Camden – Key Facts 2002

(a) Using Table 1, construct a scatter diagram for the year 2000 showing the number of people in a household and the percentage of households. Draw a line of best fit.

(4 marks)

(b) (i) What trends in household sizes might be identified from Table 1?

(2 marks)

 (ii) Table 2 shows the projection for 2011. What is the percentage increase from 1991 to 2011 for all residents?

(2 marks)

(c) Why might the data in Table 2 be of limited value?

(4 marks)

(d) Using Tables 1 and 2 and your own knowledge, what problems might arise from the need to provide extra housing?

(8 marks)

(e) The growth in the number of households means an inevitable return to high-rise housing in inner-city areas. How far is this a matter of *fact* and how far a matter of *opinion*?

(10 marks)

Total: 30 marks

AQA B January 2004

EXAMINER'S ADVICE

- The exam questions which contain mathematical applications in AQA General Studies B are all to be found in AS Unit 3. This unit tests your skills in analysing and evaluating various kinds of statistical data in mainly social and environmental contexts, for example making sense of tables of data, charts, graphs, calculating percentages, creating graphs, assessing various trends, drawing conclusions and the like. In addition to the questions given here, further examples of the questions and the techniques being tested are to be found at the end of Units 7, 10 and 26. Refer back to appropriate sections of this unit where necessary when working through these questions.
- These questions are from AS Unit 3 set in January 2004. See page 1 for more details about this paper. The unit of this book which is most relevant to the themes explored in the questions is Unit 15 'Social change'.
- If you are not sure about how to construct a scatter diagram and line of best fit for Question (a), go back to page 95. Make sure to label axes and scales, as there are marks for this.
- Two clear points should be sufficient for two marks for Question (b)(i) and remember to show your working for (b)(ii). Try to come up with four distinct points for (c).
- For this paper think in terms of number of marks = number of minutes spent on question = number of points to be made. For Question (d) consider the growth in demand and its implications and for Question (e) you should try to balance relevant facts like the growth in demand and how this may be met with past experiences of high-rise housing and attitudes and opinions towards it.
- You should allow approximately 40 minutes in total to complete these questions. When you have finished, turn to page 254 for some answer notes.

Society and Politics

Unit 14 | **The nature of society**
Unit 15 | **Social change**
Unit 16 | **Crime and deviance**
Unit 17 | **The nature of law**
Unit 18 | **Rights and responsibilities**
Unit 19 | **Power and control**
Unit 20 | **Politics**
Unit 21 | **The British Constitution**
Unit 22 | **Educational issues**

14

The nature of society

The *Oxford English Dictionary* has eight different definitions of 'society', showing how difficult it is to define the nature of society exactly. The study of the nature of society (how society originated, what it is for and how it works) is called 'sociology'. Auguste Comte first used this word in 1834 to describe the 'science of society'. He thought that this science would discover the social laws controlling the development of the human race, in the same way that the physical sciences discover the physical laws controlling the development of the earth.

Some sociologists follow Comte and believe that sociology is a science. They claim that by applying scientific methods of observation, theory and experiment to society, it is possible to discover social laws. Such sociologists are called positivists because they think of society as an objective fact, like a rock or a plant.

Other sociologists believe that sociology is about discovering how people interpret the world and how people interact with each other to form social groups. This is called 'phenomenology'.

The nature of society according to positivists

Some positivists are known as *functionalists*. They believe that each area or institution within society (such things as education, the family, and the legal system) has a function in relation to the whole of society. They often compare society to the human body and institutions to the parts of the body. Just as the heart maintains the body by pumping blood round, so the family maintains society by training children to become members of society (socialisation). The function of an institution is to contribute to the maintenance of society and to provide some of what society needs to keep it going (see Figure 14.1).

Society's needs include such things as shelter, food, socialisation and value consensus, which are often called 'functional prerequisites'. 'Value consensus' means a general agreement about what the values of society are. For example, in western society there is a value consensus that everyone should have a good supply of material goods, so the economic institutions provide a large range of goods and the family is organised to buy increasing numbers of those goods (for example CD players, camcorders, fitted kitchens).

Any society needs its members and institutions to be integrated if it is to flourish. Functionalists think that value consensus is the main means of social integration, but this is backed up by social control. Society controls the behaviour of its members by norms, which can be either formal or informal. Formal norms are the rules and the method of imposing the rules, often involving rewards or positive sanctions (for example promotion at work) and punishment or negative sanctions (for example imprisonment). Informal norms are such things as dress codes (wearing different types of clothes for work on a building site from work in an office), which are imposed by informal sanctions (smiles, frowns or comments).

Functionalists accept that there can be conflicts between different groups in society, but feel that the institutions of an effective society will soon settle these, because social groups have more in common than they have differences. This is why some people claim that civil wars are only likely to happen in the less materially advanced countries, because even the poorest people in an advanced society have an interest in maintaining the electricity supply, the water supply, television broadcasts, etc.

However, there are other positivist sociologists who take a different view of society. *Marxists* believe that society is based on conflict rather than value consensus. Karl Marx believed that the history of society is based on one group being in control until their control is challenged by another group. Marx claimed that in industrial society, the controlling group is the *bourgeoisie* (the owners of the means of production), which is trying to control the *proletariat* (the workers) to keep it from taking control. Marx claimed that society is based on economics, especially the 'forces of production' (the technology, raw materials, etc. involved in producing food, clothes, cars, etc.). The ruling class is always concerned to own the means of production. Marx was an economist and political philosopher rather than a sociologist, but Marxist sociologists have used his theories as a basis for their 'conflict theory of society'.

Marxist sociologists claim that the social institutions of society (what they call the superstructure) are used by the ruling class to keep the proletariat from revolting and taking control. They reflect the interests of the rulers rather than the workers and so there is a basic conflict. For example, educational institutions teach the ideology of the rulers and prepare children to perform the functions that will make money for the ruling class. The law is designed to protect the interests of the ruling class. For example, the laws on property usually protect the owners of property more than the interests of groups such as ramblers. Such sociologists explain value consensus in society by the idea of 'false consciousness'. This means that the ruling class is able to use such things as education and the family to make workers believe the ideology of the rulers (for example getting a mortgage and a car to give profits to the banks and car makers), when it is really in their interests to reject the ruling ideology and adopt a Marxist ideology (see 'Key terms').

The nature of society according to phenomenologists

Most phenomenologists are called *interactionists*. Functionalism and Marxism may have differences, but they agree that society is made up not only of people, but also of institutions and systems, which have a great impact on the behaviour of individuals. Interactionism is completely different in that it claims that society is made up of individuals who work out their role in society through interaction with other individuals rather than being forced into roles through institutions such as the family and education. Consequently, society for interactionists is always changing, as people negotiate their role in society.

> **DID YOU KNOW?**
>
> **On the breadline**
> There are three different ways of deciding whether people are poor:
> * By making a list of what is necessary to live – a certain number of calories and proteins per day, clean water, shelter, heating and cooking sources, medical facilities – so that anyone below this level can be said to be in 'absolute' poverty.
> * By working out the average income of a society and the normal expectations of this average (e.g. a television and video, an annual holiday) anyone who is 20 per cent or so below this can be said to be in 'relative' poverty.
> * By asking people whether they consider themselves to be poor. If they do and their behaviour reflects this, then they are 'subjectively' poor.

The nature of society according to philosophers

Philosophers would agree with interactionists that society is made up of individuals living and working together. However, they believe that any society needs laws so that people can live and work in peace. Once this happens, social institutions will be formed and society becomes a mixture of individuals and institutions. Clearly, the institutions will have functions because that is why they arose, and there is a sense in which the institution is greater than its members (your school or college was there before you started and will still be there when you leave). However, individuals do have choices about their roles, and society and its institutions change through individuals changing their roles.

So, philosophers would see society as a mixture of functionalism and interactionism, but would tend to reject Marxism because, since individuals changed society's institutions into more democratic forms, there are lots of ways in which society can be changed without conflict.

How sociologists discover facts about society

Sociologists use a variety of tools to study society.

Social surveys

These are usually conducted either by questionnaire or interview. To be absolutely accurate they would have to survey everyone in the population, but as this is impossible they should use either random sampling (which requires a large sample to make sure that all opinions are covered) or quota sampling (where the census figures are used to work out how many people in the population are in certain groups – 40–50-year-old male working class, for example – and the relevant representative quota is interviewed). Surveys have many problems, not only concerning the numbers of people interviewed (mathematicians claim that the minimum is 11 per 100,000 of population), but also in the avoidance of bias in the questions or the interviewers.

Statistical studies

These include census records and *Social Trends* (an annual publication of government figures on such things as marriages, births, employment – see Figure 14.1). Though these are more accurate than surveys, they cannot be accepted without question because there may still be some bias, for example when suicide was a crime many suicides were not recorded as suicide to save hurting the family.

Observation

Some sociologists research by studying a small group intensively over a period of time (this method is also known as ethnography). It is typically used when investigating small communities, gangs, firms, institutions, etc. The researcher usually negotiates with the group to establish their credentials and to outline how the research will be done, and how the results will be used. This type of research uses informal interviews

England		Thousands		
	1992	**1997**	**2001**	**2002**
Foster placements	32.4	33.5	38.3	39.2
Placement with parents	6.4	5.2	6.9	6.7
Children's homes[3]	–	6.6	6.8	6.8
Placed for adoption	2.8	2.4	3.4	3.6
Living independently or in residential employment	2.1	1.2	1.2	1.1
Residential schools	–	0.8	1.1	1.1
Other accommodation	2.1	1.6	1.2	1.1
All looked after children	55.5	51.2	58.9	59.7

1 Excludes children looked after under an agreed series of short-term placements.
2 At 31 March.
3 Includes local authority, voluntary and private children's homes and secure units.

Figure 14.1 Children looked after by local authorities[1] by type of accommodation[2], (Source: *Social Trends 34*)

with members of the group, participation by the researcher in the activities of the group, observation of key events/issues in the life of the group. The data is then written up in a long account which is usually qualitative rather than quantitative. Occasionally, researchers join the group without declaring their identity in the hope of their research being more objective as the members of the group do not know they are being researched.

Critics of this method claim that the data is unreliable because: either the groups know they are being studied and so behave differently, the researcher gets too close to the group and so becomes biased, the researcher tends to see causes and motives without explaining his/her reasons for doing so, and/or there is no criteria of proof for claims made from the research. Proponents say it provides a depth of insight which other methods cannot hope to achieve, especially when deviant groups such as young hooligans, drug addicts, etc. are being researched.

Activities

1. Imagine you have been asked by the government to investigate the effects of poverty on family life. How would you carry out the research and what methods would you use? (You may find the information in Figure 14.1 useful.)

2. By questionnaires or discussion, investigate whether there is a value consensus among people you know about an issue such as car ownership versus public transport.

3. Do you think that married couples should be given greater tax benefits than single people? You should think about the importance of the family in society and use information from Unit 28 ('Economic theories') on taxation.

EXAM QUESTION

Read the source below and answer the following question.

'We shall only secure the benefits of cultural diversity if members of ethnic minorities have the same job opportunities as the white majority.'
   Bearing in mind

- educational
- political
- legal
- economic

limits to what can be done, how might we ensure that ethnic minorities do not form a socio-economic underclass in Britain?

(40 marks)

AQA B June 2002

The ethnic underclass?

While some ethnic minorities are doing very well in Britain, black and Asian people often face a series of disadvantages and poorer life chances that their white counterparts do not encounter. Pakistanis, Bangladeshis, and Afro-Caribbeans, in particular, face a series of disadvantages in Britain compared with the white majority, although there are differences within each group.

- Afro-Caribbeans, Pakistanis and Bangladeshis are less likely than white people to secure the best jobs. These groups are under-represented in non-manual occupations, particularly in managerial and professional work. They are hugely under-represented in parliament and the top elite occupations.
- They are over-represented in semi-skilled and unskilled manual occupations, and often work longer and more unsociable hours (shift work and night work) than white people.
- Black and Asian people are less likely to be employed when competing with whites with the same qualifications for the same job.
- Black and Asian people have lower average earnings, even when they have the same job level as white people. Small-scale surveys have shown that male Afro-Caribbeans earn 15 per cent less and Asians 18 per cent less than whites. Ethnic minority groups are far more likely to be in the poorest fifth of the population.
- People from ethnic minorities are more likely to face unemployment, especially those of Afro-Caribbean and Pakistani/Bangladeshi origin.
- Skilled and experienced ethnic minority women are twice as likely as white women to be unemployed, according to the Equal Opportunities Commission. Black and Asian women frequently work longer hours in poorer conditions than white women or men, and receive roughly three-quarters of white women's pay, even though they are on average better educated.

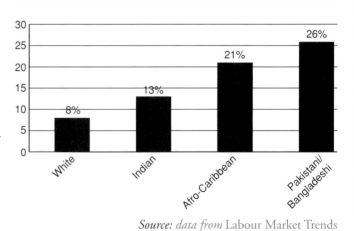

Figure 14.2 Unemployment rates by ethnic group, Great Britain 1996 (per cent)

Source: data from Labour Market Trends

Source: Ken Browne, An Introduction to Sociology *(Blackwell, 1998)*

EXAMINER'S ADVICE

- This is another question from Section A of A2 Unit 6, but this time set in June 2002. See the Examiner's Advice notes for a similar style of question at the end of Unit 31 and also page 1 for more general information about this paper.
- Make sure, as before, that you use all the prompts in the question, as well as the detail of the source. The question is structured in part to give you some ideas, but also to make sure that you address the ideas being tested. The main ideas here focus on cultural diversity, equal opportunities and the problems of disadvantage. You should attempt to set out what the benefits of cultural diversity might be, as well as the need for more opportunities for economically and socially disadvantaged groups, and the dangers of allowing an 'underclass' to develop.
- The source gives you ideas for the sort of problems to be solved and the question also mentions limits. How far can you, or should you go, in seeking to re-dress such issues as educational disadvantage? For example, how much use should be made of equal opportunities legislation and measures such as positive discrimination and economic support, for example welfare benefits?
- After researching some ideas from the previous two units of this book (you might look at Unit 22 'Educational issues' as well), plan your attempt and write your answer in no more than 35 minutes. Then turn to page 254 for some further possible points.

15 Social change

Social change means the ways in which society has and is changing, and also what possibilities there are for change in a society. Many types of social change are dealt with in other units. This unit will look at social change in terms of the family, social class, ethnicity, gender and demography.

Demographic trends in the UK

Demography is concerned with the statistics of births, deaths and population changes. When the first official census was taken in 1801, the population of the United Kingdom was 12 million, in 2002, it had risen to 59,228,900.

The UK's population grew rapidly in the nineteenth century, but slowed down in the 1920s and 1930s, perhaps because of a combination of economic depression and the new availability of contraception. After the Second World War there was a 'baby boom', but by the 1980s the UK's birth rate had fallen more quickly than the death rate, so that the population was only increasing very slightly (indeed between 1974 and 1978 the population actually fell). Today the birth rate has begun to increase and it is now expected that births will exceed deaths up to 2031.

As the birth rate has fallen, so the death rate has declined. This means that the number of under-16s in the population has fallen (25 per cent in 1961, 20 per cent in 2002), but the number of over-65s has risen (12 per cent in 1961, 18 per cent in 2002). Life expectancy has risen from 45 for men and 47 for women in 1901 to 76 for men and 81 for women in 2002.

Another trend has been for the population to move southwards. In the Industrial Revolution, it was the North of England which recorded big increases in population. However, since the collapse of heavy industry in the 1970s and 1980s, the South of England has experienced big population growth as people moved to jobs in the high-tech sector. This has been even more marked in Scotland (population 5,054,800 in 2002), Wales (population 2,918,700 in 2002) and Northern Ireland (population 1,696,600 in 2002). In 2002, 84 per cent of the UK's population lived in England and about 70 per cent of that lives south of the Wash.

As the population has moved southwards, it has also moved out of the cities. Although the population of the South East has risen fantastically in the past 30 years, the population of London has actually fallen. People have moved into the countryside in search of better living conditions. This trend was initiated by the government after the Second World War, when a New Towns policy was begun to build integrated living and work areas using the latest designs and ideas. The largest of the New Towns is Milton Keynes in Northamptonshire, which was built to take in people from London.

In the nineteenth century, the UK had more people immigrating than emigrating as there was a great demand for workers, and Britain had a tradition of taking in religious and political refugees. Between 1890 and 1955, the UK was a net exporter of people as economic problems led to massive migrations to the USA, Australia, New Zealand and Canada. In the 1950s, a shortage of labour for British industry led to workers being recruited from the new Commonwealth countries (India, Pakistan,

Bangladesh, West Africa and the Caribbean). Many of these workers had fought for the UK in the Second World War (there were more people from the Commonwealth than from the UK in the British Armed Forces in the Second World War). As these workers have settled, the UK has become a multi-ethnic society. Even so, in the 2001 census, only 7.9 per cent of the UK's population came from ethnic minorities.

The implications of these trends

Demographic trends have major implications, especially in terms of government policies. The ageing population trend has implications for the National Health Service (NHS). An ageing population is going to require the NHS to take a greater proportion of government spending. There are also major implications for the Social Security budget. If people live for longer after they retire, this means that there will be more pensioners in relation to the working population. This may mean that there will be insufficient working people to pay the pensions. This is connected with the current trend of reducing the age of the workforce by giving workers early retirement. Pensions have to be worked out on the basis of how long the pensioner is expected to live. If pensioners are living five years longer, then it may be sensible to require people to retire at 65, or even 70. There are also housing and social service issues when seaside resorts on the South Coast consist of almost 50 per cent of people over the age of 65.

The southward drift has major implications for housing and transport. More houses will need to be built in the South, putting pressure on the Green Belt. Greater numbers of people will also lead to much more transport congestion, leading to the issue of whether to increase public transport or to build new roads. Further implications are that schools and hospitals in the South are likely to be overcrowded, whereas those in the North will have surplus places. Government policies aimed at encouraging businesses to move away from the South are already in place and may have slowed down the drift.

The rural drift also has implications. People moving into the countryside are likely either to commute to work in towns or to be retired, but wealthy. This pushes up

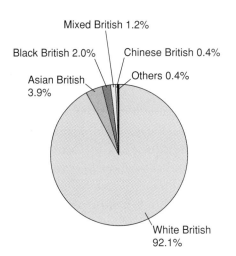

Figure 15.1 Ethnicity of UK population, Census 2001

Mixed British 1.2%
Black British 2.0% Chinese British 0.4%
Asian British 3.9% Others 0.4%
White British 92.1%

Baby boomers people born in the period 1946–53, when there was a very rapid rise in the number of births

Bourgeois members of the middle class and/or property owners

IMR infant morality rate – the number of babies who die before the age of one year per thousand births

High-rise housing blocks of flats which are many storeys high

Intergenerational mobility children moving social class compared with their parents

Intragenerational mobility people moving social class through their working life

Meritocracy a system where the top jobs are given to people on the basis of their talents and qualifications (merits) rather than their birth, wealth or the school they attended

Official census a survey of the whole of the UK's population carried out by the government every 10 years (1991, 2001) – every household has to fill in a questionnaire

Proletariat the working class

Reclaiming the inner city the practice of building new middle-class housing, shops, etc. in the inner-city so that it is no longer a slum for problem families between the CBD (Central Business District) and the suburbs

Registrar-General the civil servant in charge of the official census

Social class there are many views of social class from the basic upper, middle and working classes to the Registrar General's social classes 1–5. This classifies class 1 as professional, e.g. doctors and accountants; class 2 as intermediate, e.g. policemen, nurses; class 3 (a) as skilled non-manual, e.g. office workers; class 3 (b) as skilled manual workers, e.g. plumbers; class 4 as semi-skilled, e.g. postmen and bus drivers and class 5 as unskilled.

house prices, causing another drift away from the rural areas by people born in those areas who do not have high paying jobs. There are problems of rural deprivation as the newcomers are likely to drive to town supermarkets, doctors, etc. so that the less well-off living in rural areas suffer depleted facilities as village shops and schools close down.

The development of the UK as a multi-ethnic community has many implications because it is so varied. According to the 1991 census figures, only 4.8 per cent of the UK's population is made up of ethnic minorities. However, these ethnic minorities are not evenly spread. The immigrants of the 1950s settled where the jobs were, and where they were able to obtain housing. Consequently, there are areas with very high percentages of ethnic minorities. Racism cannot be allowed in a multi-ethnic society as it is likely to destabilise the society. Successive British Governments have tried to deal with this, leading to the Race Relations Act and the Commission for Racial Equality, both of which aim to remove racism from the UK and to give all citizens an equal chance. However, the Stephen Lawrence Inquiry Report of 1999 showed that this still has a long way to go.

Other social trends

One major trend of the twentieth century was for women to have greater participation in work and politics and for men and women to have equal rights and status. It was not until 1928 that women gained the same rights as men in voting and becoming MPs; it was 1970 before women had the right to the same pay as men for the same work; it was 1975 before it was made illegal to discriminate against people on grounds of sex. As a result of these changes, the workforce of the UK in 1997 was 14,708,000 men and 11,959,000 women. Such changes also have implications in terms of childcare and the nature of the family.

The nature of the family has been another area of social change. Marriage has become less popular (there were 405,000 marriages in 1971 and only 254,400 in 2002) whilst divorce has become more popular (25,400 1961, 153,500 in 2003). The number of households made up of cohabiting couples accounted for around 10 per cent of households in 2001, compared with just over one in 20 (5.5 per cent) households in 1991. In 2000, 39 per cent of babies were born outside marriage. Some sociologists and moral experts have used these figures to suggest that the family, as it had been known during the twentieth century, will almost disappear in the twenty-first century.

The development of a classless society has also been a feature of the twentieth century. The introduction of the Welfare State (pensions, sick pay, unemployment pay, free education and equal access to examinations and higher education, the National Health Service) by the Liberal governments of 1906–14 and the Labour government of 1945–51 removed absolute poverty and led to the rise of a meritocracy. The restriction of the power of the House of Lords in 1911 (the Lords had prevented independence for Ireland on several occasions between 1884 and 1911), the reform of the Lords in 1999, and various policies between 1945 and 1999, led to a reduction of

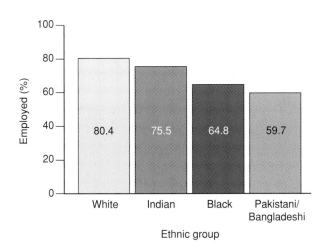

Figure 15.2 Employment rates by ethnic group (Source: *Social Trends 32*)

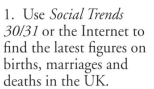

KEY TERMS

Social mobility movement from one social class, or group, to another

Suburbanisation the extension of suburbs (areas of domestic housing on the edges of towns) further and further into the countryside

the power and influence of the aristocracy at the same time that the media revolutions led to the rise of the new aristocracy of pop stars, TV and film stars and sports stars.

How equal is British society?

At first sight it might appear that major changes have been made. In 1911, 5 per cent of the population owned 87 per cent of the nation's wealth; by 1990, that figure had reduced to 40 per cent of the nation's wealth. However, that is still a large imbalance, which may be increasing due to changes in capital transfer tax and inheritance tax making it possible for people to hand down more of their wealth to their children. *Social Trends 29* (published by HMSO) compares the average gross income of the UK's population for 1996/97 in fifths and shows that the average gross income for the bottom fifth was £7080, while that for the top fifth was £45,870.

There is evidence from the latest government statistics that people from the lowest two-fifths of the income divide are much more likely to have lower educational qualifications, more health problems and lower life expectancy. A government report published in 1999 also showed wide regional variations not only in income and house prices, but also in education, health and life expectancy (income in London was 23 per cent above the average GDP, while in Northern Ireland it was 19 per cent below). There is also evidence that black people are more likely to be in the bottom two-fifths, are more likely to be arrested and are more likely to be sent to prison if they are convicted.

Activities

1. Use *Social Trends 30/31* or the Internet to find the latest figures on births, marriages and deaths in the UK.

2. Interview people from different age groups and educational backgrounds to discover what they feel about social class in the UK.

3. Research cases such as the Stephen Lawrence inquiry to discover background material on attitudes to race in the UK.

4. To what extent would you agree that the UK is an equal opportunities society?

15

EXAM QUESTION

Read the following passages and complete the tasks which follow.

Equal opportunities 'damages health of women soldiers'

An army doctor has found that women who join the Army are paying for equal opportunities with a higher risk of injury. Eight times as many women as men are discharged from the Army with injuries during basic training. The rate has more than doubled since the introduction in 1998 of identical training programmes for both sexes, from 4.6 per cent to 11.1 per cent under the new training regime, compared to below 1.5 per cent for men.

'Women face a much greater risk to their health than men,' writes Lieutenant-Colonel Ian Gemmell. 'Health and Safety guidance has been overlooked in the interests of meeting equal opportunity legislation.'

Women find the 12-week initial training tougher than men because of differences in bone mass, strength and stride length. They are more likely to suffer feet, knee, back and leg pain and stress fractures of the tibia, foot and hip.

Until 1998, female army recruits did not have to reach the same level of fitness as men. The policy changed because too many women lacked the strength for the work that they were expected to do after their training was complete.

Source: The Times, *3 January 2002*

Female fire fighter faces discrimination

A female fire fighter was removed from active service from the East Sussex Fire Authority because she was too small to do the job. At 5 feet 1 inch tall she had to stand on a stepladder to clean the fire engines and was unable to reach equipment stored high up on the tender.

Two male colleagues complained that her lack of height had led to them injuring themselves, as well as her, when they helped her remove a 45-foot ladder from the fire engine roof. She was also removed from duties that involved wearing chemical protection suits because the suits were several sizes too large for her.

As part of their training programme, fire fighters are required to perform physical tasks such as lifting a 50 kilogram weight, sprinting for half a mile, extending a ladder and rolling out lengths of hose in a prescribed period of time. A height requirement of 5 feet 6 inches was removed in 1996, but applicants have to be tall enough to 'put a ladder back on a fire engine'.

The fire fighter was assessed by senior officers who decided that her upper-body strength was insufficient and she was removed from operational duties.

Source: Daily Mail, *30 January 2002*

Write an objective report which communicates

(i) the nature of the problem outlined in these two articles

(15 marks)

(ii) which parties you consider to be responsible for the problem and why

(15 marks)

(iii) what measures might be taken to resolve the problem.

(20 marks)

A further ten marks will be awarded for communicating in a concise and logical way in a form appropriate to report writing.

(10 marks)

Total: 60 marks

AQA B June 2003

EXAMINER'S ADVICE

- This is a complete set of questions from A2 Unit 4 set in June 2003. The unit is called Conflict-Resolution, and the exercise is one of analysing the nature and source of a problem and proposing a solution. For more details on this paper check out page 1.
- The prime question requirement is to write 'an objective report' about the problem with three main components, as indicated. Use language, style and structure which is appropriate to report writing, i.e. title, headings, listed points, recommendations. The style should be detached and balanced and you should avoid a personal response in favour of ways of reconciling differences.
- In problem solving, the subject matter is less important than the ability to see both sides of a question and the ability to grasp how problems might be resolved in a realistic and effective way. Always seek to make a distinction between facts and opinions. Study the details of the problem to identify its nature and source. Look for causes and behaviour which contribute to them. This part of the question requires the ability to summarise points carefully and accurately.
- In the final part, avoid the temptation to go for 'easy solutions', for example 'remove women from

active service in the army and fire service'. That may solve one part of the problem (health and safety/ability in the job) but it doesn't address others (sex discrimination/equal opportunities legislation).
- Don't be afraid to emphasise the difficulties of conflict resolution. Most problems are more difficult than they seem. Compromise is not always easy to reach and may not satisfy the parties concerned. There is merit in recognising this and showing why some problems are difficult to resolve. You will also be able to gain AO4 marks (see introduction) by showing that you recognise the limitations of knowledge and its applications. Nevertheless the challenge is to come up with positive proposals. Negative ones will not gain many marks in this context. They are more likely to conceal the problem rather than solve it.
- You have one hour in which to complete this paper, which includes the time taken to study the passages and questions. Note the distribution of marks for the four components. Slightly more marks are given to the solution. Once again a useful guideline might be: number of marks for a question = the number of minutes to spend on it.
- When you have made your attempt, some suggested answer notes are given on page 255.

Crime and deviance

Despite the huge research, there does not appear to be a consensus of opinion about the most effective way of deterring crime or about which causal factors are most influential. Some people believe that the primary causes of crime are deep psychological states over which the criminal has no control, so that he/she cannot be held responsible or punished for his/her actions. On the other hand, the fact that many poor, unemployed, badly housed people do not commit crimes does not lead to the conclusion that these factors have no bearing on why some people become criminals.

Why do prisons fail in their aim to help offenders to return to and cope with society?

Despite the popular conception of prisons as becoming more and more like 'rest-cures' or 'holiday-camps', recent reports have described many prisons as seriously overcrowded, inhumane and uncivilised places, with insensitive and destructive regimes. If 70 to 80 per cent of offenders return to prison, then prisons obviously fail, except in the areas of revenge and protection of society. Many sociologists and criminologists have argued that prisons are the breeding grounds of criminals – universities of crime, where offenders have their self-image of deviancy reinforced and where the possibility of reform is virtually impossible. Prisons often reinforce the criminal behaviour they are designed to punish or inhibit by gathering together in tightly segregated and alienated groups those who already feel marginalised, and giving them the opportunities to teach one another the skills and attitudes of a criminal career. This is particularly true of young offenders, who may find themselves mixing with hardened criminals.

What is deviancy?

In general, what is described as deviant behaviour is decided by society itself. The American sociologist Marshall Culinary defined deviance as 'behaviour which is in a disapproved direction'. This means that behaviour acceptable in one society may not be so in another. For example, drinking alcohol is regarded as a serious offence in strict Muslim countries but is acceptable in others. Also, ideas about acceptable behaviour change over time. For example, attitudes to homosexuality changed during the twentieth century among large sections of society. Also most definitions of deviance relate to laws drawn up by only certain sections of society, i.e. powerful middle-class groups. Their norms of behaviour (table manners, for example) may be alien to other sub-cultures in society and hence are not universally agreed. Once we have labelled certain actions and those that carry them out as deviant we develop stereotypes, reinforced by the media, by which we categorise individuals. The effect of this is often to change the self-image of the criminal so that he/she is forced into the role created by society.

Physiological explanations for deviancy

These types of theory tend to assume that criminals indulge in deviant or abnormal behaviour, which can harm individuals and be socially disruptive. Since their behaviour is abnormal, they must be sick and the solution to their problem lies in diagnosing their illness. It has been suggested, for example, that stocky, well-rounded individuals tend to be particularly active and aggressive and therefore more likely to commit crimes. Other evidence suggests that a statistically significant number of violent antisocial men have an extra Y chromosome instead of the usual XY combination. Similarly, too much sugar in the blood – *hyperglycaemia* – may lead to criminal behaviour. Of course, it does not follow that everyone suffering from any of these conditions will necessarily become a criminal, but only that there is a disposition that may encourage deviancy.

Structuralism

Some sociologists argue that many criminals develop their deviant behaviour because of the way in which society is structured. Some young people belong to *sub-cultures*, which have developed different values from mainstream society. These values can develop because of educational, employment and financial deprivation and can result in people using criminal means by which to achieve high social and financial status.

Such situations could include:

- Young men who steal and joyride expensive cars in order to bolster their own status in the eyes of their peers.
- Persistent stealing to enhance the image of the thieves in the eyes of their own sub-culture – the 'respect' earned is far more important than the value of the goods stolen.

Recent trends in youth crime

The life-time likelihood of acquiring at least one criminal conviction is greater than commonly realised. Four in ten males and one in ten females are likely to be found guilty or cautioned for an indictable offence at some point during their lives. However, it is also true that a comparatively small proportion of the population – about five per cent of males – are chronic offenders who account for about half of all known offending.

Official records and 'self-report' studies also show that individuals more often break the law when they are young. The 'peak' ages at which they are most likely to be

> ### DID YOU KNOW?
>
> **Law and order**
> - *White-collar crime.* Crimes committed by high-status professionals, such as bank managers, stockbrokers, lawyers, etc. are far less likely to lead to arrests and convictions than those committed by working-class delinquents, even though such crimes can involve massive financial losses.
> - Many crime statistics are highly suspect. Many crimes involving personal injury, such as mugging, rape or domestic violence, are not reported by the victims. Many small crimes are not recorded officially at all by the local police force.
> - Despite the figures, crime is equally spread throughout society. It is just that vandalism, theft, burglary (working-class young male crimes) are easier to detect than sophisticated frauds involving money.

Crime an activity that breaks the law of the land and is subject to official punishment

Delinquency acts committed by young people, which are considered as antisocial or criminal

Deterrence the view that people will be put off committing crimes if the punishments are harsh enough

Deviance actions or attitudes that do not follow the norms and expectations of a particular social group

Rehabilitation the view that many criminals are 'sick', and therefore need therapeutic treatment rather than punishment

Retribution the theory that criminals are responsible for their actions and should be appropriately punished

Subculture certain norms, attitudes and values distinctive to a group and different to those of society as a whole

found guilty or cautioned are between 15 and 19. Criminal involvement typically starts before the age of 15, but declines markedly once young people reach their twenties. However, young people who become involved in crime at the earliest ages – before they are 14 – tend to become the most persistent offenders, with longer criminal careers.

Young offenders tend to be versatile and rarely specialise in particular types of crime, including violence. Recent research has identified features in the childhood and adult lives of violent offenders and non-violent persistent offenders that are very similar, suggesting that violent offenders are essentially frequent offenders. Studies have also found that young offenders are versatile in committing other types of antisocial behaviour, including heavy drinking, drug-taking, dangerous driving and promiscuous sex. Delinquency is, therefore, only one element in a much larger syndrome of antisocial behaviour.

Interviews with young offenders, meanwhile, suggest that their crimes are most commonly committed for material gain. However, a minority of offences, especially vandalism and taking vehicles without the owner's consent, are committed for excitement, enjoyment or to relieve boredom.

An important recent report analysed why there has been a big increase in the number of young boys carrying knives and in the number of stabbings:

- Ten per cent of boys aged 11 and 12 are reported to have carried a knife or other weapon in the previous year and eight per cent said they had attacked someone intending serious harm.
- By the age of 16, the figure had risen to 24 per cent who have carried a knife and 16 per cent who had attacked somebody intending harm.
- Pupils attending schools said that offences typically happen at school.
- Excluded young people appear more likely to experience crime in the local area where they live and are more likely to carry weapons.
- Forty-six per cent of excluded young people had admitted having carried a weapon compared to just 16 per cent of those in school. The peak age for both boys and girls committing offences is 14 to 15.
- Carrying a weapon is more common among those in Year 10 and 11 at school.
- Boys are three times more likely to carry and use knives than girls.

Understanding and preventing youth crime

The decline in the number of young offenders recorded in criminal justice statistics over the last 15 years is almost certainly illusory and due to changes in the way crimes are now reported, according to a recent MORI report. The report also stated that those people who commit crime from an early age are especially likely to become habitual offenders with long criminal records.

Major background factors associated with and contributing to youth crime include:

- low income and poor housing
- living in deteriorated inner city areas
- a high degree of impulsiveness and hyperactivity

- low intelligence and low school attainment
- poor parental supervision and harsh and erratic discipline
- parental conflict and broken families.

Research suggests that the most promising techniques for reducing the risks of young people's involvement in drug misuse, crime and other antisocial behaviour include:

- frequent home visiting by health professionals during pregnancy and infancy
- education in parenting
- high quality nursery education
- training children to 'stop and think'.

The most hopeful strategy for reducing youth crime is to identify the main risks and ways of reducing these within a community. This knowledge can be used to apply prevention techniques whose effectiveness has been demonstrated by research. Prevention is always better than either the mere suppression of criminal behaviour or punishment after the crime has happened.

Activities

1. If you were a magistrate who had to sentence two young men caught joyriding and crashing a stolen car, one of whom came from a financially comfortable home and the other from a vandalised housing estate with high unemployment, would you punish them both equally? What reasons would you use to defend your decision?

2. 'Television is responsible for the increase in crimes of violence.' To what extent do you think this statement is accurate and why?

16

EXAM QUESTION

Discuss whether we make 'the punishment fit the crime' when we commit convicted criminals to prison.

(12 marks)

AQA B January 2002

Prime Minister's prison visit

When the Prime Minister visited yesterday he mingled with inmates who improved their reading and writing, had taken a maths exam while on remand, or were taking part in the jail's 'job club'.

He was shown into the foundation English class where he sat at a tiny plastic desk before hearing from the prisoners about their experiences. In return he told them about the new 'custody of work' scheme to help offenders get jobs on release.

Source: The Guardian, *27 February 2001*

EXAMINER'S ADVICE

- This is another question from A2 Unit 5 set in January 2002 (see also Units 4, 24, 25, 27, 29, 30 and 34 of this book). It is one of five compulsory short essays, with each title taken from a different section of the specification and each worth 12 marks. Make sure that you attempt all five, so as not to lose marks unnecessarily. See page 1 for more information about this paper. Even if you are not taking A2, Unit 5 questions are similar to those set for AS Unit 1, so you should sensibly have a go at them.
- The question requires you to interpret the meaning of 'make the punishment fit the crime'. Its broader sense is: 'Is prison an appropriate sentence?' or 'Does sending criminals to prison work?' On both counts you should be thinking: 'Appropriate for what kind of crime/criminal?' and 'What are the purposes and intended benefits of sending someone to prison?'
- Once again you have some prompts to draw upon in the extract and should make use of them, for example prison can offer education and training opportunities and schemes for getting jobs on release. How do these compare with other types of sentences? You are able to state your own ideas and views, but you do not necessarily have to come down on one side or the other. With this sort of 'simple' question about a complex issue it is more than likely that there will be pros and cons. The best approach may be to set out the circumstances when you think that a prison sentence is appropriate and indeed may be necessary, and when you think other alternatives may be more effective.
- Use this unit and the next to gather further ideas about crime and punishment and then allow yourself 15 minutes to write your answer. Turn to page 255 for some further suggestions.

The nature of law

Why do we need laws?

Human beings are social creatures – they tend to live together in groups. During the thousands of years over which societies have developed, human beings have learnt that survival of the group depends on the development of a system of law. Law could be described as a way of structuring the tension between the self-interest of an individual within a group and the interests of the group as a whole. Anthropologists, historians and others who study primitive societies point out that whatever the cultural differences between different groups, they all have laws about such matters as protecting the elderly and weak, bringing up children, marriage, property rights and violence.

In a simple, small society, the population can decide its own laws and pass judgment on its lawbreakers. However, in larger, more complex societies, not only do the laws themselves become more complicated, but politicians have to be appointed to make the law, and lawyers, judges and police are needed to interpret and enforce the law. In this situation, the law is often seen as something imposed by the authorities from 'outside', or from 'above', rather than as a system of rules agreed to by every member of the community. However, most people would agree that, in general, the law provides a secure framework for society, in which human beings can flourish and exercise personal moral choice. Also, the law, in theory at least, protects the weak and vulnerable from those likely to exploit them.

Examples of laws

One of the earliest known systems of laws comes from the reign of Hammurabi, ruler of Babylon in 1790 BCE. One example of his laws is, 'If a man blinds a freeman in one eye, he shall lose his own eye.' At first glance, this law looks like a commendable attempt to deal with violence in a just manner. However, by using the word 'freeman', it implies the existence of slaves. By definition, slaves have no rights. The idea of justice, on the other hand, suggests equality and fairness for everybody. This raises the question of the relationship between law and justice. Also, this law makes no distinction between a deliberate or an accidental act. Laws tend to be very general, as it would be impossible to describe every possible situation in advance. Another issue raised here concerns the problem of violence. Should the state show its disapproval of violence by engaging in further violence? This is an important question when discussing such issues as capital punishment.

Another famous set of laws is The Ten Commandments, which appear in the Old Testament. They are claimed to be of divine origin and probably originate from before 1200 BCE. One of these laws states, 'You shall not kill.' This is obviously an essential requirement for any civilised society, but it raises many problems in interpretation. For example, does it mean that violence is ruled out in all circumstances? Does it rule out defending oneself, one's family or one's country against unprovoked attack? Does it rule out helping an elderly suffering relative who asks voluntarily for euthanasia?

Why obey the law?

Any civilised society needs *civil laws* to decide issues concerning property, taxation, child custody, etc. and *criminal laws* to deal with violence, theft, fraud, etc. Most people recognise that obeying the law produces benefits – settling disputes by non-violent means and providing a clear framework describing how people should behave as members of a civilised society, for example.

Civil disobedience or direct action?

The compulsory wearing of seat belts and the fluoridisation of water supplies are both modern examples of legislation which require individuals to give up their personal right to choose in the interests of society as a whole. However, it is clear that there may be examples of unjust laws, and this raises the issue of whether disobeying the law can ever be justified. The mediaeval theologian, *Thomas Aquinas* (1224–74), argued that an unjust law was not a proper law.

In 399 BCE, the Greek philosopher *Socrates* was unjustly condemned to death by the Athenian council on the grounds that he was subverting the state and corrupting the young with his radical ideas and questions. Despite the attempts of his friends to persuade him to escape from prison, Socrates refused, on the grounds that if one accepted the benefits of the state, so one had to abide by its decisions. Socrates was not against all forms of disobedience, however. He also argued that if someone believed that the laws of a state were corrupt then he had the right to disobey any that affected him.

John Rawls (1962) argued that any system of justice and law is to do with the concept of 'fair play'. If people agree to abide by this and recognise that it is socially necessary for everyone to obey the law, then it is not fair if someone decides to disobey the law because it is to their personal advantage. Provided that the injustice is not too great or unfairly distributed, Rawls argued that we have to accept some unjust laws. According to Rawls, the injustice of a law is not sufficient reason for disobeying it.

Many current-day practitioners of civil disobedience draw heavily on a tradition that goes back to Henry David Thoreau, a nineteenth-century US writer. In 1849, Thoreau published an essay entitled *Civil Disobedience*, where he encouraged US citizens to protest slavery, oppression and the war against Mexico by refusing to pay taxes. Though refusing to pay taxes was not a new idea (it was a tactic used by anti-slavery abolitionists), Thoreau's twist on the tactic was the punishment angle. He saw civil disobedience as an act where the punishment is as important as the act of breaking the law. Punishment, or overcoming the power of punishment, is fundamental to Thoreau's method of civil disobedience.

The *Peace Movement* has also embraced civil disobedience as a method of protest. This movement has defined the word 'civil' to mean the opposite of violence. Their philosophy states that those who are engaging in civil disobedience should do so in a 'civilised' manner, with respect for the opponent or identified target(s). Relying heavily on the teachings and philosophical thought of Mahatma Gandhi (who used the term 'passive resistance') and Martin Luther King, the Peace Movement sees the personal consequences that result from choosing to disobey as an integral component of the action.

Both of these approaches embrace civil disobedience as a tool for dialogue – primarily with the authorities that have created unjust laws – and they assume that there is a general understanding of justice. These philosophies hold that the act of creating or maintaining a conversation about an unjust law is essential to getting that law overturned. Like the actions of the Civil Rights Movement, the appeal is to the society's sense of justice.

Direct action

Direct action means acting for yourself against injustice and oppression. It can, sometimes, involve putting pressure on politicians or companies, for example, to ensure a change in an oppressive law or destructive practices. However, such appeals are direct action simply because they do not assume that the parties in question will act for us – indeed the assumption is that change only occurs when we act to create it. So, direct action is any form of activity which people themselves decide upon and organise themselves, which is based on their own collective strength and does not involve getting intermediaries to act for them. As such, direct action is a natural expression of liberty and of self-government. It is clear that by acting for yourself you are expressing the ability to govern yourself. Thus direct action is a means by which people can take control of their own lives. It is a means of self-empowerment and self-liberation.

Many direct activists had identified the US justice system, for example, as a racist, heterosexist, homophobic and sexist institution, where (at best) dialogue with the authorities has historically and repeatedly lead to misinterpretation or total destruction. US citizens, therefore, decided that they could no longer use the democratic system in which other people acted on their behalf, but would have to act directly to bring about change.

Most direct actions also work indirectly and symbolically. A strong indirect effect is to show what can be/needs to be done. When black slaves escaped from the plantations in the South, they proved that freedom was possible. When activists shut down the World Trade Organisation meetings and disrupt the smooth flow of corporate operations, they show that the empire can be ruffled.

With direct action, the participants do not necessarily welcome the consequences of their action. Unlike civil disobedience, where the resisters generally welcome the punishment as a means of furthering their message and increasing the dialogue, direct actions such as hanging a banner, spray painting a political message on a wall or damaging property are public acts of protest that can be done discreetly and in a non-public manner.

KEY TERMS

Civil disobedience a protest by a group of citizens, usually peaceful but involving illegal action against a state of affairs to which they have moral objections, e.g. hunt saboteurs and anti-abortionists

Committal proceedings a preliminary hearing, in front of magistrates, to decide whether there is sufficient evidence for the case to go to Crown Court for trial

Common law applies to laws that may be interpreted by judges in court when they have to decide on difficult or obscure cases. It also refers to ancient customs and usages that have almost acquired the status of law

Constitutional law the collection of statutes passed by Acts of Parliament down the ages. There is no one definitive written constitution in Great Britain

Counsel a lawyer qualified to represent a client in court, usually a barrister

Indictable offence an offence for which a person can be tried by jury

Judicial system the system of courts and sentencing designed to deal with civil and criminal offences

Justice of the Peace a magistrate

Lord Chancellor a member of the government and the House of Lords who is the head of the court system in the UK

Social justice the application of fairness and equal treatment to all members of a society

Activities

1. In small groups, describe six serious crimes which have been in the media recently. List them in order of seriousness, giving reasons for the order. What punishment would you consider appropriate for each of these crimes and why?

2. A recent television series showed a fictional group of animal rights protesters who planted bombs that killed two people. Do you think such illegal action can ever be justified and why?

3. Over 60% of first-time offenders return to prison. Do you think prisons should emphasise punishment or rehabilitation and why?

4. List the occasions when you think it would be reasonable to break the law, giving your reasons.

Conclusion

Despite their differences, both civil disobedience and direct action are powerful forms of resistance. They share the common aims of:

* preserving or changing a societal phenomena
* generating public debate
* empowering the practitioners and inspiring others to take action, and
* breaking the law(s), often with serious and unjust consequences for others.

Organisations which have taken part in direct action in recent years include, Greenpeace, CND, animal rights groups and other ecological movements, pro-life organisations and various terrorist groups.

To what extent can pressure groups be seen as a threat to the democratic process?

(12 marks)

AQA B June 2002

Figure 17.1 A protest organised by Greenpeace, 2004

Figure 17.2 A monument to Churchill which has been graffitied, 2001

EXAMINER'S ADVICE

- This is another question from A2 Unit 5 set in June 2002. It is one of five compulsory short essays, with each title taken from a different section of the specification and each worth 12 marks. See page 1 for more information about this paper.
- This is another typical 'to what extent/how far' General Studies question, where you are free to give your own opinions on an issue, but where arguments and opinions are finely balanced. You also need to show awareness of the existence of the opposing arguments. The visual prompts give you two examples of kinds of pressure group activity. You should think of other examples, like the ones

suggested in the unit you have just read, and also draw on ideas that follow in Units 29, 30 and 31.
- Remember that you don't have to come down on one side or the other. With this sort of 'simple' question about a complex issue, it is more than likely that there will be pros and cons. A useful approach might be to set out the circumstances when you think that pressure groups have served a useful function, and where their activities are illegal and could not be justified.
- Use this and other units to compile your arguments and examples, then allow yourself 15 minutes to write your answer. Turn to page 256 for some points for and against.

18 Rights and responsibilities

Rights

According to the *Oxford English Dictionary*, the word 'right', means 'a justifiable claim on legal or moral grounds to have or obtain something or to act in a certain way'. The question of rights can be interpreted in different ways and can be analysed from a philosophical, moral, legal or political point of view.

Many modern discussions of rights and responsibilities are a response to political situations where human rights appear to be absent. These include:

- *minority rights* – concerned with the way religious or ethnic groups are treated
- *gay rights* – concerned with discrimination against homosexuals
- *women's rights* – concerned with the role and rights of women in society, particularly in relation to less developed countries
- *animal rights* – concerned with the treatment of animals, particularly in relation to hunting, conservation and animal experimentation.

The issue of rights only arises because human beings tend to live in communities and there are often conflicts between the interests of individuals. On a desert island with only one human being present, there are no such conflicts. The status of rights is often categorised as one of the following:

- *Legal rights.* An example of a legal right would be the right of ownership to legally acquired property. This type of right can be protected by law. Legal rights also involve the right to behave in a certain way or to expect someone else to do so, such as a legally binding contract requiring someone to supply certain services in exchange for money.
- *Moral rights.* The right of an old person to care and respect is an example of a moral right, although this would not be directly enforceable in law. Similarly, one might argue for the rights of an unborn child and against the rights of the mother to choose in the context of a possible abortion. Whatever the legal status of the act of abortion itself, there is still a further moral discussion about rights involved.
- *Universal rights.* This category would include those rights with a possible moral basis but which are not necessarily legally supported in some countries or societies. For example, most people would argue that no human being should be a slave and that this right of freedom should apply universally, or that people should have the right to free speech, to express their opinions in public without fear of persecution.

In practice, rights often take the form of:

- *claims* – being owed money means that you have a claim on the debtor
- *powers* – the right to distribute your property in your will
- *liberties* – being exempt from giving evidence against a spouse in court
- *immunities* – the right not to be persecuted for joining a trade union.

The origins of human rights

Article 1 of the Universal Declaration of Human Rights produced by the United Nations in 1948 states, 'All human beings are born free and equal in dignity and rights. They are endowed with reason and conscience and should act towards each other in a spirit of brotherhood.' The Declaration goes on to specify a long list of human rights including the rights to life, liberty and security, freedom from slavery and freedom of movement across national borders. Although most civilised societies would agree to this declaration, at least in theory, there have been different views in the history of thought concerning exactly what rights human beings should have, and the basis on which such rights can be justified.

Natural rights and natural law

The phrase 'human rights' is comparatively recent. Traditionally, the phrase 'natural rights' was used, and this was often based on *natural law*. This refers to the idea that all people recognise some moral obligation, leading to generally agreeing moral principles.

- The classical Greek philosophers, *Socrates, Plato* and *Aristotle*, all argued that there is a natural justice or a right thing to do.
- In the New Testament, *Paul* spoke of those who obey, by nature, the things of the law, because they have the law written on their conscience (Romans, 11).
- *Thomas Aquinas* (1224–74) linked Christian belief with the idea of natural law in the thirteenth century. He argued that there are certain principles of true morality and justice discernible by human reason without the aid of revelation (even though they are of divine origin). Man-made laws that conflict with these principles are not valid law.
- *Thomas Hobbes* (1588–1679) argued that in its natural state, human life was 'solitary, poor, nasty, brutish and short'. In order to protect people from one another, a 'social contract' was needed, which involved the natural right not to be harmed by another.
- *John Locke* (1632–1704) had a more optimistic view of human nature. Human beings are naturally capable of acting in the interests of others and of recognising a natural law, instituted by God, which says that 'no one should harm another in his life, health, liberty or possessions'.
- The *American Declaration of Independence* (1776) is another example. It claimed to be founded on the self-evident truths that man has a right to life, liberty and the pursuit of happiness.

However, the Utilitarian philosopher, *Jeremy Bentham* (1748–1832), argued that there was no such thing as human rights. His theory was designed to cut through all the confusion and conflicts to which arguing about human rights might lead. He believed that the assertion of natural rights incites 'selfish and dissocial passions', the great enemies of public peace, and so militates against social order and the laws of the land.

DID YOU KNOW?

Moral responsibilities
- At least five different British companies provide electronic torture equipment such as cattle prods to repressive regimes.
- Official Roman Catholic teaching regards contraception as a sin because it is against their understanding of natural law.
- In 1998, at least 5,000 people died in 114 countries from torture or imprisonment.
- During the 1999 World Trade Talks, some less developed countries objected to the idea of abolishing child or slave labour.

KEY TERMS

Amnesty International a voluntary organisation, founded in 1961, which publicises and fights for the freedom of people who are unfairly imprisoned, tortured and otherwise persecuted for speaking out against corruption

Homophobia an extreme aversion to and prejudice against the idea and practice of homosexual relationships of either sex

Justice refers to the idea of fairness and equality for all and to the system of reward and punishment that helps to maintain it

Sexism the view that one sex (usually women) is inferior emotionally, intellectually or physically and the practical application of this attitude in society

Speciesism the view that animals have fewer rights than human beings and could be used for such things as experiments

Human rights were not something to which human beings were entitled by right of being human, but only permissible if they contributed more happiness than unhappiness to society.

Article 18 of the Universal Declaration of Human Rights states that everyone has the 'right to freedom of thought, conscience and religion'. It could be suggested that this is the part of the declaration that has been most flagrantly ignored and contravened since the Second World War. All over the world, the right to express political or religious views contradicting those of the prevailing authorities has been removed and those expressing such views have been imprisoned, expelled, tortured and/or killed. Examples include:

- the murder of thousands of Baha'i (a pacifist religion) in Iran in the 1980s
- the obliteration of Tibetan Buddhist culture after the Chinese invasion
- the torture of men, women and children in Bosnia in the 1990s
- the struggle for independence by the Kurds against, Iraq, Turkey and Russia.

Responsibilities

The idea of responsibility can refer to the idea that people are answerable for their behaviour, implying that they are free to choose their actions and can thus be praised or blamed for what they actually do (see Unit 17, 'The nature of law'). But it can also refer to the idea of 'duty'. Duty can be defined as 'the obligation of an individual to satisfy a claim made upon him by the community or individual or group in order to serve the common good'. In all successful societies, rights and duties have to be balanced against each other. If children have a legal and/or moral right to education, then the parents and the state have a duty to provide it. Another good example of this balance can be seen in the purchase and use of a railway ticket. The railway company has the duty to convey the passenger from one place to another and has the right to be paid for doing so. The passenger has the duty to pay for this ticket and the right to be conveyed to the destination for which they have paid.

This relationship between rights and duties has given rise to the view that all morality depends on a 'social contract'. Individuals agree to perform certain duties in exchange for the acquisition of certain rights. For example, law-abiding citizens agree to respect the property of their neighbours, in exchange for the right to have their own property protected.

What is our duty?

The philosopher *Immanuel Kant* (1724–1804) argued that human beings are rational and have the capacity to work out what their duty is and to do it. For Kant, a good action is one that involves doing what you ought to do, rather than what you want to do. Reason tells you that you ought always to treat people as ends in themselves, rather than as means to an end. This involves always telling the truth and never taking life.

Figure 18.1 Conflict of rights – these protestors feel they have the right to deny homosexuals rights

The Ten Commandments

Some lists of duties such as the Ten Commandments have stood the test of time. Whatever their religious inspiration, they seem to contain basic rules that contribute to the survival of civilised human communities. Basic human rights seem to be protected when people accept the following duties:

* Do not steal.
* Do not commit adultery.
* Do not tell lies.
* Do not kill.
* Honour your father and mother.

The problem with duties

The problem with lists of duties, however, is that they never allow for exceptional circumstances. There are always situations, for example, where one might consider that killing in self-defence or lying about the whereabouts of a relation being pursued by an assassin seems to be the right course of action. However, in general, discussing human behaviour in terms of rights and duties seems to contribute positively towards the preservation of society.

Citizenship

The 2001 General Election produced the lowest turn out of voters since 1918. Less than six out of ten of those people entitled to vote bothered to do so. This apparent apathy and disinterest in the way democracy operates and the alarming ignorance displayed during recent years regarding the whole machinery of government has led to the introduction of Citizenship as a compulsory part of the National Curriculum in schools and examinable at GCSE. Its introduction, however, has had significant effects on PSHE and Religious Education because of the time constraints already present caused by the demands of the National Curriculum.

The Department for Education and Skills (Dfes) identifies three inter-related components that should run through all education for Citizenship, as shown below:

- *Social and moral responsibility.* Pupils learning from the very beginning of their education, self-confidence and socially and morally responsible behaviour both in and beyond the classroom, towards those in authority and towards each other.
- *Community involvement.* Pupils learning about becoming helpfully involved in the life and concerns of their neighbourhood and communities, including learning through community involvement and service to the community.
- *Political literacy.* Pupils learning about the institutions, problems and practices of our democracy and how to make themselves effective in the life of the nation, locally, regionally and nationally through skills and values as well as knowledge – a concept wider than political knowledge alone.

Pupils develop skills of enquiry, communication, participation and responsible action through learning about and becoming informed and interested citizens. This will be achieved through creating links between pupils' learning in the classroom and activities that take place across the school, in the community and the wider world. The *National Curriculum Handbook* sets out what pupils should learn through citizenship education and there are now a large number of organisations supporting this project. The main emphasis of the course is on the importance of participation in the operation of a community and the development of a sense of responsibility towards the community as a whole. (Source: Dfes website)

EXAM QUESTION

'It's a free country so I can do whatever I like.' To what extent do you agree with this statement?

(12 marks)

AQA B January 2004

EXAMINER'S ADVICE

- This is a short essay question from AS Unit 1 set in January 2004. It is one of four short essays you have to write from a choice of six. Each title is taken from the five different areas of the specification, and note that from 2005 onwards they will be worth 15 marks instead of 12. See page 1 for more information about this paper. It is absolutely essential to give equal time and attention to each of your four answers, so as not to lose vital marks. There are other questions from this paper at the end of Units 9, 23, 28 and 35 of this book.

- The question is basically about rights and responsibilities as a citizen, so use the unit you have just read and Unit 17 to gather your ideas. The statement you are asked to discuss is, of course, an extreme and absurd interpretation of what is meant by 'a free country', so it would be a good idea to consider exactly what is meant when we talk about 'freedom' in this context. As citizens we have certain rights by law and custom. Set these out as part of your answer.

- At the same time, it is obvious that we can never do '*whatever* we like' in general terms. There are bound to be limits, some defined again by law and others by moral values. The limits are usually to do with the effects of our actions upon others. Again, you should set out what you think these limits are or should be.

- Only when you have done both of these can you come to a view about freedom in society. It is likely that freedom is a relative concept, but some societies may grant more to their citizens than others and some individuals may enjoy more personal freedom than others. So what is your view?

- Allow yourself no more than 15 minutes or so to write your answer. Turn to page 256 for some suggested points to make on one side or the other.

Power and control

Power can be defined on a personal level as the ability to get one's own way, even when others are opposed to one's wishes. From a wider perspective, power is about who has the authority and the capacity to change states of affairs in a society. Politics is often defined as the struggle to acquire and exercise such power. Sociologists often distinguish between two forms of power – authority and coercion:

- *Authority* refers to the exercise of legitimate power, which is accepted by everyone as right and just. For example, parliamentary decisions are accepted as lawful by members of society because they accept parliament as having legitimate authority.
- *Coercion* refers to the exercise of power that is not regarded as legitimate by those subject to it. Members of the Republican Movement in Northern Ireland, for example, do not accept the authority of the British Government and so regard the exercise of their power as coercion. Coercion may involve the use of force to overcome opposition.

The sociologist Max Weber suggested that there were three types of authority:

- *Charismatic authority* derives from those exceptional qualities displayed by some leaders which enables them to produce intense loyalty, admiration and obedience in their followers. Examples of such powerful leaders include Alexander the Great and Napoleon.
- *Traditional authority* refers to the acceptance of certain customs and traditions which have been long established. Accepting the authority of a reigning monarch because of his/her inherited status would be an example of this.
- *Rational/legal authority* is based on the fact that all the members of society accept a legal framework with a particular shared end in view. In general, people accept the authority of the legal system because they realise that it serves the goal of justice.

There is also what might be referred to as the *authority of expertise*. We tend to accept the authority of those whose expertise we recognise – doctors, teachers, solicitors, etc. Accepting their authority often means accepting their right to give us instructions.

Why do we need power?

Human beings tend to be gregarious (inclined to live in groups). The fact that virtually everyone lives together in groups immediately raises problems about how such groups should be organised. For example, the idea of 'government' usually implies either a group or an individual who is in control of the affairs of a nation. However, the way this control is exercised has profound effects on the lives of the population. Under some forms of dictatorship, a 'political discussion' might take the form of indoctrination, which justifies the authority of those in power and stifles opposition. On the other hand, you might argue that although in a democracy everyone has the right to express their views, the complicated nature of the democratic process itself prevents people's views from being heard.

Important questions raised by the discussion of power include the following:

- Who should govern and by what means?
- By what right do they exercise authority and control?
- What activities should governments be involved in?

What is a government?

A government is an organisation that has the authority to make and enforce rules and laws about important and extensive areas of human life. However, it is only a legitimate government if its authority is accepted by everybody. A government that makes laws that no one accepts, but which forces people to obey it through military might, is not a proper government because its right to enforce laws is not recognised by society. Many other organisations, such as labour unions, large corporations, religious institutions and schools, etc. exercise authority over sections of society, but what makes governments significant is the extent of their authority. This may include such areas as law and order, education, social welfare, defence, taxation, and immigration.

The purpose of government

Most political thinkers agree that some form of government is necessary and preferable to a state of *anarchy* in which there is no institutional government whatsoever. The justification for needing some form of government includes the following reasons:

- *To serve the interests of the most powerful.* This is the cynical view that government is just an organised form of domination. The most powerful group uses government agencies as a means of serving its own interests.
- *To protect people from one another.* This is the most common theory about the purpose of government. Without laws and the means to enforce them, some people would treat other people very badly and subject them to theft, personal violence and other forms of abuse. Governments exist to construct and establish a legal and social system that will provide a secure environment in which economic production and culture can flourish.
- *To promote God's will.* This ancient theory argues that governments exist to carry out the will of God and their authority consists of the fact that the government is the Earthly representative of God on Earth. This type of view can still be seen in some religiously fundamentalist societies.
- *To develop and control the economy.* This type of theory is particularly associated with *Marxism*. According to Marx, the purpose of government is to promote the

expansion of the forces of production by finding more and more effective ways of producing goods. In the final stages of history, ordinary workers finally own the means of production and control the government so that policies are all aimed towards the general welfare.

- *To bring about equality.* This theory is based on the assumption that people should have equal opportunity and equal status in a society. It is the role of government to prevent artificial social or economic distinctions and to eliminate all inequalities of property, money, achievement or power.

In practice, most governments carry out a range of functions, some of which are conflicting. While most democratic governments try to act in the interests of the general welfare of society, this may involve attacking the rights of some individuals. For example, forcing people to pay taxes or to engage in compulsory military service are attacks on individual freedom which are justified in terms of the good of society as a whole. There is a wide range of political views concerning the extent to which governments should exercise control over people's lives. *Socialist* political thinkers tend to argue that governments should own the agencies that provide education, housing, health, transport, power, etc. because these are all essential to the welfare of human beings. *Free-market/libertarian* thinkers tend to argue that governments should exercise as little control as possible in peoples' lives and that people should provide for their own welfare.

Who should have control?

The most widely accepted view is often referred to as *the consent of the governed*. A government gets its power from the fact that the people of a particular country consent to it acting on their behalf. A range of other views are presented below:

- The *American Declaration of Independence 1776* not only specified the purpose of government as the protection of natural rights and the promotion of people's happiness, but also claimed the right to abolish the authority of a particular government if it was not pursuing those purposes.
- *Thomas Hobbes (1588–1679)* argued that in their natural state, the lives of men were 'solitary, poor, nasty, brutish and short'. In order to avoid a lawless state of nature, people agree to a 'social contract', in which they give the sovereign enough power to control people's lives. This will provide a secure environment in which goods can be produced, and people can be protected from each other. However, once the sovereign has acquired this power, it cannot be claimed back, therefore government is no longer by consent.
- *Jean Jacques Rousseau (1712–78)* argued for a different type of social contract. Rousseau thought that human beings were naturally good and had kindly feelings for each other. However, he suggested that they need to live in society in order to develop their full potential and to do this they should enter into a social contract where they surrender their individual rights to the 'general will'. This is

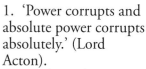

concerned with the good of the whole community, and in large communities wise legislators have to be elected to draw up laws and policies in agreement with the general will.

Democracy

Most political thinkers would argue that democracy – rule by the majority or all of a population – is the best form of government. In a democracy, the government is elected by the free choice of the population and can be removed without violence. In a modern democracy, virtually all adults can vote, irrespective of sex or status. The principal advantage of democracy is that people can exercise direct control over their policy makers by voting them out of office. Also, policies tend to reflect the interests of the majority and so receive general support. Disadvantages of democracy include the fact that non-experts often get elected to powerful positions because they are popular. Also, in a system where the majority rules, minority interests and opinions may suffer, although some definitions of democracy include human rights and individual freedom as a part of democracy. Another disadvantage is that in a system where candidates have to appeal directly to the voters, the most charismatic and financially supported public speaker may be elected rather than the most suitable person for a particular post.

Activities

1. 'Power corrupts and absolute power corrupts absolutely.' (Lord Acton).
a) Explain what you think this statement means.
b) Use your own research (Internet or library resources) to find recent examples of corruption. This might include bribery, buying votes, rigging elections, etc.

2. 'Democracy is not perfect but it is the best political system we have.' Discuss the disadvantages and advantages of democracy and say what improvements/ alterations you would like to make to the present system.

EXAM QUESTION

Read Jeremy Paxman's account of the Plowden family and complete the task below.

It could be argued either that the real power in Britain still lies with such families; or that they have lost hold of the power they once had.

Argue one way or the other, as if you were a member of such a family.

You might consider in your account

- the source, and present basis, of your wealth
- whether this wealth gives you power and influence
- where the power that you once had might have gone.

(40 marks)

AQA B May 2003

The Plowdens

William and Valerie Plowden are moving out of the house their family has occupied for the last 800 years. It is a squat, half-timbered manor house squirreled away in the blue remembered hills of A.E. Housman's *A Shropshire Lad.* There is no sign to Plowden Hall, there are no open days, no pots of National Trust jam on sale, no teas served by sturdy ladies in tweed skirts. On the drive, immature, tailless pheasants scuttle out of the way as you pass. In the drowsy fields, sheep and cattle wander aimlessly. A gardener is clipping the edges of the lawn outside the big house. Hidden away from the rest of the world, the loudest sound is the slicing of his shears. No cars, no trains, no aircraft.

The Plowden family have been 'seated' here at least since the twelfth century, when one of their ancestors fought at the Crusader siege of Acre. The Plowden family have seen it all, over the years. And still they are here, the Plowden family, living at Plowden Hall, in the village of Plowden, in a land of quiet contentment.

Their life revolves around farming, half-a-dozen black Labradors, hunting, shooting and fishing. It is not the sort of life that brings your name to the attention of editors of *Who's Who:* public service is restricted to sitting on the bench of magistrates and occasionally turning out as High Sheriff when the Queen visits the county. For the rest, it is *Farmers Weekly, Horse and Hound* and the *Shooting Times.*

The received wisdom about this type of English family is that they have been consigned to history, destroyed by the First World War, death duties, taxation, Lloyd's and congenital incompetence at handling their affairs. The image is of Evelyn Waugh's *Brideshead,* ancestral piles abandoned by families unable to meet the demands of modern life. Like all images, it is partly true. But among those who have survived, it is utterly wrong. William Plowden was 20, on army service, when his father died, leaving him Plowden Hall. There seemed little chance of hanging on to the family home and he began trying to find a tenant who would rent the Hall. But no one was prepared to take it on. So he resigned his commission, went to Oxford, 'discovered my brain wouldn't function', and took himself off to the Royal Agricultural College at Cirencester. When he took on the estate, he had 450 acres 'in hand'. Within a few years, he was running 2,000 acres. Now, the estate employs a manager, 12 people on the farm, another five in the woods, a full-time mason, a carpenter, gamekeeper, odd-job man and gardener.

Plowden and his wife are moving out of the ancestral home for a farm on the estate, so that their son can move in. Assuming William Plowden lives another seven years, Plowden Hall will pass to another generation of Plowdens, free of tax. He hands on a thriving business that gives the lie to the claim that time is up for all these old families who embody a traditional idea of Englishness.

Source: Jeremy Paxman, The English *(Penguin Books, 1999)*

EXAMINER'S ADVICE

- This extended writing question is from AS Unit 2 set in May 2003. It is the first of two pieces of extended writing you have to do in this test, the second being a more conventional essay. There is a similar type of question at the end of Unit 8 where you had to propose or oppose a motion in a debate.
- Here you have to argue a case, using the detailed prompts in the question and source, for or against the idea that long-established land-owning families still exercise real power over society. Basically, it is a question of your view of where wealth and power now reside in contemporary English society.
- However, you have to write it creatively, as if you were a member of such a family. This implies writing in the first person, but not particularly or literally in the name of William or Valerie Plowden. In other words you should take the generality of the position of families like the Plowdens and argue whether they still have the power they once had. Paxman suggests in parts of his article that their wealth, power and influence have declined, and in other parts or respects that they have not. You may wish to argue along similar lines and here the question allows for that, whereas in the debating question it did not.
- This is not an easy task and needs to be practised. Decide which case you are going to argue and use the clues in the source, plus your own ideas and knowledge from the unit you have just read, to assemble the arguments and evidence to support it.
- Allow yourself no more than 30 minutes to write your answer. Turn to page 256 for some suggested points to make on one side or the other.

Politics

What is politics?

One useful definition might be, 'Politics is the activity by which groups reach binding collective decisions through attempting to reconcile differences amongst their members.' The Greek philosopher *Aristotle* (384–322 BCE) said that 'man is by nature, a political animal'. Human beings live in groups and they can only resolve their conflicts of interest, make plans and take decisions by engaging in some sort of political activity. In this sense, all rational human beings take part in politics even if they are not professional politicians. Politics is a complex activity, which contains the following elements, to name but a few:

- *Diversity of views.* If there were no differences between people about future plans and methods of achieving them, there would be no need for political activity.
- *Reconciliation.* One of the principal functions of politics is to find an accepted solution to problems caused by major differences of points of view.
- *Decision-making.* Politics involves making decisions about future actions that will be binding on all members of a group and may be backed up with force.

Politics and government

Although some extreme political activists argue for 'anarchy' – the absence of law and government – most people recognise that in large communities individuals and institutions have to be appointed to take decisions and execute policy on their behalf. Collectively, this is referred to as the government. (Different types of government are discussed in detail in Unit 19, 'Power and control'). Governments can loosely be divided into *authoritarian* and *democratic*. Examples of authoritarian governments include the following:

- *Military rule.* In many African, Asian and Latin American countries, military leaders took over governments in response to economic and civil problems. Many of these leaders put down opposition ruthlessly and acted as a dictatorship.
- *Personal dictatorship.* Many African countries replaced colonial powers with 'hero-figures' who had fought against the colonial powers, for example, Jomo Kenyatta, President of Kenya (1962–78), and Kenneth Kaunda, who ran Zambia (1964–91). Both these leaders ended up as very autocratic, resistant to change and responsible for economic decline.
- *Dominant party rule.* Countries such as Singapore and Egypt appear democratic but in reality are run by one very powerful party, which controls the media, the economic resources and has the ability to rig elections.

Politics in Britain

Like most Western European countries, the USA, Australia, New Zealand, etc. the UK is governed as a *liberal democracy*. This can be described as a system where elected politicians act on behalf of those who elect them but within carefully defined limits, so that the rights of minorities and individuals are protected. The most important feature of democracy is the idea of *representative government*. This includes the following characteristics:

- A *Member of Parliament* who represents the interests of their constituents.
- *Freedom of expression*, meaning that people can choose their representatives freely.
- *Sovereignty of the people*, where the will of the general population is paramount.
- *Political equality*, meaning that every person's vote and right to vote is of equal value.

Parliament

In the UK, the representative government is Parliament, which consists of three parts:

- *The Monarch*, who has no real power but presents the current government's future plans in the Queen's Speech at the opening of Parliament.
- *The House of Lords* (in the process of being reformed), which has hereditary peers, life peers, archbishops, bishops, and senior members of the legal system known as Law Lords.
- *The House of Commons*, consisting of 659 elected members. Since 1872, Members of Parliament have been elected by secret ballot. Any member of the public can vote for any candidate without having to reveal their choice. Virtually all members belong to either the Conservative Party or the Labour Party (the two largest), or the Liberal Democrats. Much smaller numbers represent the Ulster Unionists and the Welsh and Scottish Nationalist parties.

The process of government

In practice, the government is made up of the Prime Minister and the Cabinet, which consists of approximately 20 of the Prime Minister's senior colleagues and their assistants who have been appointed as Ministers of State to run various departments such as defence, education, transport, etc. or to represent areas such as Scotland or Wales. This group of ministers is responsible for introducing new policies that they wish to become law. These measures are known as bills until they have passed through Parliament, after which they become *Acts of Parliament* and then law. This whole process of government involves three interlocking areas:

- *Legislature*. This describes the work of Parliament, which has the responsibility to make new laws and to change existing ones.
- *Executive*. This refers to the work of Ministers of State and the civil service departments they run. They are responsible for the execution of the wishes of Parliament, for example producing the detailed administrative framework for a change in the law affecting pensions, or raising the school-leaving age.

Globalisation the process by which social, cultural and economic trends and policies are less dependent on national power and more influenced by worldwide issues, e.g. European currency issues

Referendum a system that allows every elector to vote directly on an important national issue, such as Scottish or Welsh devolution – an example of direct rather than representative democracy

Single transferable vote an electoral system that allows voters to transfer their vote to where it will be most effective after the first ballot – used in Eire

Two-party system the traditional state of affairs in British politics, where Parliament is dominated by two strong parties with far more members than the nearest minority. This would be changed by proportional representation

- *Judiciary.* This refers to the process by which expert judges settle disputes concerning the interpretation of the law.

Acts of Parliament

In order for a bill to become an Act of Parliament, it has to have three readings. The first introduction is a formality before the second reading, where the general principles of the bill are discussed by those present in the Commons at the time. This is followed by the committee stage, where the details of the bill are examined in depth before it is sent back to the Commons for a third and final debate. Although in theory it can then be held up by the House of Lords, it will eventually become law despite their opposition, as long as a majority vote for it in the Commons. The formal Royal Assent of the sovereign is then required for it to become law. In practice, very few bills introduced by a majority government fail to become law.

Criticisms of the system

Although in theory the political process in the UK appears to be very democratic, various important weaknesses have been highlighted in recent years.

The problem of oligarchy

Oligarchy means 'rule by the few'. In the House of Commons, very few backbench MPs have any influence on government policy or the opportunity to introduce a bill dealing with the interests of their constituents, because of the pressure on parliamentary time. Backbenchers may be appointed to Parliamentary Select Committees to examine various issues, but in general, they are there to vote in accordance with party wishes. This gives the Prime Minister enormous *patronage* (the power to grant favours, including promotion in response to loyalty). Legislation is controlled by the Prime Minister and the Cabinet.

Adversarial politics

In the House of Commons, the government benches face those of the Opposition. Debates in the House tend to emphasise criticism of the other major party, and the manipulation of the process in order to gain narrow political advantage, instead of emphasising important national and social interests. Because of the shortage of parliamentary time, bills can be 'talked out' by opponents using up all the time available to pass a bill through to the next stage, sometimes involving an all-night sitting.

Conflict of interest

Unlike the USA, where the written constitution guarantees a clear distinction between the different processes of government, there has been a tendency for recent British governments to interfere with the judiciary and the executive branches of government. High-ranking members of the civil service, which is supposed to be impartial, have been replaced by people sympathetic towards government policies, and senior civil

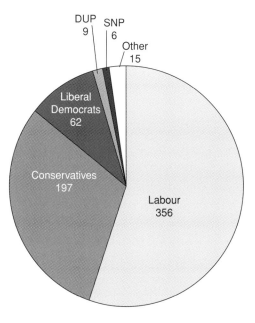

DUP
9
SNP
6
Other
15
Liberal
Democrats
62
Conservatives
197
Labour
356

Figure 20.1 Votes and seats in the 2005 election

servants have been overruled by government 'advisers'. The government also has a strong influence in the appointment of bishops and judges.

The electoral system

Proportional representation
Under this system, a large number of candidates would stand in each constituency and, according to a special formula, votes of the least supported candidates would be transferred to stronger ones. This would eventually ensure that members elected represented the number of votes cast and a much wider range of members would be elected. This would be a more representative electoral system, but it might make strong government more difficult because of the reduced possibility of a large majority for any one party and the need to accommodate a wide range of interests when making policy.

First-past-the-post
A democratic electoral system should ensure that the majority rules and that significant minorities are represented. The present system elects the candidate whose voters are in the majority in a particular geographical area. This means that a particular party may become the government because it has the most members returned in a particular election, but does not represent the total numbers of voters nationwide. In the 1987 election, the Conservative Party had a majority of 102 members but had only polled 43.4 per cent of the total vote. Under the first-past-the-post system, the government is formed by the strongest minority rather than a genuine majority. Parties such as the Liberal Democrats are under-represented in Parliament because their support is distributed evenly across the country, but not concentrated in any particular area. This means that they end up with fewer parliamentary seats than they are entitled to by their total vote.

Activities

1. Read the extract below from Lord Hailsham. What improvements do you think might make the parliamentary system more democratic?

'I have reached the conclusion that our constitution is wearing out. Its central defects are gradually coming to outweigh its merits, and its central defects consist in the absolute powers we confer on our sovereign body [parliament], and the concentration of these powers in an executive government formed out of one party which may not fairly represent the popular will.' (Lord Hailsham, 1976 Dimbleby Lecture)

2. What might be the advantages and disadvantages of closer ties with Europe?

3. Do you think Members of Parliament should be allowed to vote according to their conscience or should they always obey the party line?

4. Do you think the establishment of separate Welsh and Scottish assemblies would divide the UK or help to bring it together?

EXAM QUESTION

'Why should I vote? Voting doesn't make any difference. Politicians don't take any notice; they're all the same.' (Justin Lesbourne, aged 20)

    Discuss the consequences for democracy of widespread agreement with the view expressed above, particularly among young people.

    You might consider the following in your answer

- the 'First-Past-the-Post' voting system
- young people's knowledge and understanding of politics
- ways in which voting might be made easier
- whether voting should be made compulsory.

(30 marks)

AQA B May 2001

EXAMINER'S ADVICE

- This essay question is from AS Unit 2 set in May 2001 and is the second of two extended pieces of writing you have to do in this test. The first is compulsory and based on a passage, but for this question you will have a choice of two topics. See page 1 for more details on this paper.
- The question is based on the apparent lack of commitment to voting by young people (in the 2001 General Election less than 40 per cent of 18–25 year olds eligible to vote did so, whereas the overall turnout was 59 per cent, which was also the lowest figure for over 50 years). The main question is about the implications for democratic government and representation of the people if voters do not indicate their political preferences. Perhaps parties or individuals do not offer what young people want? Or are there other reasons?
- The quote suggests that voting doesn't make any difference and that politicians don't take any notice. Are these valid reasons or are there others? The prompts also give you some possibilities: the voting system, lack of knowledge, opportunities for voting or making opinions known, and simple apathy. Would it help to make voting compulsory, as it is in Australia? What changes could make a difference?
- For 30 marks you should expect to write a full essay of at least two pages, and in the exam proper you will have about 30–35 minutes to complete the task. When you have written your answer, turn to page 257 for some suggested arguments.

The British Constitution

It is hard to define the concept of 'constitution' and even harder to define the British Constitution. However, a generally accepted view is that, 'a constitution sets out the formal structure of government, specifying the powers and constitutions of central government, sets out the balance between central and other levels of government and specifies the rights of citizens'.

There are written and unwritten constitutions, with most modern countries having a written constitution. The constitution of the USA is contained in seven pages, while that of India is several hundred pages long. It is usually claimed that the British Constitution is unwritten, but there are several written parts of it:

- *The Bill of Rights, 1689*, is the basis of the British Constitution. It was written to justify the way in which the leaders of Parliament had removed King James II from the throne. By declaring various practices of James II illegal, it made the British monarchy constitutional. It stated that the monarch cannot raise taxes, pass or suspend laws or keep an army without the consent of parliament. It set down rules for the length of parliaments and for free elections to them. It also gave all British people the right to freedom of religion and MPs the right to complete freedom of speech in the House of Commons.
- *Habeas Corpus, 1679*, compels the authorities to bring anyone arrested before the courts, so preventing what is known as 'arbitrary arrest', where people can be arrested and kept in prison without trial.
- Various *Representation of the People Acts* have been passed so that now, by law, everyone over the age of eighteen has the right to vote and parliamentary constituencies are arranged so that a similar number of electors elect each MP.
- *The Act of Settlement, 1701*, stipulates that the monarch and the monarch's spouse must be Protestant (James II was a Catholic). This is a sign of the way in which parliament is in control of the monarchy, but also reflects the fact that the monarch is also the Head of the Church of England, which is Protestant.
- *The Parliament Act of 1911* removed the power of the House of Lords to do anything but delay legislation approved by the House of Commons.

All political power is based on the Prime Minister and the Cabinet. The monarch must act on their advice. The Cabinet controls all the government departments (run by the civil service) and the armed forces. However, the courts are independent of the government (though the Lord Chancellor, who selects judges, is a member of the government) and citizens can challenge the government through the courts (including the European Courts) if they believe the government is acting illegally.

There are other checks and balances on the power of the government. If the Prime Minister loses a vote of confidence in the House of Commons, he or she must resign. They must also hold an election at least every five years. The monarch could remove any Prime Minister who refused to do either of these things, and, as the armed forces and the civil service take their oath to the monarch, there would be the power to force their resignation. The monarch also has the final decision as to who to call as Prime Minister if no one party wins a majority in an election – this has never yet happened and no one knows what would happen if it did.

The British Constitution has considerable flexibility as parliament can adjust the constitution if conditions change.

The need for reform of the British Constitution

Many political thinkers believe that the British Constitution is in need of reform. Some feel that there is a need for a complete written constitution in one document, which should also make a clear statement of the rights of individuals. Others think that the position of the monarch needs to be more clearly defined, while others think the idea of hereditary monarchy in a democracy is contradictory and so the monarchy should be abolished. Others feel that too much power is concentrated in the hands of the Prime Minister and the Cabinet and that power should be devolved, firstly to the separate nations of the UK (Northern Ireland, Scotland and Wales), then to the

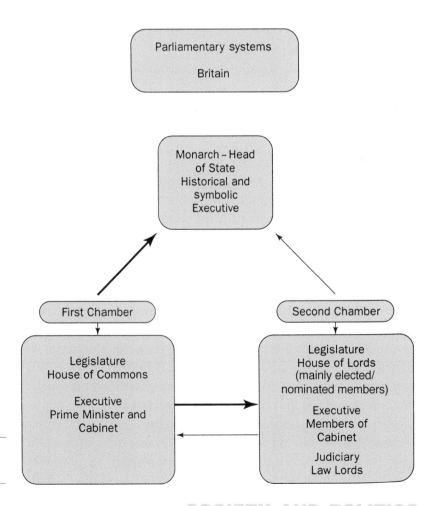

Figure 21.1 The British Constitution (Source: Barrie Axford, *Politics: An Introduction*, Routledge, 1997)

regions. It is also felt that the sovereignty of Parliament requires a second chamber to vet proposed legislation from the Commons, but this cannot be done by a chamber with an inbuilt majority of one political party (until the hereditary peers were reduced from 750 to a maximum of 92 following the *House of Lords Act*, 1999, the Conservatives could win almost any vote in the Lords).

Devolution and the House of Lords are two of the main issues concerning the British Constitution.

Figure 21.2 The House of Lords before reform

Reform of the House of Lords

The UK is the only democracy to have a second chamber where the members are unelected, but it has been difficult to find an acceptable alternative. Labour governments have recognised that while the House of Lords usually has a large Conservative majority, its undemocratic nature has meant that it has no real political authority to challenge legislation produced by a majority in the House of Commons. Replacing it with a large number of elected members would give it more power to resist government policy, while having too many directly appointed members would allow governments to put its own supporters in place. This would continue the political patronage, which appoints a majority of life peers who support the current government. The current debate initiated by the recommendations of the Wakeham Commission (2000) is focused on what proportion should be elected, what proportion should be directly appointed and for how long, how to bring in representatives from social and ethnic minorities, and what the total membership should be.

Devolution

Devolution refers to the process of transferring the power from ministers and Parliament to regional or sub-national bodies, which are subordinate to Parliament but directly elected. Unlike such countries as the USA or Germany, which operate a *federal* system where individual states have guaranteed status, in theory Parliament could abolish the powers of a region. For example, in 1972, the British Government abolished the Northern Ireland Parliament at Stormont.

Devolution has been a political issue since at least 1886, when W.E. Gladstone introduced an unsuccessful bill to give Ireland Home Rule in Dublin. In the late twentieth century, the pressure for devolution in Scotland and Wales was seen in the increased number of Members elected to Parliament representing the Scottish National Party and Plaid Cymru, the Welsh National Party.

However, since 1997 the devolution process has established assemblies in Northern Ireland, Scotland and Wales. These reforms have had far-reaching implications for the politics, policy and society in the UK. Radical institutional change, combined with a fuller capacity to express the UK's distinctive territorial identities, is reshaping the way the UK is governed and opening up new directions of public policy.

The effects of devolution so far

One of the main justifications for devolution has been the view that it might enable a fairer distribution of financial resources. What has actually happened is that there has been a wide variation in the new policies which have been developed, as shown below.

Different public policies in Scotland since devolution include:

- free long-term personal care for the elderly
- abolition of up-front tuition fees for students in higher education
- abolition of fox hunting
- abolition of the ban on 'promoting homosexuality' in schools.

Wales has fewer policy differences. But these include:

- free school milk for all children under seven
- abolition of school league tables
- free medical prescriptions for those under 25 and over 60
- free bus travel for pensioners.

Different public policies in Northern Ireland since devolution include:

- abolition of school league tables
- establishment of a commissioner for children
- free travel for the elderly.

These national differences obviously mean that some people may have financial advantages denied to others depending on where they live. Also, the introduction of some policies directly opposed to recent government legislation has caused some embarrassment and tension, for example the abolition of university fees in Scotland and school league tables in Wales. Variations in policy like this weaken central control from Westminster.

Views on further devolution

Nationalist parties – SNP and Plaid Cymru
These see devolution as a first step to complete independence, which is their ultimate goal. Plaid recognises that this goal will take time as there is considerable resistance to the idea amongst the population.

Labour party
The Labour Party sees devolution as the compromise that was necessary to satisfy demands for self-government but without granting full independence, which it does not believe a majority are in favour of. It remains committed to the UK together but with some devolved power to the regions (this may ultimately include England as well, as the party committed itself to elected regional assemblies in England in its 1997 manifesto).

Conservative party
They are very concerned that devolution will be the 'thin end of the wedge', and that it will fuel, rather than satisfy, demands for greater regional autonomy. They are committed to a unified UK and have opposed the idea of devolution in the past.

Liberal Democrat party
They see devolution as a victory as they had been campaigning for greater decentralisation of decision-making for years. They see a fully federal system as the logical outcome for the UK, with sovereignty devolved.

Regionalism

'Directly elected regional government' was a goal in Labour's 1997 manifesto, but since then the party has retreated somewhat on this issue. However, some steps have been taken already towards decentralising some power in England:

- Setting up of Regional Development Agencies (RDAs). These are unelected quangos, whose purpose is to spearhead regional economic planning and development to rejuvenate the regional economies of England.
- Reform of the voting system for European elections divided the UK into 12 constituencies, and RDAs recognise these boundaries.
- Since 2000, London has directly elected its mayor and a London Assembly. Together they control billions of pounds of funding. The most recent elections for the Mayor of London and members of the London Assembly took place on 10 June 2004. Ken Livingstone, the labour candidate, was re-elected as Mayor of London on a slightly reduced share of the vote compared with the elections in 2000. Turnout was 35.9 per cent, an increase of 2.2 percentage points compared with 2000. These low turnouts throw doubt on mayoral elections as a means of rejuvenating interest in local democracy.
- Reform of local government. The 2000 Local Government Act required local authorities with populations over 85,000 to change their management structures. One option was for a directly elected Mayor (as opposed to a Mayor or Leader chosen by the councillors) with this decision to be made by referendum. In the event, very few areas opted for this choice.

Some English regions exhibit substantial support for their own regional assembly, whilst the issue is dead in others. Recently, the North East decisively rejected the idea of a regional assembly.

The general consensus of opinion is that the process of devolution has gone very smoothly so far. This is partly due to Labour's large majority in the House of Commons and partly due to the healthy state of the economy. However, the situation could change quickly if people feel that there has been no change in the financial health of their region/country or that they are still unable to get their grievances heard and dealt with.

Activities

1. In small groups, discuss what features you think are essential in the constitution of a modern democracy. Construct a Bill of Rights that clearly lists these features.

2. Do you think that the advantages of separate Welsh and Scottish Assemblies outweigh the disadvantages and why?

3. Some MPs have been paid to ask particular questions in Parliament by powerful interest groups. Is this practice antidemocractic and why?

'Attitudes to the monarchy in the United Kingdom today mirror society's lessening of respect towards authority in general.' How far do you believe this to be a valid assertion?

(12 marks)

AQA B January 2002

Source: Larry Feign, 1999

EXAMINER'S ADVICE

- This is another question from A2 Unit 5 set in January 2002. It is one of five compulsory short essays with each title taken from a different section of the specification and each worth 12 marks. See page 1 for more information about this paper.
- This is a typical General Studies question in three respects. Firstly, although its starting point is attitude to the monarchy, which links it to this unit, its scope is wider and effectively touches on many of the themes in this Society and Politics section: the nature of society, social change, the rule of law, power and control. It requires a genuinely broad view.
- Secondly, it is another 'how far/to what extent' question, which allows you to give your own opinion but also expects that you will give it balanced consideration.
- Thirdly, it requires you to contemplate your own opinions and attitudes, the perceptions and behaviour of others and the nature and certainty of the evidence to support your beliefs in this area (AO4 once again).
- A useful approach might be to examine the extent to which you believe the claim is valid both in respect of the monarchy and then authority in society generally. Use the ideas in the cartoon as a starting point for why some attitudes may have changed. Then consider how far the change has actually gone. For example, people often talk about the 'breakdown of law and order' and how undisciplined schools have become, but does that fit with your own experiences?
- Allow yourself 15 minutes to write your answer then turn to page 257 for some further suggestions.

22 Educational issues

'Education' is a difficult word to define exactly. Almost the entire population of the UK has been to school and, in a sense, this entitles everyone who has been through the experience to express an opinion. At an individual level, education can refer to the process by which people develop their intellectual, emotional and social skills. It can also refer to the entire system of schooling within a country from nursery to university.

What are schools for?

It is usually agreed that schools have two major functions:

- to educate students in various academic or cognitive skills and knowledge
- to educate students in the personal and social skills necessary to function successfully in society.

In democratic societies, education provides the possibility of equality of opportunity and achievement. However, educational thinkers are often divided into those who think that education should serve the needs of the individual and those who think that it should serve the needs of society. Private fee-paying schools have tended to encourage individualism while, in the past, state education for the masses has emphasised the need for well-trained workers with skills relevant to the industrial demands of society.

Some important views on education

In his influential books, *The Republic* and *The Laws*, Plato (427–348 BCE) argued that philosophers should be kings. In a turbulent and unstable historical context, Plato was trying to produce a blueprint for a stable, well-ordered society in which people fulfilled the roles and functions for which they were most suited. Only those capable of understanding and discovering the real truth about things and distinguishing true knowledge from opinion and illusion should be rulers or guardians of society. However, as the development of this ability depended on a rigorous and demanding intellectual training, only a few would be successful and the rest would occupy lower but nonetheless important positions in society. Plato's views have been very influential in the history of western education. Many education systems still reflect the views that:

- Intellectual pursuits are somehow superior to practical and technical ones.
- Education should involve such processes as selection, segregation, assessment and rejection, in order to sort out potential leaders and followers.

John Locke (1632–1704) argued that the mind was like a blank sheet of paper at birth, 'a tabula rasa', devoid of innate ideas, which would acquire knowledge through experience. He emphasised the qualities of virtue, wisdom and learning amongst others. His view that 'experience' was essential to the educational process has remained very significant. The experiences or learning opportunities pupils are presented with at school may have a significant influence on their future success or failure.

In *Emile*, published in 1762, Jean-Jacques Rousseau (1712–1778) argued for a much more natural type of education. Rousseau was not impressed by the values of the civilised society in which he lived. He wanted an education system that valued and enhanced 'natural' qualities such as spontaneity, freedom, subjectivity and

Figure 22.1 A Victorian schoolroom – Shepton Mallet Grammar School, Wiltshire, 1899

simplicity, rather than the cold, impersonal values of scientific objectivity and rationalism. Feeling is much more important than thinking for Rousseau, who objected to the way in which children's development was 'over-intellectualised' at an early age. Rousseau's views have been the foundation of the debate between those *traditionalists* who argue for reason, discipline and authority in education and those *progressives* who want a system more sensitive to the idea of individual growth and development.

Karl Marx (1818–83), together with Freidrich Engels, argued that many human beings were alienated and dehumanised by the fact that the ruling classes owned the means of material production, even though it was the workers who created the wealth. Marx emphasised that the economic dimension of life was primary and that religious, political and educational values reflected the values of the ruling class. Marx wanted an education system that would produce responsible and autonomous persons who would work towards the idea of 'community' through social relationships. Marx had a vision of a system that would develop the idea that the interests of the individual and those of society are the same. However, many of his educational ideas have been distorted by Marxist or Communist societies, which have produced education systems that indoctrinate their students to accept the ideas of those in power without question and which discourage freedom of thought.

The transmission of values and beliefs and culture

Schools are often described by sociologists as 'agents of cultural transmission'. All schools transmit to their pupils, whether deliberately or not, some sense of what is acceptable in terms of behaviour and attitudes. Schools emphasise the idea of achievement through personal effort and perseverance and also community values, such as honesty and consideration for others. In some education systems, the prevailing religious beliefs of the country are built into the curriculum. There has been a strong Catholic emphasis in Irish schools in the past, and religious education with a strong Christian emphasis is compulsory by law in the UK. On the other hand, in France and the USA, for example, religious teaching is forbidden. Recently, some school boards in religiously conservative parts of the USA refused to allow the use of textbooks that taught Darwin's theory of evolution on the grounds that it contradicted the account of creation in the book of Genesis. However, many school systems encourage patriotic feelings and emphasise democracy.

Preparation for life

Traditionally, one of the most important functions of schools has been to prepare its students for a place in society. Modern governments are concerned to produce a work force with relevant and up-to-date skills so that the country can compete economically in the international market place. This requirement has resulted in different ways of organising schools and in legislation to ensure that all children receive some education. In the UK, for example, most local authorities operate a system that involves primary education until the age of 11, followed by non-selective comprehensive education until the age of at least 16. This may be followed by voluntary post-16 education either in a school sixth form, a purpose-built sixth form college or further education college, or as a preparation for university. A few local authorities still retain selective grammar schools (where the children sit an exam at eleven to decide whether they are clever enough to go to grammar school) and others operate a three-tier system, where children move from first school to middle school and on to secondary school at the age of 13. New specialist schools have also been introduced. These have a special focus on their chosen subject area but must meet the National Curriculum requirements and deliver a broad and balanced education to all pupils. Any maintained secondary school in England can apply to be designated as a specialist school in one of ten specialist areas: arts, business and enterprise, engineering, humanities, language, mathematics and computing, music, science, sports, and technology.

Recent important education debates

The gender gap

During the past few years the increasing gap in academic attainment between boys and girls has become of increasing concern and a focus for government educational initiatives. Nationally, girl's results have been improving faster than boys. In 2004, for example, 62.4 per cent of girls' exam entries achieved A*–C grade as opposed to 53.4 per cent of boys'. Various reasons have been given for this gap such as:

- Extensive use of coursework in GCSE. This is commonly thought to be a major reason for the gender divide as it rewards hard work and consistent application, which girls seem to be more content to do than boys.
- The anti-learning laddish culture.

A recent Ofsted report identified the following factors, amongst others, as significant in boys' success at school:

- Ongoing assessment procedures which value work and give clear advice on how to improve.
- A school environment where pupils and staff show respect for each other, which offers plenty of extra-curricular activities and a place where boys feel they belong.
- Teaching styles which set shorter, more frequent deadlines and encourage students to reflect on their answers and break down long written tasks into shorter sections.

The use of 'boy friendly' texts and strategies (charts, data, graphs) as well as the recruitment of male teachers have been suggested as remedies to the problem of boys' underachievement in literacy. However, while these factors do help, they do not provide a complete answer, and risk over-simplifying a very complex problem.

Research done in 2004 has found that gender gaps in performance are significantly large in virtually every country (50 researched) between boys and girls aged between nine and 15. It is felt that the change in teaching methods when children are learning to read is causing the ever-increasing gender divide in reading ability. Boys have a

DID YOU KNOW?

Schooldays
The 1988 *Education Act* initiated the following changes:
- Regular school inspections
- Qualifications and Curriculum Authority to oversee national examinations and the curriculum
- The extension of parents' right to choose schools
- The freedom of schools to 'opt out' of local authority control.

Deschooling society. In the 1970s a series of educational thinkers argued that most education systems were a waste of time. Most pupils leave school uneducated and resentful. Schools are a type of prison, operating on the assumption that education can only take place inside mass institutions and adults assume that they know what is best for young people.

Formula funding. Money for schools is based on the number of pupils enrolled. An increase/decrease of 20–30 pupils can mean the addition or loss of one teacher.

different timetable of brain development to girls. For example, the neural networks connecting the two halves of the brain develop more slowly in boys, and the implementation of more appropriate teaching methods, particularly in the area of literacy has produced significant improvements in boys' performance, both in SATs and at GCSE level.

However, while girls consistently do better at school than boys, this is not reflected in their future earnings or employment status. This is clearly a social issue rather than an educational one.

Fees in higher education

There has been much recent debate over the government's introduction of fees for students in full-time higher education.

From 1962 to 1990, students in full-time undergraduate higher education in the UK were entitled to maintenance grants, means-tested on the basis of parents' income. Between 1977 and 1998, no contributions towards university fees were payable by UK students. In 1990, student loans were introduced in addition to maintenance grants, with the intention of gradually increasing the loan amount to represent 50 per cent of the total maintenance package. The maintenance grant, including any parental contribution, was to provide the remaining 50 per cent towards support. At the same time, the value of the means-tested grant was frozen and most student entitlement to social security benefits was removed.

The Dearing Committee was appointed in 1996 'to make recommendations on how the purposes, shape, structure, size and funding of higher education, including support for students, should develop to meet the needs of the United Kingdom over the next twenty years, recognising that higher education embraces teaching, learning, scholarship and research.' The government accepted the recommendation that students should pay a contribution towards tuition fees, initially 25 per cent.

The National Union of Students published a student hardship survey which showed that three quarters of students were in debt, many up to £10,000. (In most other countries students have to pay to go to university.)

Some of the arguments for and against tuition fees

For

A university education is a valuable and expensive privilege. Why should something that is so rewarding and costly be free? It is equitable for students to make a financial contribution to their degree teaching. They stand to gain financially from a degree. Education is an investment and it is rational for students to borrow at this stage of their life cycle to finance such investment. It is rational to forgo current earnings in return for higher future earnings.

Tuition fees provide extra finance for facilities, teaching and research, allowing the government to fund an expansion of the number of students able to enter higher education thus promoting wider access. New entrants into universities under the new scheme may be drawn mainly from lower-income households as students are means-tested on what they need to pay.

Fees will encourage students to be more selective in the courses they choose and will stimulate an improvement in teaching quality of universities.

Against

It is a tax on learning.

Only seven per cent of children from families in the lowest social class currently go to university. Tuition fees will make it harder for relatively poor families to fund a degree. This will widen educational inequality and create a further widening of the two-tier education system.

Student debt may deter poorer students. Tuition fees will lead to a huge surge in student debt and hardship which in turn will have negative economic and social consequences in the long run. Seeking to expand higher education too much may work against the best interests of the economy because the graduate market may become over-crowded.

Activities

1. 'A school with poor examination results is a bad school'. What reasons would you use to either support or oppose this statement. What other information would you need to know about the school?

2. Which of the following is the most important part of school and why: the child; the curriculum, assessment?

EXAM QUESTION

Read the extracts below from a booklet published by the Independent Schools Information Service (ISIS).

The points made suggest that an independent school is 'empowering'. Imagine that you are the Head of a state-maintained school or college. Write an introduction to your prospectus in which you make the case that your school or college 'empowers' its students.

(40 marks)

AQA B May 2002

The advantage of an independent school education

How will an independent school benefit your children? What can independent schools offer them? A recent survey conducted by MORI took a random sample of parents whose children attend SC/ISIS schools. The main conclusions include:

- The **smaller class sizes** in many independent schools and increased individual attention are becoming a persuasive factor for an increasing number of parents.
- A school's **reputation**, its orderly **discipline**, its encouragement of a

responsible attitude to school work and the **fulfilment of pupils' potential** are all more important than examination results and 'league table' position.
- On almost all important measures, the parents surveyed rated their

children's current school as excellent or very good.

It is also interesting to note that more than half the children entering independent school have parents who were not educated in the independent sector.

The 'league tables'

Independent schools pride themselves on providing an 'all-round quality of education' not just academic results. Music, drama and sport can all be pursued academically by the talented, but these are also important areas for every child to develop co-operation and

teamwork skills through the club activities organised by schools.

Families should decide on the atmosphere and ethos in which they feel comfortable. Many children respond with great enthusiasm to the competitive characteristics of the highly selective schools

which dominate the top of league tables. Nonetheless, other children (and their parents!) may thrive in a less pressurised environment where the main focus is achievement measured against each individual's best.

Together, the academic and extra-curricular programme

provides a framework for developing the personal skills and experience that contribute to a sense of self-worth and confidence – the qualities that help each child become a valued member of their school community and society as a whole.

School fees

It is no secret that sending your child to an independent school is an expensive commitment. The termly fees quoted refer to Autumn Term 2000. Average fees per term (three terms each year) are as follows:

Pre-prep	(age 2–7 years)	£700 to £1200
Prep/Junior	(age 7–13 years)	£1400 to £2500 day
		£2700 to £4000 boarding
Senior	(age 11/13–18 years)	£1700 to £3000+ day
		£3200 to £5000+ boarding

You are advised to check these with the schools themselves and to enquire for details of any 'extras' – uniforms, travel, meal costs, instrumental music tuition costs, etc.

Source: Independent Schools Information Service, 2000/2001

EXAMINER'S ADVICE

- This is the third example of an extended writing question from AS Unit 2, this time set in May 2002. It is the first of two pieces of extended writing you have to do in this test, the second being a more conventional essay. Other examples of this type of 'creative writing' question can be found at the end of Units 8 and 19.

- Here you don't have a choice of which case to argue: you have to write a piece promoting the values and strengths of state education through an imaginary state school. However, you can use the article on independent schools quite creatively as suggested below, as well as some of the material in the unit you have just studied.

- You should focus on the strengths of schools which serve local communities. These too can have a good 'reputation', 'orderly discipline', encourage a 'responsible attitude to school work' and the 'fulfilment of pupils' potential'. Education is free and there is support for pupils who struggle to fund the 'extras'. As the article says, league tables are important but they are not the only factor of a good school, so stress some of these. It isn't realistic to expect a local comprehensive school to achieve better examination results than selective independent schools, but state grammar schools often do.

- This style of writing is not easy and needs to be practised. The emphasis has to be on what your school can do well for its pupils and the local community it serves. Avoid comparisons with other types of school and just focus on yours, but don't make hollow, exaggerated claims which will not be convincing. Be realistic but clear and positive about the values that should appeal to local pupils and parents.

- Allow yourself no more than 30 minutes to write your answer. Turn to page 257 for some further suggestions for points which might be made.

Arts and Media

Unit 23 | **Aesthetic evaluation**
Unit 24 | **The nature of culture**
Unit 25 | **Creativity and innovation**
Unit 26 | **The media**
Unit 27 | **Censorship**

23 Aesthetic evaluation

Aesthetics is the study of what makes something beautiful, what makes something valued as a work of art. In a sense, aesthetic evaluation is a matter of taste. We say someone has good taste or bad taste in areas such as choice of furniture, interior design, clothes, hairstyle, garden ornaments, etc. In the same way, people have good taste or bad taste in culture and the arts. However, there is more to aesthetic evaluation than taste alone. There is a connection between aesthetic values and moral values. Someone can have terrific style and taste in all the other areas previously mentioned and be thoroughly evil without it affecting their taste. However, a work of art that is evil cannot be regarded as a great work of art. Works of art are not just concerned with beauty, they are concerned with human behaviour, the nature and meaning of life, the concepts of good and evil.

Some critics have challenged this view and claim that aesthetic evaluation is solely concerned with the form of a work of art and the effect it has on the person experiencing it. They suggest that it is impossible to know what the artist had in mind when creating the work of art, so all that matters is its effects on the person experiencing it. Some critics, such as Cleanth Brooks, have gone as far as to say that nothing can be said about a work of art; it can only be experienced.

Although it is true that great works of art from the past still function for us as great works of art, even though we have no idea of their creators' reasons for creating them (e.g. pre-historic cave paintings, Greek sculptures), such a view seems to ignore many factors. If works of art can only be experienced, what is the point of their existence? There would be no greater value in Beethoven than in Sir Cliff Richard. Great art can shock, challenge, even change the lives of those who experience it. People have lost their faith in God through reading books such as Dostoevsky's *The Brothers Karamazov*. People's attitudes to the Spanish Civil War were changed by Picasso's painting, *Guernica*, which was based on an incident in the war. Dictators such as Hitler and Stalin tried to keep firm control of the arts because they saw them as dangerous in provoking criticism and questioning of the regime. The Nazis burnt books whose ideas they disagreed with and censored any art form to make sure that it was promoting the ideals of the regime. All of which indicates that there is something about the arts that can be evaluated. It is possible to draw up a set of criteria to be used when trying to determine whether something is a great work of art and whether one piece of art is better than another.

Criteria for aesthetic evaluation

1. Form
This means the method of production which varies in different art forms. The first issue is craftsmanship – is the painting well painted, is the novel well written?

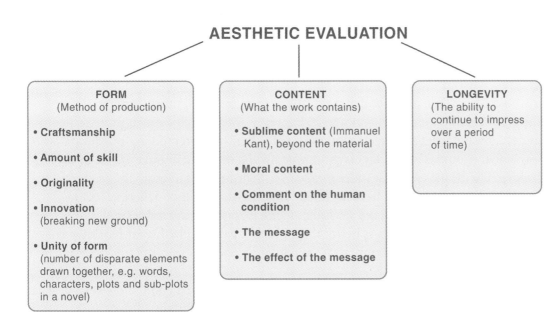

AESTHETIC EVALUATION

FORM
(Method of production)

- **Craftsmanship**

- **Amount of skill**

- **Originality**

- **Innovation**
(breaking new ground)

- **Unity of form**
(number of disparate elements drawn together, e.g. words, characters, plots and sub-plots in a novel)

CONTENT
(What the work contains)

- **Sublime content** (Immanuel Kant), beyond the material

- **Moral content**

- **Comment on the human condition**

- **The message**

- **The effect of the message**

LONGEVITY
(The ability to continue to impress over a period of time)

Figure 23.1 Elements within aesthetic evaluation

Connected with this is the amount of skill needed to produce the form, for example a symphony. A great work of art should also be original. Copying needs craftsmanship and skill, but it is not original. Connected with originality is innovation. Often the greatest works of art break new ground in the field rather than just following the tradition. Finally, the work needs a unity of form. Any work of art must bring together a great number of disparate elements (for example a novel needs good choice of words, characters, plots, sub-plots, etc. a symphony brings together lots of different instruments and even more musicians). It is often said that the more disparate elements an artist manages to unite into one work of art, the greater the work is.

2. Content

This means not only what the work contains, but also what its message and effect is. A great work of art must have some content which Kant called 'the sublime'. Something which makes the viewer/reader aware of the transcendent – the feeling that there is something beyond the obvious material world. It may be an awareness of God, or, with atheistic artists, an awareness of the wonder of the human spirit. Great works of art will also have some moral content, making the viewer/reader aware of the battle between good and evil in life. Novels, poems, plays and films will also say something about the human condition (what life is like, what it could be like and what it ought to be like).

3. Longevity

A great work of art should continue to impress people over a long period of time. This will possibly be more true of painting, sculpture and music than novels, etc. because language changes over the years. Nevertheless, great literature such as Shakespeare continues to impress even though much of the language is now unused.

Using aesthetic evaluation

The criteria for aesthetic evaluation can be used in a wide range of situations. In deciding whether classical music is more beautiful or worthwhile than popular music, it would be possible to show that, in terms of form, classical music is better because of the greater skill required to compose it. However, there may be much more difficulty in determining whether the classical music of Salieri (a contemporary of Mozart, who was equally popular in his day) is more worthwhile than the popular music of the Beatles. The Beatles were far more innovative, their music had more to say about life, and their music is likely to have far more longevity than that of Salieri.

The criteria can also be used for judging one piece of art against a similar one, for deciding whether a live play is better than a film, a painting by David Hockney is better than a painting by Rembrandt, or a song by one pop star is better than one by another.

Whenever you use the criteria, however, you should have a good knowledge of what you are applying the criteria to, and an awareness of the difficulty of drawing a boundary between popular culture and high culture (see Unit 24).

Price and value in art

There is often argument about the price paid for a work of art (particularly a painting) in auctions and whether this price reflects the true value of the work. In 1979, a painting by Modigliani could not fetch its reserve price (the minimum price the vendor is prepared to accept) of £325,000, but when it was auctioned at Sothebys, New York, in November 2004, it set a record of £17 million for any painting by the artist. At the same auction, a painting by Gauguin, which would have fetched very little 50 years ago, fetched £21.3 million.

There are several reasons why a work of art becomes more valuable:

- The artist dies, so there will be no more such works coming onto the market and they gain a rarity value.
- It is easier to see the value of an artist's work in retrospect. The originality, innovation and longevity of the artist's work cannot be fully assessed until around 50 years after their death.
- An original piece of great art is something many people would like to own, including many new public art galleries around the world. The more people there are bidding, the more the price will go up.
- Investors with no interest in art know that any work by a dead great artist is going to increase because the value is in the work of art and so will not change. The evidence of the twentieth century was that a great painting was the most secure investment of any type, as all great paintings increased in value far more than inflation plus interest.

Clearly, works of art, just like footballers, are worth what people are prepared to pay for them. It appears that some modern art such as 'installation art' (see Unit 25) may only be fetching high prices because it is a fashion accessory for super-rich people, and fashion certainly plays a part in what is regarded as valuable. Nevertheless, just as in clothes, architecture, etc. for art to be fashionable, it must have some of the criteria for form and content.

Government sponsorship of the arts

Arts such as opera, classical music, ballet, serious theatre and even serious film would not survive without government funding. The Arts Council of Great Britain receives government grants to support the arts. In 1992, museums and art galleries received £259 million, libraries received £172 million, films £22 million and other arts £490 million. By 1998, these had been reduced to £253 million for museums and art galleries, £127 million for libraries, £23 million for films and £472 million for other arts. At the same time, the cost of administering these grants rose from £16 million in 1992, to £23 million in 1998. However, the fall in government subsidy has been more than offset by the large sums given to the arts by the National Lottery.

The arguments for government sponsorship of the arts
* High culture is a vital part of a nation's culture. Popular culture can survive without subsidy precisely because it can command large audiences, but high culture is expensive to maintain and cannot be financed by the smaller numbers who attend performances.

Figure 23.2 The newly refurbished Royal Opera House, Covent Garden, London

1. Re-read the novel you studied for GCSE English and use the aesthetic evaluation criteria to explain why it is/is not a great work of art.

2. Choose an area of popular music you enjoy and explain why you enjoy it.

3. Choose a painting, piece of classical music, play or film that is considered to be a great work of art and use all the information in this unit to discuss whether it really is a great work of art (argue the points for and the points against).

4. 'Only the rich enjoy the arts so the arts should not be subsidised by government taxes.' Examine the validity of this statement. (This means just the same as discuss!)

5. 'The arts are only entertainment, and, although enjoyable, they are of no use to society.' Discuss this view with reference to more than one art-form.

- The arts are a sign of a society's civilisation. They give the members of the society an opportunity to think about the meaning of life and to experience great beauty. Arts such as sculpture and architecture make the environment more pleasant.
- The arts can make money for the country. Although the domestic performances of the Royal Shakespeare Company require subsidies, their tours abroad make a profit. More importantly, many tourists come to Britain to experience our wide range of cultural activities. Their money makes a substantial contribution to Britain's exports (money spent by tourists in Britain is an export; money spent by British tourists abroad is an import).
- The popular arts such as music and theatre depend on the training given by high culture. Many of the production teams and backing groups for pop stars have a classical music training. Actors in popular theatre and television have often had a classical training.
- There is no clear division between high culture and popular culture, and it could be that a society without high culture would also lose much of its popular culture.
- Market forces can lead to a serious downgrading of culture. The argument about the BBC being funded by licence rather than advertising (a form of subsidy because there are people who buy a licence but never watch the BBC's programmes) is usually based on a comparison between BBC programmes and those on the satellite and cable channels, which are solely determined by market forces. If quality television requires subsidy, then quality arts should also receive subsidy.
- All governments now subsidise the arts, so that if Britain stopped doing so, all the best artists would go overseas.

The arguments against government sponsorship of the arts

- The people who want high culture and who go to the opera, etc. are relatively well off, and are able to pay the market price for their seats (a French survey of the arts showed that less than ten per cent of audiences at serious theatre, opera and symphony concerts were working class).
- Most government subsidy is spent on the arts in London, which is unfair to people in the regions.
- In every other area of life, workers are paid the market rate and if their industry cannot compete it has to reduce wages and costs. The same economics should apply to serious theatre, opera, etc. Wages and costs should be reduced until subsidies are not needed.
- Writers of serious literature survive without subsidy and many serious films make profits.
- The people who decide on arts sponsorship are people from within the arts industry. Subsidies should be organised by ordinary people and the arts industries wanting the subsidy should have to justify their claims for subsidy.
- There are much more important things to spend hundreds of millions of pounds on than the arts – such as the homeless, world poverty or the National Health Service.

EXAM QUESTION

How far does the success of a piece of artwork depend upon those who view it?

(12 marks)

AQA B May 2003

EXAMINER'S ADVICE

- This question is from AS Unit 1 set in May 2003. From 2005 onwards there will be four short essays like this for you to answer from a choice of six, with each title taken from the five different areas of the specification. Note also that they will be worth 15 marks each, instead of 12. It is absolutely essential to give equal time and attention to each of your four answers, so as not to lose vital marks. See page 00 for more information about this paper. There are other example questions at the end of Units 9, 18, 28 and 35.

- This is a typical General Studies question on a standard topic about how we appreciate and judge works of art. Is it all down to the personal (subjective) opinion of the viewer and how he or she relates to the artist and the piece in question? Or are there more general or common (objective) criteria that can be applied to works of art? It is also another 'how far/to what extent' question, which means that you can argue whatever case you want but that you must support it with evidence or examples. In this case, some references to specific works of art or artists would help, although you do not have much time to develop points at length in these short essay questions.

- An important question to ask yourself is, when you appreciate a work of art, what criteria are you applying yourself and what kind of justifications would you give to explain the appeal to other people. How a piece is constructed, the moods it is reflecting and the emotions it is generating are all relevant considerations. It is unlikely that your reasons for liking something are totally individual to you, even though some may be. Your answer should contain some reference to a range of these criteria, even if you conclude that personal opinion is the key factor. Also, what does the questioner mean by 'success' in this context?

- Consider some of the arguments in the unit you have just read, as well as your own ideas and responses to works of art. Allow yourself just 15–20 minutes to write your answer, then turn to page 258 for other possible points you may not have included.

The nature of culture

Culture can be defined in a variety of ways, but it is generally agreed that culture means human beliefs, knowledge and behaviour, which form a distinctive pattern or system. Each society has its own culture based on such things as a separate language, a separate history, different rituals and customs (for example, French culture, Scottish culture, Maori culture). This idea of culture has led to stereotyping, so that Scottish culture is often seen in terms of associations such as the kilt, the bagpipes, haggis, Burns' Night and tossing the caber.

However, in the second half of the twentieth century, cultures began to mix much more and the old monocultural idea (where each society has only one culture, which everyone accepts and lives by) has been displaced, as most societies have become multicultural. In a multicultural society, there may be groups living according to a variety of ethnic cultures, but there will also be some subcultures such as teen culture, urban culture, rural culture, pop culture, mass culture, high culture. Sociologists now accept that the culture into which an individual is born may have a much smaller influence than it used to have. Individuals now have the opportunity to choose their own culture, in the sense that in a multicultural society any individual will be influenced by several cultures.

In order to help you to answer questions on culture, this unit will explain some of the more common types of culture.

Western culture

Western culture is the basic culture of Europe and the USA and has a major effect on most other cultures in the world. Much argument about culture is based around whether it is inevitable that all cultures will eventually become subcultures of western culture and whether western culture has a good or bad effect. Japan is a typical example of this argument. Its economy and media are thoroughly western culture, but Japanese culture still dominates many people's personal lives (attitudes towards and rituals concerning birth, marriage, death, festivals and so on).

The main features of western culture are:

- A concern for individual rights – free speech, freedom to choose or reject religion, free choice of marriage partner, freedom for an individual to move from the bottom to the top of society, freedom from arbitrary arrest (if arrested, people must be brought before an open court within a short length of time).
- Equality of opportunity – free education available to everyone, all jobs (especially government jobs) open to anyone, legislation against racist or sexist bias.
- Protection of the poor – healthcare and payments to the unemployed, the sick and the old through taxation.
- Democratic systems of government.

- The arts following certain forms (see 'High culture' and 'Popular culture' below).
- Dress and lifestyle based on the individual, rather the group.
- Festivals and holidays based on Christianity (for example, Christmas and Easter).
- Moral values based on Christianity (respect for monogamy, honesty, loving one's neighbour, etc.).
- The media reflecting the lifestyles and arts (especially popular culture) and having great importance in people's lives.

Many people would not accept all these features, and some critics of western culture see its key features and symbols as jeans, Coca Cola, McDonalds and pop music, which they also see as destroying the indigenous cultures of the world.

High culture

Many people link culture with the arts and use the term 'cultured person' to refer to someone who appreciates, and is knowledgeable about, classical music, opera, ballet, great literature, poetry, serious theatre and film, painting and sculpture. It is claimed that this type of culture is a sign of civilisation because these arts speak to us about the meaning of life, speak to 'the human spirit' and pass on human values.

Classical music

This includes music written either for a symphony orchestra or for groups of instruments from the orchestra. A symphony orchestra is made up of strings (violins, violas, cellos, double bass), woodwind (clarinets, oboes, bassoons, flutes, cor anglais, piccolos), brass (horns, trumpets, trombones and tubas) and percussion (drums, cymbals, etc.). The main types of music played by a symphony orchestra are symphonies, concertos (solo instrument and orchestra) and overtures. However, symphony orchestras can also be used to accompany choirs in major choral works such as Handel's *Messiah*, Bach's *St Matthew Passion* and the great masses such as the *Requiems* of Mozart and Fauré. The first great concertos were written by J. S. Bach (*Brandenburg Concertos*) and Vivaldi (*The Four Seasons*); the first great symphonies were written by Haydn (*London Symphonies*), Mozart (*Jupiter Symphony*) and Beethoven (*Eroica Symphony*). Classical music did not end with Beethoven. Mendelssohn, Lizst, Brahms, Mahler, Stravinsky, Rachmaninov, Elgar and Britten continued and evolved the tradition. There are many composers still writing classical music, such as John Taverner, whose *Requiem* was played at Princess Diana's funeral.

Opera

This can be defined as 'drama set to music where the music is essential to the drama'. The first operas were performed in Italy (Monteverdi's *Coronation of Poppea*) and developed by Glück (*Orpheus*) and Mozart (*Don Giovanni, The Marriage of Figaro, The Magic Flute*). Opera depends on the plot as well as the music, solo singers who act the main parts, often a chorus of singers and a symphony orchestra (though this is often smaller than a full orchestra). Many people see opera as the highest form of culture because it combines classical music with theatre and art in the sets and costumes. This also makes opera the most expensive art form to perform. The most popular operas today are those by Mozart, Verdi (*Nabucco, Aida, Il Traviata*), Wagner (*Die Meistersingers, The Ring*), Bizet (*Carmen, The Pearl Fishers*), and Puccini (*La Boheme, Madame Butterfly, Tosca*). Opera singers such as Caruso, Maria Callas and Luciano Pavarotti can achieve as much fame and money as great pop stars.

Ballet

This is a form of dancing to classical music that has been popular in many cultures for centuries. Ballet began in France in the late seventeenth century, with the work of the French composer Lully. Much of modern ballet developed in the nineteenth century in France, but some of the great changes to modern ballet occurred in Russia, under Diagilev, just before the communist revolution. Famous female ballet dancers include Isadora Duncan, Maria Pavlova and Margot Fonteyn. The two most famous male ballet dancers were both Russian: Vaclav Nijinsky and Rudolph Nureyev. The most popular ballets today are probably those with music by Tchaikovsky (*The Nutcracker, Swan Lake, Romeo and Juliet*), Delibes (*Coppelia*) and Stravinsky (*Petroushka, The Rite of Spring, The Firebird*). The ballet requires a symphony orchestra and so is often staged in opera houses. In England the Royal Ballet and the Royal Opera both use the New Covent Garden Opera House.

Great literature

This refers to novels or short stories that have a message about the meaning of life and say something about human nature through their characters (though their storyline may or may not stand up to scrutiny). The novel you studied for GCSE English literature will be termed as 'great literature'. The first great piece of English literature can probably be regarded as *The Canterbury Tales* by Chaucer. Novels did not evolve until the eighteenth century, when *Joseph Andrewes* by Henry Fielding and *Robinson Crusoe* by Daniel Defoe were written. The greatest nineteenth-century British novelist was Charles Dickens (*David Copperfield, Great Expectations, Oliver Twist*), though some would claim that it was Jane Austen (*Pride and Prejudice, Sense and Sensibility*) or the Brontë sisters (*Jane Eyre, Wuthering Heights*). Twentieth-century novelists such as D. H. Lawrence (*Sons and Lovers, Women in Love*), James Joyce (*Ulysses*), John Braine (*Room at the Top*) have tended to be more working class than in previous centuries. There are many contemporary novelists writing what may be considered 'great literature' such as William Trevor, Salman Rushdie (*Midnight's Children, Satanic Verses*), Martin Amis and Margaret Forster. You should be aware of great world literature such as *War and Peace* by Leo Tolstoy (about Russian aristocratic families during and after the Napoleonic Wars), *The Brothers Karamazov* by Fyodor Dostoevsky (about murder and the existence of God) and *A La Recherche du Temps Perdu* by Marcel Proust (about the decline of a group of French aristocrats at the beginning of the twentieth century).

Poetry

It is often said that 'a poem can say in a page what it takes a novel 300 pages to say'. It is also said that poetry is 'the best words in the best order'. From this it can be seen that poetry is about putting forward ideas about the meaning of life, and also about using words in special ways to give a beautiful sound, as well as a deep meaning. There is a close connection between poetry and other forms of literature. Shakespeare wrote poems as well as plays (mostly sonnets). Thomas Hardy, who wrote great novels such as *Tess of the d'Urbervilles* and *Jude the Obscure*, also wrote much poetry. One of the great periods in English poetry was the Romantic period of the early nineteenth century, whose writers included Wordsworth (*Daffodils, Upon Westminster Bridge*), Keats (*Ode to a Nightingale, Endymion*), Shelley (*Ozymandias, To a Skylark*) and Coleridge (*Kubla Khan, The Rime of the Ancient Mariner*). You will probably have studied twentieth-century poetry for GCSE English. Try re-reading some of it to see whether your views about it have changed.

Film and performing arts

This is probably the part of high culture which has the most impact on ordinary people. Although many would think only of the theatre when they think of 'performing arts', and going to the theatre to see serious drama is a minority activity, more than 50 per cent of the population is likely to come into contact with the performing arts through television drama and films.

The performing arts aim to bring imaginary situations to life so that the audience becomes involved in the situation and, through a successful portrayal, begin to look at life in different ways. Clearly the performing arts are almost totally reliant on literature through dramatists or scriptwriters.

Not many young people would go to see the RSC performing *Romeo and Juliet* for pleasure, but Baz Luhrmann's film version set in 1990s America with Leonardo di Caprio as Romeo brought Shakespeare to millions of young people worldwide. Certainly the updating made many young people think more deeply about Shakespeare's theme of institutionalised violence bringing tragedy to those who are most loved.

It is not only through performances of famous serious dramatists, such as Shakespeare, Beckett and Pinter, that the performing arts make people think deeply. Television dramas (such as *The Second Coming* about Jesus returning to contemporary society) and films (such as *Mona Lisa Smile* about feminism in the late 1950s) can enable the performing arts to encourage a lot of people to think more deeply about serious issues.

The adaptation of serious literature for film or television (or even in the case of Victor Hugo's *Les Miserables* for a musical) is a genre which does more than simply 'bring a book to life'. BBC1's adaptation of *North and South* by Elizabeth Gaskell gave a twenty-first-century interpretation of the book, helping people today to see the major problems caused to both employers and employees by the Industrial Revolution.

Of course, the performing arts do not have to be serious, Shakespeare wrote comedies. Films such as *The Full Monty, East is East,* and *Bend it Like Beckham* were box office hits seen by millions of people, but they brought serious issues to life in a less serious way.

> ### DID YOU KNOW?
>
> **'Have a bon jour'**
> The French government is worried that French culture is being taken over by American culture. The Academie Française (which is in charge of the French language) has written French words for the many English words that have come into the average French vocabulary (e.g. le jogging, le weekend, le pop music, le duty-free – such words are called Franglais). The Academie is trying to persuade French people to use the French words. In the same way, French chefs are complaining about the effects of McDonalds fast food on French restaurants and are running campaigns to persuade French people to eat French food. There are also attempts to ban British and American films and pop music in order to protect and encourage French culture. However, it appears that ordinary French people are not responding to these attempts to save French culture.

KEY TERMS

American dream the alleged basis of American culture, that any individual can do anything they want and achieve the lifestyle they desire through using market forces

Booker Prize the most important British literature award for newly written serious novels

Elitism the belief that a small, select group (e.g. advocates of high culture) is superior to the rest of society

Cultural norms standards of a culture, e.g. the norms of western culture are individual rights, equal opportunity, etc.

Cultural values what is regarded as important in culture (very similar to cultural norms)

Ethnic originally connected with race, it is now used to refer more to a cultural group, which may have certain racial characteristics (e.g. gypsies, Sikhs)

Grand opera opera in which there is no spoken dialogue; everything is set to music

Indigenous culture the culture that is native to the area (e.g. the culture of the native Americans is the indigenous culture of the USA)

Monoculture a society based on only one culture

Multiculture a society with several different cultures

Multiethnic a society with different races and cultures connected with those races

Pop art serious art based on popular culture and the mass media, e.g. Andy Warhol's painting of a can of Campbell's soup

Turner Prize the most important British award for contemporary art

Whitbread Prize a British award for the best book of the year

Youth icon an object of admiration reflecting what is regarded as important by young people

Painting and sculpture

These have been part of human life from prehistoric times. Some of the earliest examples of human culture are cave paintings, the most famous being those from northern Spain and southwest France, dating from over 40,000 years ago. The Egyptian civilisation is remembered both by its sculpture, such as the huge statues of pharaohs, and by the intricate paintings on the walls of the tombs and on the sarcophagi (coffins of the mummies). Of course, painting and sculpture is joined together in architecture, which often reflects the spirit of an age. The most famous ancient sculptures come from Greece (*Venus de Milo*), where sculptures began to be made from bronze as well as marble. In western Europe, most art took the form of architecture until the Renaissance, when painting and sculpture enjoyed a rebirth. Michelangelo is famous not only for the paintings on the ceiling of the Sistine Chapel (frescoes depicting Christianity from Adam to the final judgement), but also great sculptures such as *David* and *Pieta*. After the Renaissance, there have been several different periods and styles: Baroque (Bernini, El Greco, Carravaggio, Rembrandt), Rococo (Canaletto, Watteau), Romantic (Goya, Turner), Impressionist (Renoir, Degas, Monet, Cezanne), Expressionist (Van Gogh, Roualt, Munch and abstract expressionist in Jackson Pollock), Surrealist (Klee, Magritte, Dali). The most famous sculptors of these periods have been Bernini, Rodin and Henry Moore.

Popular culture

Popular culture is often used in a derogatory sense to indicate the type of culture that is less educated and less valuable than high culture. However, each area of high culture has a corresponding feature in popular culture. Music is perhaps the easiest example, where popular music is a major business worldwide. Groups and popstars can attract massive audiences at concerts almost anywhere in the world and their records sell millions of copies. Closely connected with popular music are a variety of dance forms, from ordinary people dancing in a nightclub to professional dancers in modern dance shows. Popular literature ranges from thrillers and romances to biographies of sports and pop stars. Theatres and cinemas make their money from the popular shows and films they put on. Andy Warhol developed a form of painting that he called pop art, but no painting can ever be popular in one sense because only the rich can afford to buy original paintings. However, most homes will have some cheap reproductions of famous paintings, which may reveal that paintings are often more a part of popular culture than high culture, e.g. Constable's *Haywain*. Many modern sculptures are publicly funded and can become popular because they are in places frequented by the public. *The Angel of the North* in Gateshead seems to be more popular with ordinary people than with those who consider themselves 'cultured', and as such is perhaps an example of popular sculpture.

This sculpture also identifies a major problem with trying to make a division between high culture and popular culture, as there are so many fringe areas. James Horner's theme music for *Titanic* appeared in both the pop music charts and the classical music charts. Serious films such as *Brassed Off* and *The Full Monty* have also

Figure 24.1 The Angel of the North by Antony Gormley, created by a high culture sculptor, but most admired by ordinary people who follow popular culture

been hugely popular. Perhaps this is more easily seen in television, where traditionally ITV is the popular culture channel with BBC 2 and Channel 4 as the high culture channels, although it is ITV that screens *The South Bank Show*, a programme dedicated to culture. The differences between high and popular culture (and the fact that high culture can only survive through subsidies from the taxes of people who do not like it) are all dealt with at greater length in Unit 23.

Activities

1. Interview people of a variety of ages and social situations to discover what they consider to be the key features of British culture.

2. Use the Internet to discover the main features of popular culture.

3. Listen to 30 minutes of Classic FM, 30 minutes of Radio 1 and 30 minutes of an Asian radio programme. Decide whether the music played on Classic FM or the Asian station has most in common with the music of Radio 1 and why.

4. Make a list of the arguments for and against western culture being adopted throughout the world.

EXAM QUESTION

The Elgin Marbles are part of the frieze from the Parthenon in Athens which were purchased by Lord Elgin in the early nineteenth century and are part of a permanent collection in The British Museum.

To what extent do you believe that the UK still has the right to retain artefacts, such as the Elgin Marbles, which originally belonged to other countries?

(12 marks)

AQA B June 2003

Figure 24.2

EXAMINER'S ADVICE

- This is another question from A2 Unit 5, this time from June 2003. It is one of five compulsory short essays, with each title taken from a different section of the specification and each worth 12 marks. Make sure that you attempt all five in the test, so as not to lose marks unnecessarily. See page 1 for more information about this paper. Even if you are not taking A2, Unit 5 questions are similar to those set for AS Unit 1, so you should sensibly have a go at them.
- The question may seem a slightly unusual one, but the topic had been in the news leading up to this examination, and you may expect some topical themes to appear, although questions are usually set 12 to 18 months ahead. It is essential to keep informed about controversial issues which arise during your course, and this one has certainly been discussed between the UK and Greek Governments. So far, the UK Government has declined to return the sculptures.
- The issue is presented as an ethical one ('To what extent do you believe the UK has the right …'), so you can make up your own mind on what you think is right. However, even if you see this as a simple issue, and think the pieces should be returned, you must also consider the reasons why this has been resisted, at least to show your awareness of the arguments. Before you commit yourself you should perhaps find out more.
- Try a quick Internet or encyclopaedia search, then allow yourself 15 minutes to write your answer. Turn to page 258 for some suggested arguments on both sides.

Creativity and innovation

Creativity can have many meanings. There is a sense in which everyone is creative. Anyone who has written a letter, decorated a room or planted a garden has been creative. However, calling someone creative is usually taken to mean more than this – it is used to refer to people who write books, paint pictures or create designer gardens.

Innovation is more clearcut. To count as an innovation, what is created must be different from what has gone before. It must break new ground, by starting a new school of art as the Impressionists Renoir and Degas did, developing the form of the symphony as Beethoven did, or, like the Beatles, changing the direction of popular music.

Creativity and ordinary people

Many experts believe that all human beings have a creative urge and so they believe that education should give people the opportunity to develop that creativity. The purpose of art, music, cookery, woodwork, metalwork, needlework, drama, and design lessons at school is to encourage creativity, and also to give young people the opportunity to discover whether they have particular creative gifts and to give them the skills to use their gifts. It is often argued that many great artists will never be able to reveal their creative gifts if they are not given skills and opportunities in creative subjects. In just the same way that Shakespeare could not have written his plays if he had not been taught to read and write, likewise no one can become a great violinist if they never have the chance to learn to play a violin or become a great designer if they are not given the necessary basic skills. This is seen very clearly in the case of Sir Paul McCartney, who composed all the music for his classical piece *Standing Stones*, but had to have expert help to write it into an orchestral score because he had never actually been taught musical composition.

It is also argued that those who take part in the arts, in even the most basic way, are more able to appreciate them than those who only go to watch. Someone who has played in a school orchestra knows how hard it is to get a group of musicians to play correctly. They also have some understanding of musical forms, and so are more able to appreciate great music. Someone who has tried to paint or sculpt is likely to have far more appreciation of a painting or sculpture than someone who has not, because they are aware of the technical problems involved. Likewise, people who have sung in choirs or acted in school plays are likely to have a better appreciation of choral music or theatre than someone who has not.

However, it can also be argued that anyone who has creative urges and skills will be driven to use them. Sir Paul McCartney may not have written and performed great pop music if he had been trained in music. It can be argued that if he had been trained, he would not have had the originality or the desire to perform that a great pop musician needs. He has been a great musician without training. In the same way,

Makes you think

Creativity and innovation is a vital part of science, maths and philosophy, as well the arts. René Descartes (1596–1650) is known as the father of modern philosophy. When he read about the ideas of Copernicus and Galileo, he realised that all he had been taught at school about science was wrong. This also led him to realise that he had accepted what other people told him without trying to find out for himself whether it was true, so that everything he had learned might be false. This led Descartes to develop what has become known as 'systematic doubt'. This means doubting everything until you come to what cannot be doubted. In the process of doubting everything, Descartes realised that he could not doubt his own existence because there must be something to be doing the doubting. From this came Descartes' famous statement, 'Cogito ergo sum' ('I think therefore I am'). The creativity and innovation of Descartes led to later philosophical and scientific ideas about truth, the importance of maths for science and the scientific method.

artists like van Gogh and Gauguin had no formal art training, but felt a compelling urge to paint. Very few novelists have any formal training in literature.

In the same way, it is possible that music lessons and art lessons put many young people off the arts in the same way that teaching Shakespeare, rather than going to see performances of his plays, puts young people off Shakespeare for life.

Le Corbusier and modern architecture

Charles Jeanneret (1887–1965), who adopted the pseudonym Le Corbusier (the name of one of his ancestors) when he started writing, was the most famous of a group of artists and architects who wanted to break away from traditional forms. In *Towards a New Architecture*, Le Corbusier put forward the view that architecture should be functional, rather than decorated – 'A house is a machine for living in', 'a curved street is a donkey track, a straight street, a road for men'. Le Corbusier utilised the new invention of reinforced concrete to build a shell of concrete floors resting on steel girders so that the outside of his buildings could be of any material – he most often used glass – that would keep plain vertical and horizontal lines. He also believed that the city of the future would be full of green areas and parks with all the living spaces and offices being in skyscrapers.

Le Corbusier found it difficult to get his designs built (a workers' city he built in Pessac, France, in 1926, was so hated by the local authority that it refused to pipe water to it), but his books illustrated with his designs had a tremendous impact on young and trainee architects. By 1950, his ideas had become so influential that he was

Figure 25.1 A building by Le Corbusier

able to design a complex of housing and shops for 1800 people in Marseilles. In 1951, he was made architectural adviser for the construction of Chandigarh, the brand new capital of the Punjab Province of India. His use of unfinished concrete for the principal buildings of the city had an immediate impact on architecture around the world. What is often called 'modern architecture', high rise, straight line, functional buildings using concrete and glass, is the result of Le Corbusier's successful fight against the conservative forces of architecture.

Monet and Impressionism

Claude Monet (1840–1926) was the son of a successful grocer and ship's chandler in Le Havre. He began painting in his mid-teens, and, though he went to Paris, he refused the formal art training his father wanted to pay for, preferring to work with artists. Throughout his life Monet was fascinated by the *effects of light* on how objects are perceived. Oil painted landscapes were painted in studios after remembrances or sketches of the real thing. Monet insisted on painting his landscapes outdoors so that the perception could be put onto canvas immediately.

In 1869, Monet went to La Grenouillère, a resort on the Seine, to paint with Renoir. Together they painted what were to be regarded as the first Impressionist paintings, recording on the spot the impression of a scene rather than a detailed study. This was done by interpreting the light and movement by *rapid, short strokes and fairly vivid colours*. It was Monet's painting, *Impression: Sunrise*, shown at an exhibition in Paris in 1874, which led the critics to call this school of painting 'Impressionism'. Other famous painters worked in the same style and exhibited with Monet and Renoir (for example Degas, Pissarro, Cezanne). However, the artists gradually drew apart and began to develop different styles. The last Impressionist exhibition was held in 1886.

Monet himself continued to paint in his impressionistic style through paintings that studied a single subject through varying lights. As he became more famous, he used the money to develop a garden at his new home in Giverny (now a French national monument), which he painted in his later years. Between 1906 and 1926 he painted a series called *Water Lilies*, in which the actual features become more and more indistinct, with just a shimmering series of colours giving the overall impression of sunlight playing on a lily pond.

Monet was not only an innovative creator – his ideas have had an influence on all the modern schools of art. The exhibition of his paintings at London's Royal Academy in 1999 was a sell-out, the most successful art exhibition ever held in London.

Modern art

Innovation and creativity is particularly concerned with what is termed 'modern art'. This was most connected with abstract art when artists like Wassily Kandinsky and Jackson Pollock began to paint pictures whose content was shapes and colour rather than anything which could be directly connected with the 'real world'. However,

KEY TERMS

Abstract art art which does not represent recognisable objects from the world (e.g. Kandinsky, Pollock)

Barbican the City of London Arts centre, where the Royal Shakespeare Company and the Royal Philharmonic Orchestra perform

Bauhaus new-style art college founded in Berlin by Walter Gropius after the First World War, connected with minimalism and functionalism in design

Cartesian anything connected with Descartes

Denouement the unravelling of the plot at the end of a play/film/novel

Dewey decimal the most used system of classifying books in libraries

Iconoclast someone who breaks down accepted traditions or statues

Left Bank area of Paris associated with artists and intellectuals

Minimalism style of art with no decoration or ornaments

RADA the Royal Academy of Dramatic Art

Representational art art which represents recognisable objects from the world (e.g. Da Vinci, Rembrandt)

Royal Academy society to encourage painting, sculpture and architecture

RSC the Royal Shakespeare Company

Royalties payments made to authors for sales of their books

South Bank the area south of the Thames, housing the Royal Festival Hall and the National Theatre

Symposium a collection of articles on the same subject by different authors

Thespian an actor

1. Think of any creative activity you have ever been involved in (especially to do with music, art or drama – remember what you did at Junior School) and try to analyse its good and bad effects on you.

2. Find examples of the work of either Le Corbusier or Monet and use the criteria from Unit 23 ('Aesthetic evaluation') and the knowledge from this unit to assess their greatness.

3. Work out the arguments for and against giving every school child the right to learn a musical instrument.

4. 'Only those who have participated in the arts can understand the arts.' To what extent do you agree with this statement?

5. Many works of art (novels, films, plays, paintings, etc.) are created as vehicles for political, social and/or moral comment. Choose any one work of art that has influenced your thinking about life and society, and explain its purposes and impact on you.

abstract artists had to have considerable artistic skill in terms of the 'form' of aesthetic evaluation. Moreover, modern artists like Pablo Picasso and David Hockney often moved between representational and abstract art.

A major issue in the contemporary art world is whether 'conceptual installation art' is art at all. This type of art has featured in the Turner Prize and is typified by: Tracey Emin's unmade bed; Martin Creed's empty room with the lights going on and off; Damien Hirst's dead sheep in a glass case filled with formaldehyde. Many people argue that such things are not art at all. The 81-year-old-Welsh painter, Sir Kyffin Williams, has said, 'Much of modern art is totally unbelievable . . . Conceptual installation art is worthless and people don't want it.' (BBC News, 14 January 2004)

However, a very different view is given by *The Guardian*'s art critic, Adrian Searle, 'Maybe Creed wanted to give us a prolonged moment of expectation (in the empty room with the lights going on and off) . . . The more I thought about them (Tom Friedman's empty cups) the more associations piled up: from the manufacture of the cups themselves; to the water cooler culture of the office; the fact that the ring of cups on the floor was more beautiful and shimmering than I would have thought possible; that it looked like a sci-fi halo . . . Some people are undoubtedly afraid – both of the feelings art provokes and of having their preconceptions of what art ought to be upset. They want meaning on a plate, served up the way it always has been.' (*The Guardian*, 11 December 2001)

EXAM QUESTION

To what extent does the Hollywood domination of the film industry cause concern for the future of film-making?

(12 marks)

AQA B June 2002

Why it's Bridget, Corelli or a video

Moviegoers wanting to see something less mainstream than Bridget Jones's thighs or Harry Potter's broomstick are out of luck. New research shows that Britain has become the most blockbuster-obsessed nation in the western world.

While cinemas in France, Germany and America still show a diverse mix, the horizons of British cinema-owners rarely stretch beyond showing *Gladiator* or *Captain Corelli* in Screens One, Two, Three and Four of the local multiplex.

Source: The Independent on Sunday, *22 April 2001*

EXAMINER'S ADVICE

- This is another question from A2 Unit 5, this time from June 2002. It is one of five compulsory short essays, with each title taken from a different section of the specification and each worth 12 marks. Make sure that you attempt all five in the test, so as not to lose marks unnecessarily. See page 1 for more information about this paper. Even if you are not taking A2, Unit 5 questions are similar to those set for AS Unit 1, so you should sensibly have a go at them.
- This is also another 'to what extent/how far' question, typical of General Studies, that enables you to argue the case as you wish. It also allows you to present a balanced view without committing yourself wholly to one side or the other, which is usually the better strategy unless you have a strong conviction that you can back up with evidence.

- The best supporting evidence you can provide in this question are some examples of films, both of the 'blockbuster' type and more independent studio productions, that might be more up to date than the ones suggested in the extract above. Of course, you need to have seen or at least know of some to write a convincing answer.
- Hollywood has, of course, been a dominant force throughout the history of film-making, promoting American cultural values in the process, but that has not prevented successful films being made in Europe and elsewhere. Consider the recent successes of British films in the Oscar awards.
- When you have assembled some examples you would like to use, allow yourself 15 minutes to write your answer. Turn to page 258 for some suggested arguments on both sides.

The media

The word 'media' relates to any form of communication between a small group and a larger group. It is usually thought of in terms of the mass media, i.e. communication with a mass audience. The most important forms of mass media are: the press (newspapers), radio and television. However, it is important to remember that cinema, magazines and books are also part of the media. The most important recent addition to mass media is the Internet, which enables individuals anywhere in the world to communicate with a worldwide mass audience (see Unit 11, 'Computers').

The press

In the UK, the press is dominated by the national press. There are regional daily morning newspapers such as the *Northern Echo* and the *Yorkshire Post* and regional evening papers such as the *Manchester Evening News*, but over 90 per cent of the morning newspaper market belongs to the nationals.

The national press is traditionally divided into 'popular' and 'quality'. The popular press aims at a large circulation (85 per cent of sales go to the popular press). The popular press is largely represented by *The Sun*, *The Daily Mirror*, *The Daily Star*, *The Express* and *The Daily Mail*, although the latter two regard themselves as in between popular and quality and are aimed at a more educated and discerning reader than the

Figure 26.1 The journalist who took this photo regarded it as legitimate news because one of the prices of fame is that anything that famous people do is news. However, others call this 'intrusive journalism' and think that famous people are only news when they are doing the work for which they became famous

other three. Sometimes the popular press is called 'the gutter press' because of its tendency to publish sensational stories about the private lives of the rich and famous. These five dailies are also called 'tabloid' because of the size of the paper.

The quality press is represented by *The Times*, *The Guardian*, *The Daily Telegraph*, *The Independent* and *The Financial Times*. These newspapers are aimed at an educated, middle-class market and are often called 'broadsheets' because they have larger pages with much more print than the tabloids. They rely heavily on advertising for their income (as do the tabloids, but not as much).

Newspapers as we know them began in the seventeenth century and the first English newspaper was *The Weekly Newes*, which appeared in 1622. Although gimmicks and sensational reporting are generally thought of as something new, they are not. (In 1890, *The Daily Mail* offered £1 a week for life to any reader who could guess the value of the gold in the Bank of England.) However, all journalists see that the press has an important role to play in informing the public and in ensuring that the government and political parties are subjected to regular scrutiny.

The press is controlled by the Press Complaints Council (run by the press itself), D-notices and the laws of libel (see Unit 27, 'Censorship').

Radio

Radio in the UK is divided into those stations funded by the BBC (through money raised by the television licence) and independent stations funded by advertising. Both BBC and independent radio are also divided into national and local stations. The BBC's national stations are Radio 1 (mainly popular music), Radio 2 (light music and entertainment), Radio 3 (classical music and cultural programmes), Radio 4 (news and spoken word programmes) and Radio 5 (sport and current affairs). The BBC's 30 local radio stations use Radio 2 or 4 when not broadcasting their own programmes.

There are over 50 local independent FM radio stations, and two national independent FM stations – Virgin Radio and Classic FM (Britain's first national independent radio station and now the largest classical music radio station in the world).

Digital radio (DAB) began in 1999 and now covers 80 per cent of the country (as well as being available via digital television and worldwide through radio station websites). As well as the BBC stations, DAB has several national stations – Prime Time, Talk Sport, Life, Planet Rock, One Word, Core – as well as Virgin Radio and Classic FM. DAB requires no tuning, has a much clearer signal and can be paused and replayed. Interactivity is a future possibility.

Both BBC and Independent Radio can have their licences revoked by the government, so it can be claimed they are not completely free (see Unit 27).

Television

Television is the most rapidly expanding form of the media. In the UK, the most watched television is still provided by the terrestrial stations (the BBC provides

Channels 1 and 2 from the licence fee, independent regionally based stations provide ITV, and Channels 4 and 5 are both separate national independent stations). However, the growth of satellite, cable and digital broadcasting has led to many more stations being available and also to links between television and the Internet. The Independent Television Commission (ITC) is responsible for licensing all independent television stations, including cable and satellite. It awards licences to the regional ITV companies on the basis of their past record, their proposed schedules and the amount of revenue they intend to give to the government. The ITC is responsible for the content of the programmes and advertising put out by ITV, Channel 4 and 5 and enforces government codes on advertising and violence. The terrestrial independent stations are funded solely from revenue from advertising during 'natural breaks', whereas cable and satellite are funded from a mixture of advertising and subscription.

Fifty-five per cent of households now have digital television and this has led to a great growth in channels. The BBC has introduced BBC 3 and 4 and other new channels. Programmes and films can be bought by using a digital handset, the Internet can be accessed and e-mails sent, Sky Plus allows recording while watching, pausing and a whole range of facilities to put the viewer in charge. These changes, plus the huge increase in channels, have led to a great change in viewing habits. Twenty years ago it was normal for a popular BBC 1 or ITV programme to attract twenty million viewers, now an audience of ten million is regarded as exceptional. Moreover, the BBC's entry into digital, cable and satellite television means it is gaining money from subscriptions as well as the licence fee, leading recent reports to suggest scrapping the licence fee so putting the BBC on a similar footing to the other television companies.

Both the BBC and ITC have to produce a mixture of types of programme. Figure 26.2 shows the BBC hours of output of different types of programme for 2003/4. Can you work out the percentage of output for each different type?

	Total	
	2003/2004	**2002/2003**
First Transmission: Originated programmes Network BBC 1 and BBC 2		
Factual and learning	**1,667**	1,488
Education for children	**56**	83
News and weather	**3,083**	3,151
Current affairs	**426**	433
Entertainment	**774**	802
Sport	**1,241**	1,446
Children's	**438**	473
Drama	**498**	487
Music and arts	**201**	258
Film	**5**	17
Religion	**116**	116
Subtotal	**8,505**	8,754

Figure 26.2 BBC Television hours of output by origin
(Source: Table 8, BBC Annual Report and Accounts, 2003/2004)

The influence of the media

Some sociologists believe that the media are used by the Establishment to influence people's behaviour. They claim that almost everyone in the top positions in the media belong to the ruling group. They went to public schools and pass on to the public the ideals of a bourgeois society through the media. The media encourage people to follow certain ways of life and to buy certain goods. Capitalist society is always portrayed in a good light, even in programmes such as soaps and sitcoms.

Other people believe that the media's use of sex and violence has an influence on behaviour. Some psychologists have claimed that the rise in sex crimes and crimes of violence can be directly linked to the rise in the portrayal of sex and violence in the media. (For example, the young boy killers of James Bulger were alleged to have been watching, and possibly copying, a very violent film.)

However, others believe that although the media clearly have some influence, otherwise advertisers would not use them, the audience has just as much effect on the media as the media have on the audience. *The Simpsons* is one of the most popular shows worldwide, but it makes fun of capitalist society. Television and newspapers are in competition and need to keep their viewers and readers. If a programme does not attract viewers, it will be dropped, showing that it has not had the intended influence on the audience. *The Sun* had supported the Conservatives until 1996, when it saw that most people were now supporting Labour. It changed its support to Labour to keep its readers, rather than to influence them. In the same way, *The Sun* adopted 'Page 3 girls' to attract a mass male readership, but is beginning to change this due to fears that 'Page 3' might now lose readers for the paper.

You should also be aware that TV and newspapers have been responsible for uncovering lots of things the government and capitalists would like to keep secret such as whether there were weapons of mass destruction in Iraq.

Some experts feel that there are now so many different elements to the media that the audience can pick and choose, so that they have more influence on the media than the media have on them.

Bias in the media

It is often argued that the media are biased, an issue closely connected to the media's influence. Most newspapers have a particular political bias (i.e. they support one of the political parties). It is also claimed that certain television programmes are biased for or against a political party (for example, that *Panorama* is biased against the Conservatives and *Today* on Radio 4 is biased against Labour).

'Bias' means a prejudiced view. In the media, it occurs when one side of an argument or one point of view is given an unfair advantage by lots of coverage or ignoring its bad points. Bias can be very difficult to uncover, but a typical example is the word 'terrorist' compared with 'freedom fighter'. If a newspaper calls someone a terrorist, this predisposes the reader to think that their cause is wrong, whereas calling them a freedom fighter predisposes the reader to think that they are right.

KEY TERMS

Broadsheet the name given in the UK to 'quality' newspapers

Elite a small group that considers itself/is considered superior to the rest of society

Establishment social group exercising control over the rest of society

Hard news newspaper stories about real issues which would make TV news headlines, compared with soft news which is more 'magaz, iney'

Hyper-reality believing that television programmes, especially soaps, are more real than reality

Investigative journalism journalists creating news by investigating illegal or scandalous activities

IRN Independent Radio News, an independent company producing news for independent radio stations

ITN Independent Television News, a similar company for television

ITC Independent Television Commission, the body in charge of Channels 3, 4 and 5

New technology in the media this is used to refer especially to computerised printing so that journalists can type in their stories directly

Paparazzi news photographers and journalists who try to get unexpected photos of famous people

Pulitzer Prize American prize awarded for investigative journalism

Reuters the largest of the news agencies, with journalists worldwide and which sells its stories and photos to newspapers and magazines that cannot afford to fund so many journalists

Tabloid name given to popular newspapers in Britain

Activities

1. Use the Internet to discover the names of the Sunday national papers, their circulation figures, their owners and what other papers they own.

2. Use the Internet to discover the Channel 3 TV stations, who owns them and how near their owners are to the legal limit of 25 per cent of ITV advertising revenue ownable by any one company.

3. Use the Internet to find one recent case referred to the Press Complaints Council, why it was referred and what was done about it.

4. Video the news on BBC 1, BBC 2, Channel 3, Channel 4 and Channel 5 on the same night. Watch them, noting the differences in coverage of the same story and stories carried by some channels but not others, and suggest reasons to explain the differences.

5. Try to find any notes you have on media bias from your GCSE English course.

Media ownership

Many people are worried that the ownership of the media is in the hands of too few. Rupert Murdoch, through his News International Corporation, owns *The Sun*, *The Times* and BSkyB, as well as newspapers and television stations in Australia and the USA. This is now a typical situation as communications multinational companies develop. People think that someone like Murdoch must be able to manipulate public opinion and that he is too powerful to be opposed by governments. He was regularly consulted by the Conservative Prime Minister, Mrs Thatcher, and Tony Blair was criticised in 1999 for discussing Murdoch's commercial interests in Italy with the Italian Prime Minister.

However, Murdoch was banned by the ITC from making a bid for Channel 5, and when he refused to publish a book on China (because it was critical of the Chinese Government and his companies were just about to sign a deal with China), it provoked an outcry and was criticised not only in the rest of the media, but also by *The Times*, which Murdoch owns. The UK does have monopoly laws that prevent any one company owning too much of the media, but the arrival of the Internet is going to make it much more difficult for any group to manipulate people through the media.

EXAM QUESTIONS

Look carefully at Tables 1, 2 and 3 below. Table 1 shows information about the daily news circulation of some newspapers. Table 2 shows the most visited websites for news (given by page impression) for 2001 and Table 3 shows the websites for e-commerce domains in May 2001.

Having studied the tables answer all of the questions which follow.

Table 1 Daily circulation of newspapers, January–June 2001

	Thousands	Type of newspaper
Daily Mail	2400	Tabloid
Daily Mirror	2200	Tabloid
The Daily Telegraph	1000	Broadsheet
Daily Express	900	Tabloid
Financial Times	500	Broadsheet
The Guardian	400	Broadsheet
The Independent	200	Broadsheet
The Sun	3500	Tabloid
The Times	720	Broadsheet
Total	**11,820**	

Table 2 Most visited websites for news, 2001 (by number of page impressions)

Website	Visits (millions)
www.bbc.co.uk/news	207
www.ft.com	40
www.guardian.co.uk	30
www.cnn.com	29
www.telegraph.co.uk	27
www.ireland.com	25
www.thetimes.co.uk	18
www.ananova.com	16
www.independent.co.uk	15
www.teletext.co.uk	13

Table 3 Top 10 European e-commerce domains, May 2001

Rank	Domain	Site description	Unique visitors (1000s)	Average minutes per visitor per month
1	amazon.de	Books, etc. – Germany	2567	10.8
2	bahn.de	Rail Travel – Germany	1887	14.0
3	amazon.com	Books, etc. – USA	1672	6.7
4	amazon.co.uk	Books, etc. – UK	1588	11.8
5	bonzi.com	Search engine	1432	3.3
6	apple.com	Computers	1274	6.3
7	register.com	Domain names	1135	1.5
8	comdirect.de	Finance – Germany	1131	33.1
9	lastminute.com	Travel and leisure	1073	7.6
10	adobe.com	Software	1025	3.8

This ranking includes data from Denmark, France, Germany, Norway, Spain, Sweden and the UK.

Source: all data taken from Carel Fact Files 2002

(a) Using Table 1, construct a bar graph to show the circulation of the broadsheet newspapers.

(4 marks)

(b) (i) Calculate the mean circulation for the tabloid newspapers. Show your working.

(2 marks)

(ii) What percentage of the total daily circulation is accounted for by the *Financial Times*? Show your working.

(2 marks)

(c) What could be concluded from Tables 1 and 2 about the use of the Internet compared with newspapers?

(4 marks)

(d) Why might the information in Table 3 be of limited value?

(8 marks)

(e) With the increasing use of the Internet as a means of accessing information, we may soon be a 'book-free' society. How valid is this claim?

(10 marks)

Total: 30 marks

AQA B May 2003

EXAMINER'S ADVICE
- This question is from AS Unit 3 set in May 2003. See page 1 for more details about this paper and see the other example questions at the end of Units 7, 10 and 13.
- Questions (a) and (b) are very straightforward and should present no problems, but make sure to label axes and scales on your graph and to show your working, as there are marks for these details. Don't spend too much time on the graph for only four marks.
- Try to come up with four distinct points for (c), remembering that part of the question is about comparing Tables 1 and 2. What can you say for definite about the data in each table? What does comparing the two tables tell you? If you think that it doesn't tell you much, explain why.
- Most time should be spent on Questions (d) and (e) as they are worth more than half the marks. Think in terms of: number of marks = number of minutes spent on question = number of points to be made. For Question (d) think about why Table 3 doesn't tell you much (it only shows May 2001) and what additional information you would like to have in order to make it more meaningful. In Question (e) you should consider whether the Internet will really mean 'no more books'. In theory it could do, but is it likely? What arguments are there on each side?
- You should allow approximately 40 minutes in total to complete your answers to these questions. When you have finished, turn to page 259 for the answer notes.

Censorship

Forms of censorship

When westerners think of censorship, they tend to think of the type of censorship that once existed in the Soviet Union and still exists, to a certain extent, in countries such as the People's Republic of China. Under such governments, the media are owned by the government and only publish the views of the government. Plays and books have to be submitted to a government censor prior to publication.

The justification for such a form of censorship is to protect the state from being weakened, either by hostile powers being given access to its secrets, or by its institutions being weakened by criticism. If you believe that your form of government and its institutions are the best (as most communist or totalitarian governments do), then you will believe that they should not be weakened in any way. Such governments also feel that the people who live in their society should be protected from the misinformation that capitalist societies try to feed to them in order to bring them back under the control of capitalism. Non-communist governments opposed to freedom of information and so imposing media censorship may do so because they think their people should be protected from lies. A fundamentalist Muslim government may feel that anything not based on the *Qur'an* is untrue and that the citizens should be protected from it.

The United States Constitution states that there should be a right to freedom of speech and freedom of the press, and this is why all societies with democratic forms of government (as in western society) claim to believe in freedom of expression. In order for democracy to work, the electorate has to be able to make informed choices before they vote. For this, they need a free press so that they can know what is going on in the world and in their own country and can work out which political party will deal best with the problems of the country and the world.

Even so, most democracies have forms of censorship in certain areas.

Censorship and the press

In some countries, especially France, there are privacy laws preventing the press from publishing any stories that infringe upon an individual's right to privacy. It is sometimes claimed that this law is the reason why French politicians are not as worried by the press as British politicians. In Britain there are three forms of press censorship.

- *D-notices.* The government can issue the press with a D-notice under the Official Secrets Act to prevent them from publishing anything classed as an official secret. There have been a few occasions when a newspaper has ignored a D-notice in the public interest, for example when a civil servant has leaked a piece of information showing the government to be breaking the law.
- *Obscene Publications Act.* Under this act, a newspaper or publisher can be charged with a criminal offence if they publish something that is obscene. The definition of

'obscene' varies, from the 1868 British definition – 'whatever has a tendency to deprave and corrupt those whose minds are open to such immoral influences' – to the 1973 American definition – 'works which portray sexual conduct in a patently offensive way, and which, taken as a whole, do not have serious literary, artistic, political or scientific value'.

- *Defamation of character* (libel when written, slander when spoken). If the press publishes an article defaming someone's character, and it is untrue, then they can be sued for damages. The damages can be huge (Jeffrey Archer received £3 million from the *Daily Star* when they accused him of having sex with a prostitute and could not prove it).

Censorship and television

Television is covered by all the same censorship regulations as the press, but has some additional regulations.

The 'watershed' is a voluntary code of practice under which the television companies agree only to screen programmes of 'a family nature' before 9.00 p.m. This is self-censorship, aimed at the protection of children.

In addition, there are extra requirements for the self-censorship of ITV. The Broadcasting Act requires the Independent Television Committee (ITC) to ensure that nothing is included in programmes that 'offends against good taste or decency'. The ITC's own code of conduct requires that there should be no abusive treatment of religious views or beliefs and no 'improper exploitation of any susceptibilities of those watching programmes'. Furthermore, the ITC requires that any adverts shown on television must be 'legal, decent, honest and truthful' and that companies sponsoring programmes must be suitable for the subject content of the programme.

The BBC is controlled by its charter, which requires it to produce a range of programmes that uphold the standards of public decency. After the 1990 Broadcasting Act, which established the ITC, the BBC set up its own Programme Complaints Unit, to which the public can complain if they think programmes have offended standards of decency or have been biased. The BBC has also published a set of *Producers' Guidelines* showing how producers are prevented from producing programmes which give an unbalanced view of a political issue or offend public decency.

Censorship and the arts

The Lord Chamberlain's Office used to view all theatre productions and censor them for obscenity, until this was ended by the Labour Government of 1966–70. Today, the theatre is only censored by the same obscenity and defamation laws as the press and television. However, many theatres operate a voluntary policy of indicating to the public if a performance may cause offence or is unsuitable for children.

All films must be submitted to the British Board of Film Classification for a viewing category. The categories must be enforced by cinema owners who can be prosecuted if

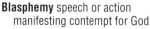

under-age children are watching '12', '15' or '18' films. The Board can also cut scenes from films if it considers that they are too graphic in their portrayal of sex or violence. It is also possible for the Board to refuse to grant a certificate to a film, and local councils can refuse permission for such films to be shown in their area. The Board used to justify its work in terms of 'preserving public decency', but now justifies it in terms of the guidance its categories give to parents and cinema owners.

In a question on censorship in the arts, the information on television could also be used.

The case for censorship

The amount of censorship currently existing in the UK is usually justified by some or all of the following arguments:

- Children have a right to be protected from adult material. There is evidence of children being influenced by what they see because they are too young and inexperienced to have worked out their own ideas and opinions on adult issues. (You could quote the Jamie Bulger case or the Helen Mirren film *Killing Mrs Tingle*, which was banned in Germany after children plotted to kill their teachers when they received low grades, like the children in the film.)
- People have a right not to have their sensibilities offended. So, people have a right not to be confronted by graphic sex scenes, obscene language, etc. on their televisions; members of religions have a right not to see their beliefs ridiculed, etc. People who argue for censorship in this way claim that there is a difference between 'free-to-air' television, radio and the Internet, where people have no control over what is on and 'pay-to-view' television and the theatre, where subscribers only see what they have paid to see. They argue that there is much less need for censorship when there is no free access.
- Film and television directors, newspaper publishers, etc. are motivated by greed and profit and should not be able to make money by gratifying people's baser desires.
- The press needs to be prevented from intruding on people's privacy. Famous people should have a right to a private life and the *paparazzi* should be banned from taking photographs without permission. In the same way, people should have a right to freedom from press intrusion in moments of family crisis, such as after a murder or a plane crash.

The case against censorship

Those who argue against censorship are often in favour of a system such as film categories in order to protect children and people's sensibilities. They also accept the need for defamation laws to protect people from untrue things being published about them. However, they would oppose all other forms of censorship, including the Official Secrets Act. They hold the following views:

KEY TERMS

Blasphemy speech or action manifesting contempt for God

Index a list, which used to be compiled by the Roman Catholic Church until 1966, of books that Catholics were not allowed to read

Libel defaming a person in writing

Official Secrets Act makes it an offence for anyone who has ever served the Crown (civil servants, armed forces, etc.) to communicate any information acquired in that service, whether harmful to the state or not

Pornography the representation of erotic behaviour in books, pictures, films, etc. that is intended to arouse sexual excitement

Pre-publication censorship censorship imposed before people have a chance to see an item, e.g. film censorship, D-notices

Press self-restraint the idea that the press will regulate each other and so not print things which are libellous or offensive (e.g. the Press Complaints Commission)

Post-publication censorship censorship imposed after people have seen an item, e.g. libel and slander laws

Quis custodet ipsos custodes? literally, 'Who guards the guardians?' It comes from Plato's *Republic*, where Plato suggested that a perfect society would have a group of guardians who would protect the people from harmful ideas

Slander defaming a person in speech – there is a legal argument as to whether defamation on radio or television is libel or slander

Watch-dog committee a group of people monitoring other people's activities, e.g. National Viewers and Listeners Association which monitors sex and violence on televison

- Any democracy needs freedom of information. How can voters make informed decisions in elections and referenda if facts are kept from them?
- Who decides what needs to be kept secret or what needs to be censored, and, perhaps even more importantly, who is there to check that their decision is correct?
- If obscenity and violence are corrupting, then the censors, who spend their lives watching such things to decide that other people cannot see them ought to be very corrupt.
- Censorship has always been impossible to impose completely. The rich and powerful have always been able to gain access to what was denied to the mass of the population. Nowadays, with new technology and the advent of the Internet, effective censorship is impossible.
- Privacy laws can be, and have been, used by the powerful to cover up their misdeeds. Who is to decide whether a politician having an affair is in the public interest, other than the press?

Is it censorship?

Not everything that happens reaches the pages of the newspapers or the screens of our televisions. Someone has to decide which of the many items are to be published and in what prominence. Local newspapers, for example, attend the Magistrates Courts, but only a fraction of the cases reach the pages of the local newspaper. First the journalist, then the sub-editors and finally the editor decide which cases are newsworthy and which are not. However, is it censorship if the case of shop-lifting by the editor's mother-in-law is not reported, while the case of under-age drinking by youths from the local council estate is?

Experts in Communications and Cultural Studies have called this selection of news 'gatekeeping' and the people doing the selecting 'gatekeepers'. Of course, there are many more gatekeepers than newspaper journalists and editors:

- Laws passed by the government, the EU and the UN can prevent some news stories from being published. For example, privacy laws meant that newspapers did not report on David Blunkett's affair in 2004 until he went to court to gain access to his son, thus ending his right to privacy.
- Libel laws can make it difficult for newspapers to publish stories unless they can prove them to be true without any doubt, for example the *Daily Telegraph* and George Galloway in 2004.
- Pressure groups can affect news organisations and broadcasters. For example, The National Viewers and Listeners Association can make television companies reluctant to screen programmes with sex and violence; animal rights groups can make journalists reluctant to report on animal experiments which might reveal the identities or addresses of scientists.

The question is whether gatekeeping is censorship or just an inevitable feature of living in a society.

Often connected with gatekeeping is 'government spin'. If the government publishes a decision to end free school meals on the same day that it publishes its decision to abolish the House of Lords, is that a form of censorship, because the free school meals will get little media attention compared with the abolition of the House of Lords? The Hutton Inquiry into the death of Dr Kelly revealed a large amount of gatekeeping by both the BBC and the government.

Activities

5. Blasphemy against the Christian religion is still a criminal offence. It is rarely used and some members of ethnic communities have suggested that it should be extended to make it an offence to denigrate any religion. What problems can you see in trying to impose such a law in a multifaith community?

6. Interview people from varying age groups to see what they would regard as a programme which 'offended public decency'.

EXAM QUESTION

In spite of the Code of Practice below, many would argue that the press is still too intrusive. To what extent do you share this view?

(12 marks)

AQA B June 2004

Code of Practice

The current Code of Practice covering the behaviour of newspapers includes areas such as

- accuracy of material printed

- opportunity to reply by the individual concerned
- distinguishing between comment, conjecture and fact
- privacy of persons
- the use of listening devices

- the use of misrepresentation by journalists
- harassment by journalists
- payment for articles
- intrusion into grief or shock

- interviewing or photographing children.

Source: adapted from Press Complaints Commission – Code of Practice, *1997*

EXAMINER'S ADVICE

- This is another question from A2 Unit 5, this time from June 2004. It is one of five compulsory short essays, with each title taken from a different section of the specification and each worth 12 marks. Make sure that you attempt all five essays in the test, so as not to lose marks unnecessarily. See page 1 for more information about this paper. Even if you are not taking A2, Unit 5 questions are similar to those set for AS Unit 1, so you should sensibly have a go at them.
- You should be familiar with the existence of the Press Complaints Council's Code of Practice from studying Units 26 and 27 of this book. One major issue is that it is operated by the press itself, as a code that members have drawn up voluntarily, and only has censure or criticism as its main weapon. Editors have to take it seriously, however, to forestall stricter laws that the government might threaten from time to time.
- Once again this is a question where the arguments for press freedom need to be balanced against the rights of law-abiding citizens to lead their own private lives without intrusion and interference. You should state what you think the arguments are on both sides, before you attempt to reach a view about whether the press is 'still too intrusive'. Examples to illustrate your points will also help you to gain marks.
- When you have thought about the question, allow yourself 15 minutes to write your answer. Turn to page 259 for some arguments on both sides.

Industry and Commerce

Unit 28 | **Economic theories**
Unit 29 | **Economic issues**
Unit 30 | **The European Union**
Unit 31 | **Rich world, poor world**

Economic theories

According to the *Oxford English Dictionary*, 'economics' is 'the science of the production and distribution of wealth'.

If human beings were self-sufficient, there would be no need for economics, but as soon as a farmer could produce more food than he needed, and another farmer, who made pots, discovered that people wanted the pots he made, economics was needed so that the potter-farmer could become a full-time potter. Specialisation or division of labour (certain people producing certain goods rather than each person producing everything they needed for themselves) is one of the bases of economics. Although economics in the form of the production and distribution of wealth has been around since the beginning of society, theories of economics did not develop until the eighteenth century.

Adam Smith (Professor of Moral Philosophy at Edinburgh University) wrote *The Wealth of Nations* in 1776, in which he worked out how the human desire for self-betterment will lead to changes in society and a gradual increase in wealth. Although written over 200 years ago, Smith's book contains most of the economic theories now accepted by the vast majority of economists.

Money and exchange rates

In the early stages of human development, specialisation was needed for civilisation to occur. However, there was then the problem of how the potter and the farmer were to exchange their surplus products. At first this was done by *bartering* (I will give you 'x' beans and 'y' chickens for 'x' plates). However, as society became more complex (it is difficult for people like teachers and poets to barter), some other system was needed. Money was developed as a system, which gave an external value to bartering.

Money has no *intrinsic value* (a pound coin has no value in itself, unlike a plate) but is based on the value or resources of the government or bank that issues the money. These resources must have intrinsic value and if that value goes down, the value of the money will go down. Money works on the law of supply and demand, so that a currency in high demand will have a high value, and one in low demand, a low value.

This can be seen clearly in the exchange rate of a currency. The exchange rate is the value given on the world markets to one currency in terms of another currency (the exchange rates of the world currencies in terms of sterling – the British pound – are on the business pages of newspapers every day). Until 1972 there were fixed exchange rates made under the Bretton Woods Agreement, 1944. This meant that everyone knew the value of goods worldwide and manufacturers exporting goods knew exactly what their profits would be. However, the drawback was that if a country was not doing as well as expected, it would have to *devalue* its currency by negotiating a new exchange rate. Since 1972, there has been a *floating exchange rate*, where the market decides the value of a currency.

If the value of a currency goes up, this means you can buy more with it abroad, but manufacturers will find it more difficult to sell abroad as their products will be more expensive. However, imports will be much cheaper (if the value of the pound against the euro increases by 10 per cent, a French car that cost £10,000 in Britain will now cost £9000, but a British car of the same value will now cost £11,000 in France).

The law of supply and demand

This says that if there is a low supply of a product and a high demand, the price will rise. Conversely, if there is a high supply and a low demand, the price will fall. This is why brain surgeons are paid more than factory workers (there is a high demand and a low supply of brain surgeons; there is a low demand and a high supply of factory workers, who require less training and intelligence than brain surgeons).

Economists believe that the forces of supply and demand create an equilibrium (where supply and demand are mainly equal) through the price people are prepared to pay meeting the price for which the supplier is prepared to sell.

Market forces

Closely connected with supply and demand are market forces. The market means the place where consumers and suppliers meet. A supplier can keep the price of a product artificially high by restricting the supply, or by creating a *monopoly* (a market where there is only one supplier). However, in a *free market*, it will always be possible for another supplier to come along and offer the product at a lower price. This is competition, and is associated with a theory of economics known, from Adam Smith, as *laissez-faire economics*, where the role of a government is to prevent monopolies occurring so that market forces can determine prices and wages and what is produced.

There are lots of market forces that can affect the basic law of supply and demand:

- Changes in income (if wages or taxes fall or rise, people will have less or more money to spend and so demand will fall or rise).
- Changes in price of connected goods (if the cost of CD players falls, the demand for CDs will rise).
- Taste and fashion (BSE caused a fall in demand for British beef; the introduction of mountain bikes caused a fall in demand for ordinary bikes).
- Competition (a new firm producing the same product will increase the supply and reduce the price).
- Population changes (as people live longer, and there are more people over the age of 65 in the population, there will be a rise in demand for Saga holidays and pensions).

Competition Commission

In 1999 the Competition Commission replaced the Monopolies and Mergers Commission. It is the duty of the Commission to implement the Enterprise Act of 2002 to ensure that mergers and markets in the UK remain fair and competitive. Members are appointed by the Secretary of State for Trade and Industry for an eight-year term on the basis of their experience, ability and diversity of background. There are special committees for utilities, telecommunications, water and newspapers. When a merger or takeover is announced which might lead to unfair competition, the Chairman of the Commission appoints a special committee from the members to make a decision. For example, when Morrisons supermarkets wanted to take over Safeway supermarkets, the Competition Commission had to decide whether this would be in the public interest and, in allowing the Morrison bid to go ahead, it stipulated that Morrisons must sell certain Safeway stores where Morrisons already had a number of stores. The Commission was making sure that the demise of Safeway was used to increase competition in the supermarket business rather than reduce it.

Consumerism

This is the word used to describe the economic conditions which encourage people to buy things so that the economy thrives. Clearly if everyone was a miser spending (consuming) as little as possible and saving as much as possible, then money (and the savings) would become worthless. If people do not buy goods, firms cannot sell goods and so they have to make their workforce redundant. If firms do not sell anything, their shares become worthless and if all the firms in a country do not sell anything, then the country's money becomes worthless. This means it is important for a country to make sure that consumers have sufficient money to consume goods.

In modern western society, consumers have much more choice and therefore can be more discriminating in their choices. One of the main consumer changes in the last 15 years has been the rise of ethical consumerism. This means buying products which were ethically produced and/or which are not harmful to the environment and society. It can be buying free-range eggs produced by hens that live a normal life, rather than those produced by battery hens (the market for battery eggs in supermarkets has virtually died out in the last five years). It can be refusing to buy goods which have been produced by child labour (a much more complex process – do you know where your trainers were produced and whether they used child-labour?). The Ethical Consumer Research Association publishes details of ethical and non-ethical goods in its magazine. Its major success was in virtually ending the sale of GM foods in the UK. However, although 35 per cent of the UK population claim to be concerned about ethical consumption, only three per cent of the UK market is devoted to the production of ethical goods.

Keynesianism

This is an economic theory based on the ideas of J.M. Keynes (1883–1946), who claimed that Smith's ideas on market forces producing full employment were wrong. He said that in times of high unemployment, the government should increase spending to increase national output and so increase employment. In times of full employment and inflation, governments should reduce expenditure. This was the economic theory behind Roosevelt's New Deal in America, which led to the recovery of the American economy after the Wall Street Crash of 1929 and the Depression of the 1930s.

Monetarism

This is an economic theory connected with the American economist Milton Friedman, who claims that any economic problems such as inflation or unemployment are caused by the government producing too much money (the *money supply*), and that by restricting the money supply, firms will have to lower wages and cut staff to become more productive. This will eventually lead to greater profits and so there will be more resources and the money supply can be increased.

Often connected with monetarism is the concept of *privatisation*. This is the idea that industries run by the government (nationalised industries) are not as efficient as private industries. In the 1980s, the Conservative monetarist government led by Mrs Thatcher privatised water, electricity, gas, telephones, railways and buses. There is evidence both for and against whether this was effective. Although gas, water and electricity might be slightly cheaper than they would otherwise have been, there are problems with the number of power stations and the ease of reducing pollution in the power industries when dealing with several private companies. Some people feel that these utility industries are so important to the nation that they should be in national control (see also Unit 10 for issues involved in the privatisation of transport).

Figure 28.1 Mrs Thatcher, Conservative Prime Minister, 1979–1992, claimed to be using the principles of monetarism and market forces to reduce the power of trade unions

EXAM QUESTION

'Lloyds TSB to bid for Abbey National.' Why might the takeover of one company by another **not** be in the public interest?

(12 marks)

AQA B May 2002

Economic issues

Economic issues are problems or arguments about issues concerning money or the state of the economy. The main ones you are likely to be asked questions about are covered in this unit.

Taxation

In any country, the government requires money to provide services. This money is raised by levying taxes on the population.

In the UK in 2004–5, the government expects to spend £455 billion (around £5900 for each person in the country – see Figures 29.1 and 29.2).

Total managed expenditure: £488 billion

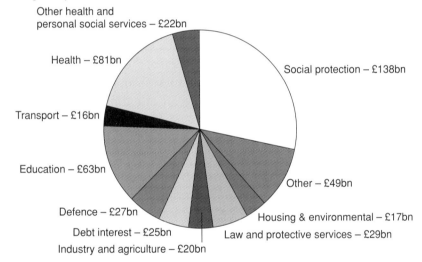

Figure 29.1 Government spending by function

Total receipts: £455 billion

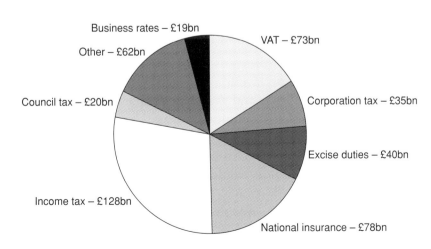

Figure 29.2 Government receipts

Arguments about taxation come in three forms:

1. *Whether the taxes are being spent in the right way.* One of the main debates between political parties is how much money should be spent on *social security.* The reforms of disability allowance and the work of the Child Support Agency are aimed at reducing the amount spent on social security. Any changes in employment will affect the social security spending (the more people who are unemployed, the more benefits have to be paid out). Changes in the population can also affect the budget (an increase in the number of old people will increase expenditure on pensions and health, a decrease in children will reduce expenditure on child benefit and education).

   There are also arguments about whether more or less should be spent on defence than education, etc. Any political party that suggests that there should be more police on the streets is also suggesting that the amount of taxation spent on law and order should be increased, which will mean either increasing taxes or reducing the amount spent in some other area.

2. *Whether taxation should be direct or indirect.* *Direct taxes* are those collected directly by the government. Income tax is a direct tax, which the Inland Revenue collects from every adult. It is *means tested* (the more you earn, the more you pay) and is a percentage of your earnings, capital gains and interest from savings above a certain allowance. *National insurance* and *corporation tax* are also direct taxes collected by the government. Council tax and business rates are direct taxes collected by the local council.

   Indirect taxes are often called hidden taxes. They are a percentage of the cost of various goods, which are collected by shopkeepers, etc. and then paid to the government. *Value added tax* (VAT) is 17.5 per cent of all goods sold in shops except food, newspapers and books. *Excise duties* are paid on petrol, alcohol, tobacco and are much more than 17.5 per cent.

   Some people claim that indirect taxes are unfair because everyone pays the same amount whatever they earn. Other people claim that indirect taxes are the fairest taxes because rich people can find ways of not paying direct taxes (some of the richest people in the country pay no direct taxes). There is no way of avoiding indirect taxes, but the rich spend more than the poor, so they will pay more taxes.

3. *What the level of taxation should be.* There are many arguments between politicians as to what percentage of the gross domestic product (GDP) should be paid to the government. Those who favour a free market approach believe that the percentage should be much lower and that most people should have to pay for such things as their own health and education needs. Those who believe in a mixed economy (see below) would be happy to see taxation at between 35 and 40 per cent of GDP because of the benefits of giving everyone the same opportunities and care. Some socialists would want much higher taxation in order to redistribute wealth from the rich to the poor, but many economists believe that if taxation is too high, people stop doing any extra work and the economy slows down.

Inflation

Inflation is the rising of prices. It is measured by the Retail Price Index (RPI), where a representative sample of things people have to buy is measured on a baseline of a particular year. This can give an annual inflation rate (the percentage by which prices have risen over 1 year).

Inflation is caused by:

- the value of the currency falling
- pay rises not being supported by increases in productivity
- demand for goods being greater than the supply.

The effects of inflation are:

- a rise in interest rates
- businesses going bankrupt because they cannot afford the interest, or their customers cannot afford the much higher prices they have to charge
- people's standard of living going down because their wages have not increased as much as the prices
- people saving more because the interest rates are high, so they do not buy goods, so firms cannot sell goods and have to sack workers, thereby increasing unemployment.

Governments try to reduce inflation by reducing demand. They may do this by *monetary policy* (restricting credit and increasing interest rates) or *fiscal policy* (increasing taxes and reducing government spending).

Although all economists agree that high inflation is bad for the economy, some economists believe that a medium rate of inflation is better than high unemployment and lower living standards.

Types of economy

In any society there are scarce goods and scarce resources and there has to be a mechanism for allocating them.

In a *market economy*, the scarcities are allocated by market forces. The price mechanism of supply and demand is regarded as sufficient to run the economy. The market economy is favoured by right-wing political parties who claim it is the most efficient way of producing and allocating goods and gives the consumer greater power.

The disadvantages are that social costs are ignored and poor people get no help. If there is no public sector health, education, etc. everything has to be paid for by the private individual buying from the private sector.

Left-wing parties tend to favour the *command economy*, where all production is in the hands of the state (private companies are nationalised). They claim that this is more efficient because people can be given what they need, income can be distributed fairly and industry can be made to be aware of social costs, for example by reducing pollution. The disadvantage is that by ignoring the laws of supply and demand and keeping all decisions in the hands of the government, massive mistakes can be made (for example, making shoes that no one wants to buy) – the Soviet Union had a command economy that collapsed, leading to the collapse of the Soviet Union itself.

Centre parties usually operate a *mixed economy*, where there is a public and a private sector. In many ways, this is a market economy that is controlled by the government to remove the disadvantages. Public goods such as health and education are provided by the state. A 'safety net' is run by the state to provide money for those who are unwanted by the market (the old, the unemployed, the sick and the young). The government also forces firms to pay attention to the social costs of their production.

Industrial location

There are many factors involved in a company deciding where to build its business. Clearly it depends on the type of business:

- A distribution centre needs to be close to the motorway network and probably in the North Midlands for national coverage.
- Some firms need access to raw materials, for example Birds Eye is located in East Anglia for the fish and vegetables to be frozen immediately.
- Some firms locate in particular areas because of the availability of a skilled workforce, for example computer industries in the Thames Valley M4 corridor.
- Some firms need to locate near their market (market gardeners) or near a port (for example Nissan Sunderland to export to Europe).
- The availability and cost of land will affect the choice of a new site. Sometimes a firm may prefer to take over an existing factory/warehouse because this will be a quicker move, whereas other firms may want empty land because they want the building and facilities to be exactly to their specifications.
- Government or EU policies may affect their location, for example if grants are being offered to locate in areas of high unemployment.
- If a firm is thinking of re-locating to a new area, they will have to make sure that any essential staff who need to move with them are happy to re-locate.
- Many larger companies have moved their manufacturing and even service sectors, overseas because of much cheaper labour costs.

Employment and unemployment

During the 1980s and early 1990s, unemployment was a major issue in the UK as around 12 per cent of the workforce was without work. A variety of issues arise when there is a high rate of unemployment:

- Many people are living on state benefits and so are living close to the poverty line.
- Those who are in work have to pay higher taxes to pay for the benefits of the unemployed.
- Social tensions arise between the employed who can have a good lifestyle and the unemployed who face the prospect of life with few, if any, luxuries.

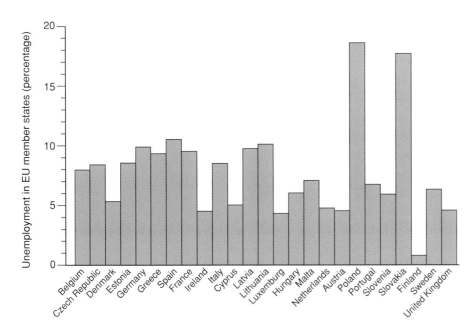

Figure 29.3 Unemployment in EU member states, December 2004

- Wages tend to be kept low because employers can always find people to fill job vacancies.
- Young people see little point in gaining qualifications when there are no jobs at the end of the training.
- Young people who do gain qualifications will be tempted to leave the country to find work.

The UK unemployment rate has fallen since 1997 and is now one of the lowest in Europe at 4.5 per cent. Many economists believe that this is because business rules and opportunities are more flexible in the United Kingdom (for example, longer hours can be worked). However, having a low rate of unemployment also brings problems:

- There is likely to be a shortage of skilled labour as the unemployed tend to be those who have no skills to offer an employer (the UK is dealing with this problem by increased levels of immigration, especially from Eastern Europe).
- Wages may have to rise in certain firms to keep workers or attract new ones.
- Young people may be less inclined to undergo extensive training if they know they can get a job without it.
- Prices may rise because people have more money to spend so there may be a greater demand for the same supply of goods (though often low unemployment leads to an increase of production as more people have more money to buy the goods).

For comparison, the figure for the USA is 5.5 per cent and for Japan 4.7 per cent.

> **DID YOU KNOW?**
>
> **Who wants to be a millionaire?**
> Hyperinflation is when inflation becomes so high that it has to be calculated on a daily rather than a yearly basis, and the government has to issue larger denomination notes weekly. For example, during the Yugoslavian Civil War in 1993 the daily rate of inflation in Serbia became 50 per cent (something costing £1 on Monday cost £1.50 on Tuesday). In eight weeks, one million dinar notes had become 50 million dinar notes.

KEY TERMS

Balance of payments the difference between what a country imports (buys from other countries) and what it exports (sells to other countries)

Fiscal policy decisions on taxation and public spending

GATT General Agreement of Tariffs and Trade – since 1948 the main countries have met to agree on trading with each other

GDP Gross Domestic Product – the total value of the goods and services produced by a country in a year

GNP Gross National Product – the GDP plus any income from investments abroad

IMF International Monetary Fund

Monetary policy decisions on interest rates and the amount of the money supply

OECD Organisation for Economic Co-operation and Development established by the industrialised nations in 1961 to achieve the highest growth and living standards in member countries

Science/technology parks industrial estates for small industries specialising in products connected with science or technology, e.g. research firms, computer firms

Social costs the costs of producing goods, which the producer does not have to pay, e.g. the education of the workforce, the transport systems being used, the costs of the pollution caused by the production

Stake-holding having an interest in a business or other enterprise which brings with it certain responsibilities (e.g. all citizens of the UK are stake-holders in the state pension system and so have an interest in who forms the government, and a responsibility to pay national insurance/taxes for their pension)

Tariffs customs duties placed on goods being bought from abroad usually to protect the country's own suppliers

Rural development issues

Demographic and economic changes have led to rural problems in the United Kingdom. The fact that better roads and the Internet have made working from home possible, have led to the urban middle-class moving into the countryside, this has driven up the price of housing in the countryside so that people in lower paid jobs (especially young people) cannot find affordable housing. Many young families have migrated to the towns so that there are insufficient school-age children to keep village schools open. The reliance of the farming community on EU subsidies (Common Agricultural Policy) and the EU's attempts to reduce the subsidies have led to business and economic problems in the countryside.

Defra (the Department for Environment, Farming and Rural Affairs) has established the England Rural Development Programme (ERDP), a programme which will provide £1.6 billion of government and EU money from 2000–6 and €14 billion per year throughout the EU from 2007–13 for rural development. The programme provides:

- Hill Farm Allowance for beef and sheep farmers in difficult farming areas in recognition of their vital role in maintaining the landscape and rural communities of the uplands.
- The Organic Farming Scheme provides funding to convert to organic farming methods which are more environmentally friendly and provide higher returns from shops.
- Farm Woodland Schemes encourage farmers to change farmland to woodland for both commercial and environmental purposes.
- The Countryside Stewardship Scheme is the government's main scheme. It pays grants to farmers to follow more traditional farming methods that enhance the landscape, encourage wildlife and protect historical features. Over 1000 miles of dry stone walls, 9000 miles of hedgerow and 16,500 miles of grass margins in intensive arable farming areas have led to an increase in a variety of bird species (for example bittern, lapwing, wagtail) that were in serious decline.
- The Environmentally Sensitive Areas Scheme gives grants to farmers to manage areas of the countryside where the landscape, wildlife or historic interest is of national importance (a quarter of the South Downs is now in the scheme).
- The Vocational Training Scheme offers grants of up to 75 per cent of the costs of improving the skills of those involved in forestry and farming activities.
- The Energy Crops Scheme provides grants for farmers to grow coppice and miscanthus which are carbon neutral producers of heat or energy so reducing greenhouse emissions.
- The Rural Enterprise Scheme provides assistance in setting up new businesses to help farmers diversify (for example turning a piggery into a nursery).

In addition, the Office of the Deputy Prime Minister, which looks after housing policy, is setting up schemes to provide affordable housing in rural areas.

There are arguments within the rural communities as to whether these measures are the right ones.

Marketing and advertising

In a consumer society, businesses have to make sure that the consumer buys their products rather than those of a rival. They also have to make sure that the consumer knows about any new products they want to bring onto the market. Achieving these things is known as marketing. Marketing has two processes:

1. *Market research* to determine what consumers want so that the firm makes a product that will sell. Connected with this will be determining the design and packaging of the product so that it has maximum saleability.
2. *Promotion* to: increase sales of existing products; introduce a new product onto the market; maintain or increase market share; and improve the image of the company. Promotion includes what is called 'below-the-line promotion', for example free samples, special offers, premium offers (collecting labels to get gifts), competitions, point of sale advertising (special displays of a product in a shop). However, the best known, and most argued about promotion method, is advertising. When a firm decides to advertise, it has to decide on a form to choose:

Figure 29.4 The Chancellor of the Exchequer, Gordon Brown, on budget day, 1998. The budget is the government's statement on what it intends to spend and what taxation will be for the coming year

1. Use the Internet to find the proportion of taxation to GNP for the UK, the USA, France and Germany.

2. Using the Internet and discussion, make a list of the arguments for and against indirect taxation.

3. Should taxation be used to implement social policies? You may like to think about such issues as the government ending the tax allowance for married couples, the government giving tax allowances for working mothers to pay for childcare, but not for the wage earner if one of the parents stays at home to look after the children.

4. How would you change the public spending and taxation figures given in the 1999 Pre-Budget Report? Give reasons for your answers.

- Television provides mass coverage, but it is expensive and digital television and video machines are making it easier to avoid the adverts.
- Radio also provides mass coverage (especially during the day) but is also expensive and the adverts are very temporary.
- Newspapers and magazines have a more permanent nature, allow coverage of selected markets (for example, certain social classes read *The Times*, certain interest groups read *Cricket Monthly*) and are less expensive, but lack the impact of sound, vision and movement.
- Posters give mass coverage, but may not really target vehicle drivers.
- Cinema advertising is less expensive and can use the same film as the television adverts.
- Mail shots (junk mail) reach a mass audience but can be ignored easily by the recipient throwing them in the bin.

Many people argue that advertising is manipulating consumers (especially groups like children) and makes unfair claims which consumers cannot verify. But advertising is checked by the Advertising Standards Authority and it provides the service of not only letting us know what products are on offer, but also of allowing us to have a wide range of television, radio, newspapers and magazines which would otherwise be financially unviable.

EXAM QUESTION

Discuss whether the UK tax system is fair.

(12 marks)

AQA B January 2003

What is tax?

It's the government's way of raising money. Wherever it comes from – deducted from your pay, from the profits of companies or business, from VAT or customs duties – it pays for services like health, education, defence, and social security. The charts on the right show how the money coming in and going out is divided up.

What is income tax?

Income tax is your contribution to government spending. Everyone who earns or receives income over a certain amount in the tax year pays income tax, and the more you earn the more you pay. A tax year starts on 6 April in one year and ends on 5 April the following year.

How will I pay income tax?

If you work for someone else, your employer will usually take the tax from your earnings each day and pass it to us. This is known as the Pay As You Earn (PAYE) system. It takes care of your tax automatically, and saves you having to pay tax in one go at the end of the year.

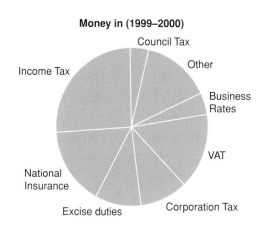

Money in (1999–2000)

Council Tax, Other, Business Rates, VAT, Corporation Tax, Excise duties, National Insurance, Income Tax

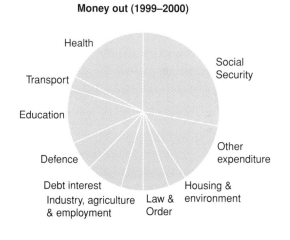

Money out (1999–2000)

Health, Social Security, Transport, Education, Other expenditure, Defence, Housing & environment, Debt interest, Law & Order, Industry, agriculture & employment

Source: Inland Revenue Series (IR33)

EXAMINER'S ADVICE

- This is another question from A2 Unit 5, this time from January 2003. It is one of five compulsory short essays, with each title taken from a different section of the specification and each worth 12 marks. Make sure that you answer all five in the test, so as not to lose marks unnecessarily. See page 1 for more information about this paper. Even if you are not taking A2, Unit 5 questions are similar to those set for AS Unit 1, so you should sensibly have a go at them.
- The question says 'discuss whether the UK tax system is fair' which means that you should consider both the proposition that it is and that it isn't. Use the information you are given in the Inland Revenue document, which is fairly neutral in the information it gives, but its explanations are there to support the system. The first part of the unit you have just read gives you more information and some of the arguments both for and against the way that taxes are levied in the UK.
- You are entitled to state your view and argue your case – for some people it depends on their political leanings – but in a question like this make sure that you show awareness of other views even if you do not agree with them. You can do this by using phrases like 'some people claim that the UK tax system is fair because … but I do not agree because …'. Always give reasons and examples where you can.
- When you have thought about the question, allow yourself 15 minutes to write your answer. Turn to page 260 for some answer notes.

The European Union

In the first half of the twentieth century, Europe was the cause of two world wars, which killed millions of people and weakened European economies. After the Second World War, European leaders met to work out ways of preventing Europe ever again going to war against itself. Out of the various options, West Germany, France, Italy, The Netherlands, Belgium and Luxembourg signed the Treaty of Rome in 1957 to form the European Economic Community (EEC). The aims of the EEC as expressed in the Treaty were to:

- remove barriers to trade among member nations
- establish a single commercial policy towards non-member countries
- co-ordinate members' general economic and agricultural policies
- co-ordinate member states' transport systems
- remove all national barriers to free trade and competition
- establish free movement of labour and capital throughout the EEC.

The first successful policies were concerned with the removal of tariffs and quotas between members, with the result that between 1957 and 1968, trade between the member states quadrupled. Indeed, the EEC was so successful that in 1973, the UK, Ireland and Denmark also joined. Greece joined in 1981, followed by Spain and Portugal in 1986. East Germany entered as part of the re-unification of Germany in 1990 and Austria, Finland and Sweden joined in 1995. These 15 states were joined in May 2004 by Cyprus, the Czech Republic, Estonia, Hungary, Latvia, Lithuania, Malta, Poland, Slovakia and Slovenia into what is now known as the European Union. Turkey is also actively seeking membership.

Any new countries wishing to join the EU must fulfil the following conditions:

- have a stable democracy
- have a free market economy
- be prepared to accept all the EU laws.

How the EU is organised

Ultimate power in the EU lies with the *Council of Ministers*, which consists of a representative from each member government, and can be called for meetings at any time to make a decision. The European Council, by contrast, meets three times every year and is made up of the heads of governments of the member states. The system is set up to ensure that no member state can be forced to do things it does not agree with, as each member has a right of veto in the Council of Ministers (though there was some agreement at the meeting in Finland in December 1999 for limited areas where majority voting would be introduced).

Decisions made by the Council of Ministers are implemented by the *European Commission*. This is the EU civil service. The President and Commissioners (each responsible for a policy area, for example Peter Mandelson is responsible for trade) are selected by the Council of Ministers for a four-year term and no more than two may be of the same nationality. It is the role of the Commission to ensure that the policies of the Council of Ministers are put into practice. They also award EU grants to member states and draw up acts for the European Parliament or the Council of Ministers to debate.

The *European Parliament* has 500 members, with each member state having its number of MEPs determined by its population as a proportion of the total EU population. All MEPs have to be elected by proportional representation and the election of 1998 was the first proportional representation (PR) election in the UK. (This system is different from most other elections in the UK which are based on political party rather than personalities – see Unit 20, 'Politics' and Unit 21, 'The British Constitution'.) The Parliament has 12 one-week sessions during the year, but members are also expected to serve on standing committees responsible for checking the work of the Commissioners. The Council of Ministers has to consult the Parliament on various matters, but the Parliament's main function and importance is to keep democratic control of the European Commission. It has to approve the Budget of the EU and can force the resignation of commission members if they have behaved improperly (Jaques Santer, a President of the Commission, was forced to resign by the European Parliament).

The *European Court of Justice* has 11 judges appointed by the consent of all the members states for a period of six years. There are many situations where EU law overrules national law and there have been several instances where individual UK citizens have taken the UK government to the European Court of Justice and the government has been forced to change policy (for example, homosexuals being allowed to serve in the Armed Forces, men having the same rights as women to cold weather payments over the age of 60).

Main EU policy areas

When the EEC was established, all the member states supported agriculture, but in different ways. The first major success was to bring all national agriculture policies into the *Common Agricultural Policy* (CAP). This bans all tariffs and quota restrictions between member states and a common tariff system is applied to agricultural products from non-member countries. An EU price is set for all agricultural products and if the market price falls below this, the EU buys from the farmers at the EU price. Although this policy was a major success, and made the EU agriculturally self-sufficient, it also led to huge surpluses (as farmers produced more when the price was high) which are often referred to as butter mountains and wine lakes. It has also led to conflict between countries such as the UK and Germany, which are net importers of food (and so pay into CAP much more than they receive) and Italy and France which are net exporters (and so receive much more from CAP than they pay in). One of the provisions of the *Maastricht Treaty,* 1991, was the reform of CAP and the reduction of both subsidies and surpluses. This is a major area of concern in the EU.

Another area of concern has been that of *foreign policy*. If the EU has common economic and agricultural policies, it should have a common foreign policy. Matters of foreign policy are regularly debated at the Council of Ministers, and the Kosovo intervention in 1999 showed that it is possible for all the member states to work together on foreign policy. It would seem impossible now for EU members to take different sides in a war, but without any machinery for a common foreign policy, this is still possible in theory. Several decisions were made in 1999 by the Council of Ministers that make a common foreign policy more likely.

In the same way, *defence* should be a common matter. Most, but not all, of the EU states are members of NATO, a common defence group between Europe and North America. It would appear that the EU should have a common defence policy and an agreement to defend any member state that is attacked. The Maastricht Treaty committed the EU to formulating a common foreign and security policy, but by the end of the 1990s, little had been done. The Kosovo intervention in 1999 showed the need for this and there were subsequent agreements for member states to contribute forces to a European rapid deployment force. The European defence industries now work together to produce European fighter aircraft, tanks, etc.

The *Single Market* was established by the Maastricht Treaty. This treaty established the *Single European Act* and changed the law so that all citizens of member states became European Union citizens. All restrictions on mobility of labour, exchange controls, Europe-wide banking and other financial services were outlawed.

> ## DID YOU KNOW?
>
> **Can we join your club?**
> The UK did not apply to join the EEC until 1961 because it did not think it would be a success. However, since 1953, the UK's production had only risen by 30 per cent, compared with France's 75 per cent and West Germany's 90 per cent. The French President, de Gaulle, said in 1963 that the UK was not yet ready to join and so the UK's application was rejected. In 1970, the new Conservative Prime Minister, Edward Heath, applied again. France now had a new president, Pompidou, and the UK, along with Ireland and Denmark, entered the EC on 1 January 1973. The Labour Party promised a referendum on the UK's membership of the EC in the election of 1974. As they won that election, a referendum was held in 1975, when 67 per cent of those who voted were in favour of the UK being a part of the European Community.

The EU Constitution

In June 2004 the member states of the EU agreed a treaty establishing a Constitution for the EU. According to the leaders, the Constitution will not alter the relationships between the member states, rather it is intended to clarify the present complex structure of laws and treaties agreed at different times during the EU's history to 'make its institutions more transparent, more accountable, more efficient and better able to meet the challenges of the twenty-first century' (British government statement).

The draft Constitution has ten main points:

- Consolidates existing Treaties into a single text.
- Creates a President of the European Council and a minister for Foreign Affairs.
- Introduces a system of double majority voting from November 2009 where decisions made by QMV (Qualified Majority Voting) will need the support of 55 per cent of the EU states representing at least 65 per cent of the EU population.
- Extends QMV to 15 policy areas.
- Makes clear that member states can leave the EU if they wish.
- Includes a new role for national parliaments to give opinions on Commission proposals.

Brussels often used as a synonym for the European Commission, whose headquarters are in Brussels

ECB the European Central Bank

EMU European Monetary Union, the idea behind the euro

Federal state the idea of a European central government, with the national governments becoming similar to the state governments in the USA

Free trade the idea of countries having no trade tariffs against each other's goods, but not having common laws

National sovereignty a nation having control of all its affairs

QMV Qualified Majority Voting – the idea that members of the EC should not be able to use the veto to hold up progress in certain areas

Rotating presidency the presidency of the Council of Ministers moves from one member state to another so that every state has a turn

Strasbourg the headquarters of the European Parliament (it is in France, but right on the border with Germany)

- Carries over the UK protocol so that the UK can opt-in where it wants to for immigration, asylum and civil justice issues.
- Incorporates the Charter of Fundamental Rights.
- Gives a procedure for opting out of QMV on criminal procedural law.

The Conservative Party and UKIP feel that the new Constitution hands too much British sovereignty to the EU and so the Labour Party has promised a referendum on the new Constitution before it is adopted by the UK (as has the French Government).

The euro

A *European monetary system* was begun in 1979 to avoid day-to-day fluctuations in the money markets affecting trade between member states. This was based on the value of the German Mark and meant that members had to make sure (by interest rates, taxation, etc. – see Unit 28, 'Economic theories', and Unit 29, 'Economic issues') that the value of their currencies stayed within a percentage band of the mark. This system was known as the ERM (exchange rate mechanism) and the UK initially took part in it. However, the value of the pound declined rapidly in 1992 and the UK was forced to withdraw from the ERM.

Maastricht had set 1999 as the deadline for introducing the euro. In order for the euro to work, interest rates, inflation rates and public sector borrowing rate (PSBR – the difference between what a government receives in taxes and spends) in states joining the euro had to be equalised (as well as the currencies being in their correct band in ERM). Those members who met the criteria and wanted to join locked their currencies into fixed parities on 31 December 1998, and on the first of January 1999, Austria, Belgium, Finland, France, Germany, Ireland, Italy, Luxembourg, the Netherlands, Portugal and Spain became part of the European Monetary Union (Eurozone). The European Central Bank took over the functions of the national banks to control the exchange rate and interest rates.

The strict rules for the EMU on interest rates, tax and spending have led the euro to increase in value compared with the dollar, the pound and the yen, but this has also led to low growth and high unemployment in many of the countries in the Eurozone.

The UK has not yet joined the Euro and Denmark and Sweden have rejected membership in national referendums. The Chancellor of the Exchequer has set out five tests which must be met before the UK could join:

1. Are the business cycles and economic structures compatible so that the UK could live with euro interest rates? (UK interest rates tend to be higher than the Eurozone because the UK has a much larger private housing market and if interest rates go too low the cost of houses rises – very fast.)
2. If problems emerge is there sufficient flexibility to deal with them? (The British labour market is much more flexible than the Eurozone's, making the UK's unemployment rate far lower than the Eurozone's.)

3. Would joining the euro make firms more likely to make long-term investments in the UK? (This is the easiest test to say yes to as several multi-nationals have decided not to invest in the UK because it is outside the huge market of the Eurozone.)

4. What impact would joining the euro have on the UK's financial services industry? (The UK has the strongest financial services industry in Europe and it is now reckoned to be so strong that joining the euro would have little effect.)

5. Will joining the euro promote higher growth, stability and a lasting increase in jobs? (This is likely to remain an issue whilst the UK's growth rate is much higher than that of the Eurozone.)

Tests 1, 2, and 5 are the strongest factors keeping the UK outside the Eurozone, but there are many in Britain (such as UKIP) who would oppose joining the euro even if it brought great financial benefits to the UK because they see the pound as the final sign of national sovereignty.

Activities

1. Read as much as you can in the newspapers, or use the Internet, to discover more detailed information on the arguments for and against the euro.

2. Consult the Business Studies Department to find out the effects of EC legislation on business.

3. Consult the Health and Safety Committee to discover the effects of the EC on Health and Safety legislation.

4. 'Being part of a European Federal State would be better than being dependent on American multi-nationals.' Examine the arguments for and against this view.

EXAM QUESTION

How far is it true to say that free trade is always beneficial to everyone concerned?

(12 marks)

AQA B June 2003

The Law of Comparative Advantage states that a country should specialise in the output of those products in which it has the greatest comparative advantage over other countries (other things being equal). Thus countries with tropical climates produce tropical foodstuffs, island nations tend to have fishing industries and so on. The Law of Comparative Advantage benefits consumers, as they can consume more and they get more choice. Yet for the benefits of specialisation to accrue in full, free trade has to exist. Free trade means trade with no artificial restrictions or barriers, a free market system in fact. In the real world, however, free trade does not always exist. Instead, countries may protect their own industries and discriminate against those of other countries.

Source: D. I. Browne, Economics, Theory and Practice *(Edward Arnold, 1989)*

EXAMINER'S ADVICE

- This is another question from A2 Unit 5, this time from June 2003. It is one of five compulsory short essays, with each title taken from a different section of the specification and each worth 12 marks. Make sure that you attempt all five, so as not to lose marks unnecessarily. See page 1 for more information about this paper. Even if you are not taking A2, Unit 5 questions are similar to those set for AS Unit 1, so you should sensibly have a go at them.
- It is also another 'how far/to what extent' question, typical of General Studies, that enables you to argue the case as you wish. You can also present a balanced view without committing yourself wholly to one side or the other, which is usually the better strategy, unless you have a strong conviction that you can back up with argument and evidence.
- Before you tackle the question it would be a good idea to study both this unit on the EU and the next on the developing world, as the issues spread over both areas. They also touch on economic issues discussed in earlier units of this book. The EU is a free trade area for its own internal markets. This should give you some idea of the benefits of free trade in terms of expanding markets and maximising competition and efficiency.
- The next unit gives some indications of the problems caused by protectionist policies and the economic strength and purchasing power of the richer nations. So the EU supports both free trade and protectionism – arguably the 'best of both worlds', but at some cost to poorer and less powerful trading nations.
- When you have assembled some ideas, allow yourself 15 minutes to write your answer. Then turn to page 260 for some suggested arguments on both sides.

Rich world, poor world

In 1980, world leaders expressed their concern about the growing division between the rich countries of the mainly northern hemisphere and the poor countries of the southern hemisphere. The *Brandt Report* (named after the former chancellor of West Germany, who was its chairman), identified the difference in living standards between countries. For example, in North America living standards are 40 times higher than in many parts of India and Africa. These countries are often referred to as *less economically developed countries* or *LEDCs* because they have not benefited from the effects of technology and the Industrial Revolution in the same way as the more developed countries in the North.

Poverty

The most important characteristic of LEDCs is *poverty*. It has been argued by many voluntary and United Nations aid agencies that poverty is the fundamental cause of many other problems. Poverty traps millions of people in a cycle of malnutrition, disease, illiteracy, large families, etc. often limiting their capacity to work hard enough to grow enough food to live on or to earn sufficient wages. Poverty produces powerlessness so that people are incapable of removing themselves from this cycle of deprivation (see Figure 31.1). For example, many southern hemisphere farmers only grow enough food to feed their own families. If the crop fails, they either starve or have to borrow the cost of new seed from money lenders at exorbitant rates of interest. Farmers who operate at this level of *subsistence farming*, often because they are using pre-industrial technology, such as mule-drawn wooden ploughs, and planting low-yield, disease-susceptible and unfertilised crops, never produce a surplus that they can convert into cash in order to buy more modern farming technology.

Definitions of poverty

Poverty is defined in relation to the *average* wealth of a country. In many poor countries, such as India and some South American countries, some people are extremely rich and some areas are heavily industrialised and intensively farmed. But these conditions are not uniformly spread throughout the countries as a whole and there is a great contrast between the rich and the poor.

The average wealth of different countries, however, can be measured against each other statistically. Countries produce wealth through agriculture, mining, industry and trade. This total is referred to as the Gross Domestic Product (GDP). But countries also have other financial activities, such as banking and insurance, which generate national and international revenues. This is added to the GDP to produce the Gross National Product (GNP). Both the GDP and the GNP of a country can be measured against another country by dividing it by the population. In 2003, Bangladesh, for example, had a GDP of around $385 per head, while the USA had a GDP of around $36,924 per head.

Figure 31.1 The unending cycle of poverty

The unending cycle of poverty

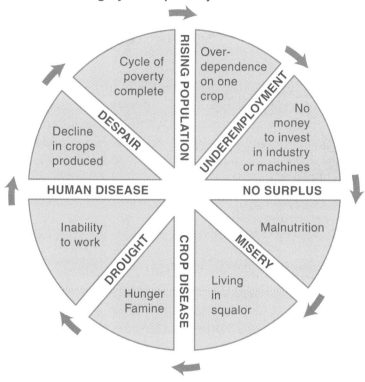

The effects of poverty

There are many conditions associated with absolute poverty that affect the lives of about 300 million people worldwide:

- *Malnutrition and hunger.* Many people live on the edge of starvation and do not have properly balanced diets, lacking protein in particular.
- *Disease.* Poor diet and bad water contribute to the many diseases associated with poverty. Diseases such as malaria, sleeping sickness, river-blindness and bilharzia, etc. affect 200 million people annually. It is estimated that 20,000 children die every day from diarrhoea.
- *Mortality rates.* The average age of death in LEDCs is between 40 and 50. (In Britain, it is about 76.) This is caused by a high infant mortality rate and the effects of endemic diseases on many adults.
- *Environment.* Many people live in slums in vast urbanised areas such as the shanty towns of Manila in the Philippines, Mexico City and Calcutta. Most of these areas lack clean drinking water, proper sanitation, power for heating, cooking and lighting and community health care or leisure facilities.
- *Illiteracy.* Across the world, 800 million people worldwide can neither read nor write. Many poor countries cannot afford to build schools or pay teachers, but they cannot increase their wealth without a more skilled work force.

INDUSTRY AND COMMERCE

Figure 31.2 Starving children

The causes of poverty

Physical causes

- *Heat.* Many LEDCs have extremely hot, humid climates which not only make it impossible to work efficiently in the daytime heat but also encourage diseases such as malaria.

- *Desertification.* Due to climatic changes, extensive deforestation of land and other land mismanagement, huge areas of once-fertile land are becoming desert. (The Sahel region in North Africa is a good example of this.) This reduces the food-growing and wealth-producing capacity of a particular country. Although other parts of the world also suffer from the climatic and physical conditions described below, the difference lies in the economic capacity to cope with such conditions. Rich countries cope much better with flood, drought, earthquake, crop failure and the effects of typhoons because they can store or buy in food and technology to reconstruct their society.

- *Lack of natural resources.* Some poor countries not only have the problems of a subsistence level and unmechanised agricultural system, but they have no other natural resources such as oil or other valuable minerals, such as rare metals or coal. (Japan's enormous development with no natural resources is an exception.)

- *The population explosion.* One of the most serious problems facing not just poor countries but the world as a whole, is the problem of increasing population. One million people are added to the population every five days and the current total figure is six billion. This is not just a cause of poverty but also a result of it. Poor families tend to have the largest number of children, partly because they lack access to family planning information and also because high infant mortality rates encourage the need for several children, so that there is someone to look after the parents when they are old. However, in many developed countries such as Sweden, Switzerland and Japan, there has been a drastic decline in the birth rate, raising concerns about their future capacity to generate enough wealth to maintain current standards of living.

- *Distribution of wealth and resources.* One of the major causes of poverty is the unfair distribution of wealth. Poor countries are often exploited by richer countries who pay very low prices for exports of raw materials and set up unreasonable tariffs to make manufactured goods produced by LEDCs, uncompetitive in price. Powerful multinational companies have engaged in economic *neo-colonialism* by controlling what poorer countries produce and paying very low wages to people desperate for work. International banks have also contributed to the continuing poverty of many LEDCs by lending them vast sums of money, the interest payments on which are quite beyond the capacity of the country to pay. Thus, no spare capital is generated for development. Unfair distribution also applies to crucial resources such as food. Despite the increases in population, there is enough food to go round but it is unfairly distributed. The rich northern hemisphere, for example, has only 25 per cent of the world's population but consumes over 70 per cent of the world's resources (see also Unit 7 'Agriculture and food production').

Possible solutions

The Brandt Report suggested that drastic action needed to be taken in order to alleviate the dire conditions in which huge numbers of people lived. Its recommendations included the following:

- An increase to 0.7 per cent of GNP by rich countries to spend on aid to less developed countries (in fact, the contribution of countries such as the USA and the UK has gone down since 1980).
- A diversion of the enormous international expenditure on arms production into improving the quality of peoples' lives instead of trying to destroy them.
- An immediate emergency aid programme to help the worst cases of starvation and disease (short-term aid).
- A massive development programme for agricultural techniques such as irrigation, fertilisation, pest control, crop storage and mechanisation in order to help poor countries to become self-sufficient in food (long-term aid).
- Greater support for and emphasis on family planning techniques.
- A drastic re-organisation of the world trading system so that developing countries are not exploited by richer countries in terms of the prices paid for their raw materials and crops, the prices they are charged for manufactured goods or the way in which cheap labour is manipulated.

- A greater emphasis on education programmes in order to improve the possibility of LEDCs competing in the technology race, organising their own international marketing and equipping themselves with the legal expertise to fight corruption in their own countries.
- A reform of the International Monetary Fund, so that poor countries benefit, and a cancellation of the huge debts owed to international banks by some countries, which have crippled their chances of development.
- Education programmes, which will inform the population of richer countries about the effects of poverty and the need for more international cooperation.

The global economy

Is globalisation benefiting the poor?

Economic experts and some political leaders have been calling for radical changes in the direction of world economic policy to overcome the negative effects of globalisation. Major changes in trade and immigration policy are needed if the world's poor are to share in the benefits of globalisation, according to a recent UN report.

The report says that only a dozen developing countries have benefited from the increasing integration of the world economy. Those who have lost out include the poor, the asset-less, illiterate and unskilled workers, and indigenous peoples. Income per person in the world's 20 poorest countries has barely changed in the last 40 years, from $212 in 1960–62 to $267 in 2000–02, while income in the richest 20 nations has tripled, from $11,417 to $32,339. The report said globalisation's 'potential for good is immense', but 'the advantages are too distant for too many, while the risks are all too real'.

The president of Tanzania and co-chair of the report, Benjamin Mkapa, said the situation was 'untenable' and that 'countries with impoverished, disadvantaged and desperate populations are breeding grounds for present and future terrorists'.

Important changes called for are:

- An international agreement on migration.
- Fairer trade agreements that open Western markets to agricultural and textile products from developing countries.
- An agreement on a 'balanced framework' for foreign direct investment that will ensure that developing countries benefit.
- Enforcement of labour laws and trade union rights especially in export processing zones.
- Better coordination between world institutions like the IMF, World Bank, ILO, and World Trade Organisation in ensuring that job creation is the central economic policy goal.

The report also says that the fundamental problem is that 'global markets have grown rapidly without the parallel development of economic and social institutions necessary for their smooth and effective functioning'.

Activities

1. 'Many people talk about the poor. Very few people talk to them' (Mother Teresa). What measures would you put in place to overcome this criticism?

2. Charity begins at home.' What arguments could be used to support or oppose the view that we should solve our own problems before we help other countries?

3. Which five courses of action taken by rich countries might be most effective in changing the lives of some absolutely poor people and why?

4. Research the work of one major charitable organisation and describe in detail one major overseas project they have carried out recently.

The distribution of wealth in Britain

We tend to assume that inequality of wealth distribution is a function of less developed countries. However, according to some expert observers, including the journalist Polly Toynbee, Britain has one of the world's worst distributions of wealth. Income inequality in Britain is the worst in Europe and the minimum wage virtually the lowest (£4.85 in 2004). The argument against raising the minimum wage is fear of job loss. At some levels, jobs would be lost, but it is difficult to predict at what level or in which sectors. All predictions about job losses when the minimum wage was introduced turned out to be wrong. The lowest paid jobs tend to be in the service industries and there is an argument that this is because women traditionally fulfil these roles (such as catering, caring or cleaning).

Read the source below and answer the question which follows.

War of pledges gives hope to world's poor

George Bush will arrive in Monterrey, Mexico, tonight for this week's United Nations summit on tackling global poverty in an unusual position for a Republican president – locked in an argument with his European allies about whose plans to boost aid spending are the most generous.

Just days before the summit, Mr Bush announced a $5bn (£3.6bn) package of help for the poorest countries spread over three years, while in Europe, finance ministers overcame opposition from the cash-strapped German government and pledged an increase in European aid of $7bn a year by 2006.

With Mr Bush due to give a keynote speech to the conference tomorrow, the White House is now saying that the American aid package will be double the size of the original announcement. The confusion over the size of the US package was apparently due to an 'internal mix-up' in the White House, prompting one aid campaigner to note ruefully yesterday: 'These kinds of numbers are just spare change to them.' Officials are now saying the US will gradually boost aid spending from 2004 to an extra $5bn a year by 2006 and make the increase permanent.

Many development charities were preparing the usual press releases trashing the summit as yet another UN talk-fest. But with a multi-billion dollar pledge from the US, matched by a similar sized undertaking from the European Union, the UN can at least claim it has started to reverse rich-country indifference to poverty.

Two years ago at the UN's millennium summit, world leaders re-committed themselves to longstanding international goals of halving extreme poverty, getting every child in the developing world into primary school and reducing infant and maternal mortality by 2015. Meeting those goals would cost $40–65bn extra in aid a year, says the World Bank – roughly double current spending. But the combined American and EU announcements will add only about an extra $12bn a year to aid spending by 2006.

The cost of western miserliness can be measured in children's lives, according to Oxfam. The UN predicts that by 2015, about ten million children a year will be dying before their fifth birthday, compared with a target of 4.2 million. Campaigners point out that even assuming the US president manages to push his ambitious aid increases through Congress and that the EU succeeds in persuading aid laggards such as Italy and Greece to boost their budgets, the world's leading economies will still be spending far less on aid than the UN target of 0.7 per cent of national income. The US spends just 0.11 per cent of national income on aid. The EU average is three times that, while Denmark spends ten times as much as a proportion of national income.

Among the big donors, the US has the worst record for spending its aid budget on itself – 70 per cent of its aid is spent on US goods and services. And more than half is spent in middle income countries in the Middle East. Only $3bn a year goes to South Asia and sub-Saharan Africa.

The US intention to restrict the new money to countries which implement its preferred economic reforms is also alarming campaigners. 'Do you judge countries on the basis of their success in reducing poverty or on what the US thinks is good for the world's poor?' asks Kevin Watkins, senior policy adviser at Oxfam.

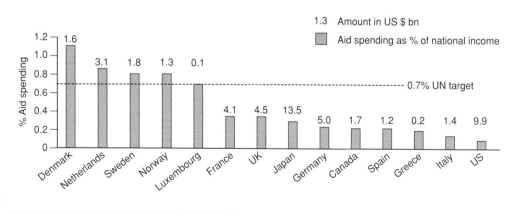

Figure 31.2

Source: The Guardian, *March 21 2002*

Source: Julian Borger and Charlotte Denny, The Guardian, *March 21 2002*

The passage is about how much aid wealthy nations should give to countries in need. The bar graph shows how much is given by 14 donor nations. For what

- political
- economic
- social
- moral

reasons might donor nations give, or not give, such aid? Should we pass judgement on those countries that are less generous than others?

(40 marks)

AQA B January 2004

EXAMINER'S ADVICE

- This question is from A2 Unit 6 set in January 2004. It is another example of the compulsory question in this paper (Section A), which is based on a single source and requires an answer in essay form. The second question (Section B) is also an essay, but is based typically on a comparison, or bringing together, of two sources and offers a choice of two questions. See page 1 for more information about this paper and also the end of Unit 11 for another example. There are examples of Section B questions at the end of Units 1 and 2.
- Remember that Unit 6 is the synoptic paper, which means that it brings together different sorts of knowledge, ideas and skills from the whole subject. It is therefore the most demanding part of the examination and you can expect to find it hard, particularly in terms of the ideas under discussion. You have 1¾ hours for the whole test, but quite a lot of material to read through before you tackle the questions, and each question is worth 40 marks.
- Good planning and detailed study of the extracts is essential before you start to write your answer, so

don't be afraid to spend at least 20 minutes planning your answer. This will still leave around 35 minutes for writing, which is plenty of time, if you have worked out what you are going to say.

- Also make sure that you use the prompts in the question. The question is structured in part to give you some ideas, but also to make you address the ideas being tested. For example, in response to the first part of the question you should attempt to give at least one example for each of the bullet points.
- The second part of the question is asking you what you think is the ethically correct position on aid – remember that there are different kinds of aid – and what criteria there might be for some countries giving more or less than others. You should obviously make extensive use of the passage in your answer, but the highest marks will go to those that are able to draw on ideas, information and examples that are outside the passage.
- When you have made your attempt, turn to page 261 for some ideas and arguments.

Beliefs and Values

Unit 32 | **The nature of religion**

Unit 33 | **Why people have religious belief**

Unit 34 | **The need for morality and the nature of ethical theories**

Unit 35 | **Ethical issues**

The nature of religion

Religion is one of the oldest of human activities. As far back as anthropologists (people who study the origins of humanity) can go, they find evidence of the existence of religion.

According to the *Oxford English Dictionary*, 'religion' is:

- the belief in a superhuman controlling power especially in a personal God or gods entitled to obedience and worship
- the expression of this in worship
- a particular system of faith and worship.

Major world religions

When most people use the word 'religion' they tend to use it in the third sense as the Christian religion, the Jewish religion, etc. You should be aware of the basic beliefs of each of the major world religions. All the religions have groups within them that have different interpretations or emphases (such as Catholics and Protestants in Christianity).

Buddhism

Buddhism was founded by an Indian prince, Siddhartha Gautama, known as the Buddha (the Enlightened One), in the seventh century BCE. It is based on the Four Noble Truths, which say that life is suffering and that humans are stuck on a wheel of life – they live, they die, they are reborn. Humans keep being reborn, and so suffering, because they crave life. The way out of suffering and rebirth is to follow the way of the Buddha in the Noble Eightfold Path, which, by meditation, ends craving and leads to *nirvana* (paradise). Buddhism does not necessarily involve belief in God or worship, though many Buddhists do both. The teachings of Buddhism are found in three holy books known as the *Tripitaka*.

Christianity

Christianity was founded by a Jewish teacher, Jesus of Nazareth, known as the Christ (God's Anointed One), in about 30 CE. It is based on the belief that Jesus was the Son of God who showed humans what God is like. Christians believe that humans fall short of what God wants them to be and so at the end of life (Christians do not believe in reincarnation), they will not go to heaven as God wants them to. However, if they follow the Christian way of love of God and love of neighbour set out by Jesus they will spend eternity in paradise as shown in the life and resurrection of Jesus. The teachings of Christianity are found in the *Bible*, especially in the *Gospels* of the *New Testament*, which contain the life and teachings of Jesus.

Hinduism

Hinduism originated in India around 1500 BCE. Many Hindus say there is no such thing as Hinduism, only Hinduisms, as there are so many variations of belief. Nevertheless, there are certain beliefs that most Hindus have in common. All Hindus believe in reincarnation and karma (the law of cause and effect which states that what you do in this life determines what you will be born as in your next life). They also agree that the aim of life is to escape from rebirth into *nirvana*. Different Hindu groups teach different ways to gain this freedom from rebirth, known as *moksha*. It can be achieved through fulfilling your duty as a member of a caste and so moving up the castes from the *shudras* to the *brahmins* and then to *nirvana*; through knowledge of God, through devotion to God, or through the way of yoga. Hindus believe in one universal spirit, Brahman, who is seen by humans in many different forms such as Shiva, Vishnu and Krishna. The teachings of Hinduism are found in the *Vedas*, *Upanishads*, *Ramayana* and *Bhagavad Gita*.

Islam

Muslims believe that Islam was the original religion founded by the prophet Adam at the beginning of creation, which was distorted and then given back its original form by the Prophet Muhammad in the seventh century. Muslims do not believe in reincarnation. They believe that there is only one God (who is referred to as *Allah*, the Arabic for 'the one God'). They feel that the purpose of life is to look after the world as stewards (*khalifah*) of God's creation by following the way of Islam as set out in the *Qur'an* (the word of God given directly by God to Muhammad) and in the *Sunnah* (examples and sayings of Muhammad, as recorded in the *Hadith*). This way of life is the Five Pillars (belief, prayer, charity, fasting, pilgrimage) and the *Shari'ah* (the laws of Islam, which cover every aspect of life). If this way of life is followed, God will reward Muslims with paradise after death.

Judaism

The fathers of Judaism are Abraham (1500 BCE) and Moses (1200 BCE). Jews believe in one God, who they call the Almighty because the name of God is too holy to say. They believe that God chose the Jewish people and gave his laws to the Jews so that they could be God's holy nation and bring the rest of the world to true worship of God. The laws are in the *Torah* (the first five books of the Bible) and are explained in the *Talmud* and the teachings of the *rabbis*. Jews do not believe in reincarnation. They believe that if they obey the commandments of God they will go to heaven.

Sikhism

Sikhism is based on the teachings of ten *gurus* (teachers) and especially the first *guru*, Guru Nanak (1469–1539). It is the youngest of the world religions and began in the Punjab area of India, where Hindus and Muslims were fighting each other. Sikhs believe that humans are self-centred rather than God-centred, and that this causes them to be reborn. So Sikhs believe in reincarnation, but they also believe that by becoming a Sikh you will not be reborn. By following the Sikh way of life of service and equality (there are no castes and no differences between men and women in Sikhism) and devotion to God, you will go to heaven. The teachings of Sikhism are found in the holy book, the *Guru Granth Sahib*.

Conclusion

This brief run-down has provided a summary of the major world religions, using 'religion' in its main dictionary sense (definition 3 page 224). All the religions except Buddhism believe in a supreme being, God, who has created the universe (definition 2 page 224). They all believe that there is a purpose in life and that by following certain rules and teachings (definition 1 page 224), humans will have eternity in paradise.

Sociologists study religion and look at how it operates in society. Functionalist sociologists (see Unit 14, 'The nature of society') give a definition of religion in general, which can be useful in answering questions about the importance of religion. They claim that the key feature of religion is to answer the major and ultimate questions of a society (for example, 'What is the purpose of life?') and to establish a value system that unifies the members of the society. Although such a definition can be criticised because religious groups are often at the forefront of trying to change society's attitudes (for example, Christians and the antislavery movement), it does seem that people are attracted to religion because it offers answers to the ultimate questions and gives a sense of belonging.

Symbolism and ceremony in religion

As religion is concerned with the intangible (things that cannot be tested by the senses), it uses symbolism to express ideas and beliefs that are difficult to express in straightforward language.

Some of the symbolism is in language. For Christians, the word 'father' symbolises the creativity, care and concern of God for his children; it also symbolises the relationship existing between humans and God. The word 'love' symbolises the care of God for humans, the emotions Christians should feel for God, the care and concern Christians should have for their neighbours, the relationship of God to Jesus and through Jesus to the world, etc. Some religious thinkers believe that all words used in religion are symbolic because it is impossible for anyone to describe God using human language.

Religious beliefs are also expressed symbolically in religious ceremonies and rituals. In the Christian service of the Eucharist (Holy communion), the main symbolism is the bread and wine, representative of the body and blood of Jesus. They are used to make worshippers aware of the presence of Jesus, who is regarded as an eternal spirit. The rituals of prayers and actions in a Eucharist service are intended to help the worshippers in their lives (for example, confessing and being forgiven for sins) and to bring them into a closer relationship with God (for example, through taking Jesus into their body through the symbols of bread and wine).

Figure 32.1 Coventry Cathedral Sutherland tapestry. What symbols can you see and what meaning might they have?

Agnostic someone who is not sure whether God exists

Atheist someone who believes that God does not exist

Benevolent the belief that God is all-loving and forgiving

Ecumenical Movement a Christian movement to bring the different Christian churches (denominations) together (Christian unity)

Gurdwara a Sikh place of worship

Immortality the belief that humans have a soul that lives on forever after the death of the body

Inter-faith understanding the attempt by religious people living in multi-faith societies to bring different religions together by understanding each other and working together

Mandir a Hindu place of worship

Monotheism the belief in one God

Mosque a Muslim place of worship

Omnipotent the belief that God is all-powerful

Omniscient the belief that God is all-knowing

Polytheism belief in many gods

Religious fundamentalism the belief of certain groups in many religions that: their basic beliefs cannot be adapted or changed; the teachings and customs set down in the scriptures must be strictly maintained; all other religions are wrong

Resurrection the belief that the body will come back to life at some point after death

Secularism the belief that religion and religious belief are unimportant and should not affect society's institutions

Synagogue a Jewish place of worship

The effects of religion on everyday life

Holding a religious belief is likely to have a huge effect on the way a person lives their life. However, it should always be remembered that people have different levels of commitment to their faith, and different members of the same faith regard different beliefs in the religion as more and less important.

Activities

1. Interview a religious believer and ask them why they believe and what effects their belief has on their way of life.

2. Survey your friends to find out how many of them are atheists.

3. Use the Internet to find how many religious websites there are.

4. Explain why some religious thinkers believe that all religious language is symbolic.

Consider the influence that religion has on the everyday life of a Muslim. Muslims believe that there is only one God who gave Muhammad the *Qur'an* in a form that can never be changed. This means that Muslims must do everything the *Qur'an* says. Also, as there can be no prophets after Muhammad, Muslims must follow the example of Muhammad as set out in the *Shari'ah* (Muslim holy law). So Muslims should:

* pray five times a day
* go to mosque every Friday lunchtime
* refrain from food and drink during daylight hours in Ramadan
* give two per cent of their wealth to the poor every year
* only eat halal food
* not drink alcohol
* not gamble
* neither pay nor receive interest on loans and many, many more things.

Clearly these are major effects, symbolising that Islam means submission to God and that a Muslim is one who has submitted to the will of God. However, not all Muslims do all of these things. Some feel that God cannot expect all of these instructions to be followed, so they decide which are the most important and follow only this selection.

'The Queen is Defender of the Faith; the Prince of Wales aspires to be 'defender of faiths' – yet neither has the power to do any such thing.'

Discuss the view that religious leaders in the UK no longer have the power and influence they once had.

You might consider the following in your answer:

- the decline in numbers of church-goers
- the growth in numbers of followers of other faiths
- the extent to which science and technology have supplanted religion
- the emergence of other non-religious sources of power.

(30 marks)

AQA B January 2002

EXAMINER'S ADVICE

- This essay question is from AS Unit 2 set in January 2002 and is the second of two extended pieces of writing you have to do in this test. The first is compulsory and based on a passage, but for this question you will have a choice of two topics. See page 1 for more details on this paper.
- The basic question here is on the importance of religious authority, its influence over people's lives, and the extent to which these have declined. Here you have the option to agree with the proposition, or to disagree with it, or to take a balanced view with some points for and others against. You will see that in the next unit there is a question on a similar theme where you are required to argue just one case. Always pay close attention to the wording of questions to see exactly what is required.
- The introduction to the question is a reference to the role of the established church in the UK (the traditional relationship between Church and State) and a more modern view that Prince Charles has put forward. The question also suggests a range of points to consider in your discussion. What are the implications of the suggested bullet points? There are also ideas and pointers in the unit you have just read which it will help to draw on. Finally, remember that the specific question is about the power and influence of religious leaders in the UK, so focus your responses on the roles of such people as bishops, the clergy and their equivalents in other faiths.
- For 30 marks you should expect to write a full essay of at least two to three pages, and in the exam proper you will have about 30–35 minutes to complete the task. When you have assembled your ideas and written your answer, turn to page 261 for some suggested arguments for and against the proposition.

Why people have religious belief

It is one of the remarkable characteristics of all human beings that they claim to have religious beliefs. The word 'belief' itself can have several different meanings:

- 'Belief' might mean trust or confidence in something, for example believing in a person or believing in justice.
- 'Belief' might mean accepting that a particular state of affairs is actually the case, for example believing that there are tigers in India.

Religious beliefs, which can be defined as any belief that is distinctive to members of a particular religious group or denomination, are often a mixture of both types, for example:

- 'Belief that' something is true, for example a factual proposition such as, 'Jesus was a messenger from God'.
- 'Belief in', which is to do with the trust and commitment people experience in their relationship with God.

Often these beliefs are interdependent. You cannot believe *in* God in the sense of trust and commitment, for example, unless you first believe *that* his existence is a fact.

Problems with religious beliefs

One of the fundamental beliefs common to most religions is the belief in some divine being or beings. In the modern world this belief raises serious problems. How can someone claim that some special knowledge or message that he or she believes they have received from God is real knowledge? How do we know, for example, that *Mother Theresa* or *St Francis of Assisi* were not mistaken about their belief that God spoke to them? We cannot prove the existence of God by either rational or empirical means – the two generally acceptable methods of establishing proof of the existence of something.

Types of knowledge

Particularly since the work of *René Descartes* (1596–1650), a *rationalist* philosopher, there has been a strong tradition arguing that to know something is to be able to prove it: to reach a conclusion by logical inferences from self-evident premises. In practice, this means proving things by using your reason, for example proving that 2 + 2 = 4 or proving Pythagoras' theorem. However, *rational knowledge* cannot tell us anything about the real world. *Empirical knowledge*, however, is based on sense-experience, our

BELIEFS AND VALUES

perceptions of the real world. But the problem with sense-experiences is that they may be mistaken. For example, railway lines appear to converge in the distance even though they are actually parallel. So rational knowledge is certain knowledge, but it is only about logic, and empirical knowledge is about the real world, but it may be mistaken. Religious believers usually claim that their religious beliefs are *real* but are not simply matters of logic or ideas, or mistaken sense-impressions.

Where do religious beliefs come from?

There are various answers to this question including the religious, the sociological and the psychological.

Religious explanations for religious belief

Many religious believers would claim that their religious belief is based on a *religious experience* which led to their *conversion*. Conversion often involves a dramatic change of attitude, beliefs and behaviour. The best known example of this is *Paul* on the road to Damascus, who changed suddenly from being a persecutor of the early Christian Church into its greatest missionary after experiencing a blinding light and hearing a voice.

Other religious experiences might take the form of an appearance by a saint or a divine figure, hearing voices or experiencing some strange phenomena, such as:

- Moses and the burning bush
- the Virgin Mary appearing to Bernadette of Lourdes
- the angel Gabriel appearing to the prophet Muhammad.

The problem for religious believers is that, although they are usually certain about their beliefs, it is difficult to establish the authenticity of these events by the usual methods. Also, the claim that a particular experience is an experience of God may simply be self-deception. The experience may be self-generated, i.e. arise in the imagination of the person having the experience, rather than having been caused by a source outside.

Peter Sutcliffe, '*the Yorkshire Ripper*', claimed that God told him to murder 13 women. Joan of Arc claimed that the saints spoke to her and told her to save France. It is extremely difficult to prove or disprove the authenticity of these claims as they are intensely personal, private, 'inner' experiences, which, by their very nature, cannot be shared.

Some religious believers claim that their belief is based on a religious book, such as the Bible or the Qur'an. This raises several problems:

- Some passages in these religious texts seem to contradict each other.
- It is often not clear whether particular passages have divine or human origins, despite the claims made by some believers that their scriptures are inspired by God (see 'Did you know?' box).

- Most religious texts reflect the social/cultural conditions of their own time and it can be difficult to see how they can be the basis of religious faith 2000 years later.
- Only one religious book can be true and there is no way of deciding which it is.

Sociological explanations for religious belief (see also Unit 14)

Sociological theories tend to assume that the explanation for religious belief lies in society itself, rather than in the idea that there is some external divine reality responsible for the experiences that believers claim to have had. Sociologists are interested in *belief systems* rather than individual beliefs, because most religious believers have an interlocking set of beliefs, rather than individual ones. They are also interested in the way in which religious beliefs reflect and are part of the *culture* of a particular society. Indian children are more likely to be Hindus than European children because their religious beliefs have been learnt within a Hindu culture. In 1912, the French sociologist *Emile Durkheim* offered a *functionalist* analysis of religion in terms of what purposes religion serves in society. These include:

Figure 33.1 Hindus bathing in The Ganges – many religions see water as purifying sin and bringing people closer to God

- *Social solidarity.* Social life is impossible without shared values and moral beliefs. Religion reinforces those values and collective religious worship is a way of bringing people together so that they can integrate and strengthen the moral values that unite them.
- *Reverence for society.* Durkheim argued that when people have the experience of standing before the divine or some greater power, what they are really doing is worshipping society itself. People use religious ideas as a symbol of what they hold most sacred, which is the tribe or clan and its values and customs to which they belong.

There are other functions of religious belief identified by sociologists:

- *Crisis management.* Religious belief and ritual help people to deal with life crises such as birth, puberty, marriage and death. The religious services surrounding such events help people to cope with the disruption of their lives caused by such things as death and to support each other. This support helps to reintegrate society and to provide solidarity.
- *Meaning of life.* Religion also helps people to cope with uncertainty in life. It helps them to answer difficult questions like why there is evil and suffering and whether there is life after death.
- *Continuity.* Religious ceremonies help to maintain a sense of history and link together different generations.

Critics have pointed out, however, that if religious belief is merely a reinforcement and reflection of the values of society as a whole, it is hard to see where revolutionaries or prophets come from in the first place. If religion were no more than a reflection of society's values, the ability to criticise the values of the society in which they have grown up or to develop a more universal perspective on life would never have developed.

Psychological explanations for religious belief

Sigmund Freud (1856–1939), the originator of psychoanalysis, regarded religious beliefs as 'illusions, fulfilments of the oldest, strongest and most insistent wishes of mankind'. He regarded them as a mental defence against the more threatening aspects of nature, floods, death and disease, etc. According to Freud, human beings project onto the universe the memory of their father as a great projecting power in order to cope with the threat of these natural forces. Although much of Freud's explanation is rejected by modern critics, his view of religious belief as a kind of 'psychological crutch' is accepted by many religious thinkers as a true description of some aspects of religion.

Karl Marx (1818–83) described religion as 'the opiate of the masses'. As an atheist, he argued that there is no God except the God that man creates for himself. Religious belief encourages human beings to put up with intolerable conditions and obscures the fact that history is controlled by human interests and desires. Religion does not help human beings, but chains them.

KEY TERMS

Charismatic a Christian who believes in the gifts of the Holy Spirit, such as speaking in tongues and the power to heal (fundamentalism, evangelism and charisma are often found together)

Conversion the often intense emotional and dramatic process by which someone may become a religious believer

Evangelical Christians who place a particular emphasis on preaching the faith to others and who regard the Bible and a pious moral way of life as very important

Fundamentalism the view held by many Christians that every word in the Bible is true – usually associated with the views that the words of the Bible are 'divinely inspired' and should be taken literally

Providence the belief that there is a God who created, maintains and is responsible for everything that happens in the world

Religion and terrorism

Modern terrorism is increasingly motivated by extremist religious rather than political points of view. The most worrisome example is the worldwide *Jihad* phenomenon. There are two main trends in modern terrorism. The first is the tendency toward higher-casualty attacks, and the second is a far-reaching change in the motivation behind terrorist attacks. Today's terrorist is much more likely to be driven by extremist religious beliefs than by a wish to gain political concessions – the Islamic extremist al-Qaeda network is a prime example of this. The aim of such groups is to win converts among potential supporters, to intimidate potential enemies, and to punish actual enemies.

The rise of religiously-motivated terrorism has been accompanied by a rise in suicide attacks. This is particularly true of extremist Islamist terrorism, where the image of the suicide bomber, or 'Shahid', carries great power and prestige.

The vast majority of Muslims are hospitable, compassionate and tolerant, with very little hatred in their hearts. During the past century, the mass of suffering that the West has inflicted on Muslims, especially the Arabs, has given them reason to hate. Yet, only a few have developed blind hatred.

There appear to be three schools of Muslim thought on the subject of the relationship between Islam and other religions. The majority group believes that it is the sacred mission of Islam to rule the world by use of the sword if necessary – the Jihad or holy war mentality. Another group accepts cohabitation with other religions as long as Islam is the world's pre-eminent religion. A third group, the moderates, advocates co-existence primarily because of the economic benefits it brings.

Many Arabs hate the United States because of its military and political support of modern Israel, a state which was created after the Second World War in response to the need for a homeland for displaced Jews. This involved, however, the loss of statehood and the actual homes of thousands of native Muslim Palestinians who have been fighting for justice ever since. Until very recently, most Arab countries have refused to recognise the State of Israel. Wars have been fought in 1948–49, 1956, 1967 (The Six Day War), 1973–74 (The Yom Kippur War), and 1982 between Israel and the Arab states.

The religious backdrop to the situation is heavily mixed with anti-US sentiment, where the US is seen as supporting Israel only because of American oil interests. Further, the US is seen as being responsible for militarising the region (the Middle East is the most militarised region in the world) and propping up corrupt Arab governments in order to guarantee secure oil supplies. The US is accused of double standards because it uses the support of freedom and democracy as justification to invade some countries such as Iraq but ignores the suffering of the Palestinians.

Islamic groups which simply hate Israel and want to destroy it include *Hamas, Hezbollah*, the *Popular Front for the Liberation of Palestine*, and the *Palestinian Liberation Front. The Palestine Liberation Organisation* (PLO) is the co-ordinating council for all Palestinian organisations, founded in 1964 at the first Arab summit meeting. The dominant group is *Al Fatah*, until recently headed by Yasser Arafat who formed a group of warriors known as *fedayeen*, and became chairman of the

PLO in 1968. Since its founding, the PLO has been committed to the destruction of Israel, and over the years has been involved in acts of terrorism. It toned down its rhetoric and acts of terrorism in 1974 when it received UN recognition as a government in exile.

Activities

1. Research the life of Jackie Pullinger in Hong Kong or Camillo Torres in Colombia. What effect do you think their religious beliefs have had on their lives?

2. 'Religious beliefs are an essential part of a society's culture.' What evidence is there to support or oppose this point of view?

3. 'Religious beliefs do not have to be true. They just have be important to the believer.' Evaluate this statement, giving reasons for your answer.

EXAM QUESTION

'Three or four generations ago, religion made a powerful contribution to people's lives. It shaped their thinking and their conduct. Today, religion has lost its hold on people: it has ceased to be relevant, or to matter.'

Argue **either** for **or** against this view. You might consider the following in your argument:

- religious education in school
- religion in the media
- the influence of religious leaders
- whether science has all the answers.

(30 marks)

AQA B May 2004

EXAMINER'S ADVICE
- This essay question is from AS Unit 2 set in May 2004 and is the second of two extended pieces of writing you have to do in this test. The first is compulsory and based on a passage, but for this question you have a choice of two topics. See page 1 for more details on this paper.
- The basic question here is on the importance of religion and whether it has declined. Note that on this occasion you have to argue either that it has or it hasn't. The statements, however, are very sweeping generalisations, based on an historical view, and would not apply to everybody, so the extent to which they apply to the majority is what you should base your answer on. If you choose to support the proposition, it may still help to make the point that you are dealing with generalisations that not everyone or all groups would accept and to clarify what you mean and give examples.
- The bullet points also suggest a range of areas to include in your discussion as evidence to support your case one way or the other, so it makes sense to use them as well as raising the expectation that you will. There are also ideas and pointers in the unit you have just read which it will help to draw on.
- For 30 marks you should expect to write a full essay of at least two to three pages, and in the exam proper you will have about 30–35 minutes to complete the task. When you have assembled your ideas and written your answer, turn to page 261 for some suggested arguments for or against the proposition.

The need for morality and the nature of ethical theories

Why morality is important

Human beings are gregarious – they like to be with other people and they like to live in groups or societies. If you live in a society, then you need to know how other people are likely to act, and you need some method of balancing one person's self-interest against the self-interests of others.

A set of moral principles is known as a moral code. Sociologists sometimes call this 'a shared value system'. They feel that any society needs to have shared values if it is to survive, because without shared values there will be conflict.

As societies have come together and changed, there can be several value systems at work and this is why there is now debate about moral issues. There are no longer shared values about issues such as cohabitation (living together without being married), divorce, abortion, fighting for your country, etc.

Even though there are such differences about what is right and what is wrong, we all make moral judgements saying, 'this is right' or 'that is wrong'. In fact, we have to do this. If you are offered drugs, if your boyfriend/girlfriend wants to sleep with you, you have to make a moral choice. If you are a scientist cloning sheep, or a doctor killing human embryos in order to give a couple a baby through IVF, you are making a moral decision. Studying ethics should help you to make informed moral choices and moral judgements.

Ethical theories

There are many different theories on what makes an action right or wrong. You should use at least some of these theories when you are answering questions on ethical issues in the exam.

Utilitarianism

This is the view that you decide whether an action is right or wrong by looking at the consequences. If you have a choice of actions, you should choose the one that will produce the most happiness or the least suffering to the people who will be affected by the action. For example, if you had to decide whether to ban smoking in public places, you would weigh the suffering caused to the smokers by having to wait for a cigarette against the suffering caused to non-smokers by passive smoking (lung cancer,

KEY TERMS

Amoral outside morality, or having no moral principles

Conscience an inner feeling about good and bad, which makes you feel you ought to do the good and makes you feel guilty if you do the bad

Consequential an ethical theory, which says that what makes an act good or bad is the effects or consequences of the action

Deontological an ethical theory based on rules rather than the effects of an action, which says some things are absolutely right and others are absolutely wrong

Duty following your conscience by doing what you feel you ought to do

Immoral having moral principles, but going against them

Objective morality an ethical theory based on outside facts, which are independent of an individual

Shared values the idea that for society to function, members of that society must share similar ideas on what is right and what is wrong

Subjective morality an ethical theory based on the ideas of an individual

heart disease, bronchial problems, etc.) and decide that the least suffering would be caused by banning smoking.

This theory is associated with *Jeremy Bentham* (1748–1832) and *John Stuart Mill* (1806–73) and the phrase 'a good action is one that brings about the greatest happiness of the greatest number'.

Religious morality

Almost all religions argue that it is God who decides what is right and what is wrong and that humans discover how to behave from finding out God's will. Christians believe that this comes from the teachings of the Bible and the decisions of the Church. Muslims believe that God's will was revealed through the *Qur'an* and the Prophet Muhammad, and from these Muslim lawyers have worked out the *Shari'ah*, a holy law covering every aspect of life. So, if Muslims are faced with a moral choice, they find out what the *Shari'ah* says. Orthodox Jews consult the laws of God found in the *Torah* (the first five books of the Old Testament). Buddhists would look at the moral precepts laid down by the Buddha. In all these cases, there is no looking at consequences, what makes something right or wrong is decided by God.

So, if faced with the issue of whether homosexuals should be allowed to marry, Christians would look at the Bible and say that homosexuality is condemned, therefore homosexuality is wrong and there can be no marriage. A Muslim would make a similar statement, based on the teachings of the *Qur'an*.

However, not all religious people would make moral decisions in this way. Many feel that the consequences must be looked at and that some of the laws in the holy books were only intended for the time when they were written. If two people love each other and want to commit themselves to each other in marriage, then allowing them to do so is the most loving thing, so homosexual marriage should be allowed.

Activities

1. Make two lists of arguments for and against cloning animals. Read the key terms definitions, then go through your lists and work out which of your arguments are deontological and which are consequential. Do you think your lists make you agree or disagree with cloning?

Figure 34.1 Making moral decisions

Natural law

Thomas Aquinas (1224–74) used the earlier work of Aristotle to claim that just as there are natural laws of science, so there is a natural law of morality. Just as scientists can study the world and find the principles on which it is based, so moral philosophers can study humans and society and find out what is the 'natural' form of behaviour, which will lead to a perfect society if everyone follows it.

Aquinas believed that God created everything with a final cause or purpose and that discovering this tells you what is right. For example, the final cause of sex is the creation of children, so any form of sex that does not involve the creation of children is wrong. Those who follow natural law today tend to relate behaviour to the place of humans in the world and the basic requirements for humans to survive.

To take another example, if making a decision about homosexual marriage, they would say that heterosexuality is natural because it is a basic requirement for humans to survive and so homosexuality must be wrong and homosexual marriage cannot be allowed.

Social contract theory

This is a view first put forward by Plato, but very much connected with *Thomas Hobbes* (1588–1679) and *Jean-Jacques Rousseau* (1712–78). It claims that laws and morals are a human invention upon which we agree to make life better for ourselves. As Hobbes said, 'Life without laws would be nasty, brutish and short.' Rousseau claimed that if governments or rulers do not make life better for their subjects, then the subjects have a right to overthrow the government.

If making a decision about homosexuality, social contract theorists would say, 'What would be the impact on society? Is it something like adultery, which we can't have laws about without being too restrictive on people's freedom?' They would then probably agree to homosexual marriage because it will make the couple more stable and therefore make society more stable.

'There is an inescapable sense that events are somehow influenced by human choice. Without that, there would be no sense of morality' (Mel Thompson, *Teach Yourself Ethics*).

Activities

2. Make a list of the morals and laws you would put forward if you were in Rawls' 'original position'. Are they similar to those Rawls suggests? Write down what you think of Rawls' ideas and why.

3. Read through the ethical theories in this unit again. Using the key term definitions, work out which theories are objective and which are subjective. Then work out which theories are deontological and which are consequential. Decide which theory you would find most useful in making a moral decision and why.

4. Use the Internet to identify a country with a high population growth. Also find out its gross national product (GNP) and per capita income. Then use the ethical theories and your own ideas to discuss whether the country should adopt a policy of compulsory sterilisation for couples after they have had one baby.

5. On the basis of all the work you have done, answer the question 'Is it ever justifiable to break the law?'

EXAM QUESTION

Discuss how people learn to make moral judgements.

(12 marks)

AQA B June 2004

When faced with a question such as 'What is morality?' one may be stumped. Is morality an idea? Or is it an institution? Perhaps it is a set of rules. Some may say that morality is a feeling or a kind of behaviour.

The word 'morality' is a noun. It is related to the adjective 'moral', hence we refer to 'moral act', 'moral choice', etc. If we asked instead, 'What is a moral judgement?' it should be a far more manageable question.

The following sentences express moral judgements:

- Abortion is always wrong.
- Under certain circumstances, killing is right.
- Torture is always wrong.

Source: *adapted from Fred Feldman,* Introducing Ethics *(Prentice Hall Inc)*

EXAMINER'S ADVICE

- This is another question from A2 Unit 5, this time from June 2004. It is one of five compulsory short essays, with each title taken from a different section of the specification and each worth 12 marks. Make sure that you answer all five in the test, so as not to lose marks unnecessarily. See page 1 for more information about this paper. Even if you are not taking A2, Unit 5 questions are similar to those set for AS Unit 1, so you should sensibly have a go at them.
- The question says 'discuss how people **learn** to make moral judgements'. The emphasis is therefore not so much on what morality is, but on how we acquire moral values and apply them in our lives. Nevertheless, you have to have a clear view of what morality is to answer the question coherently. The arguments in the extract are designed here to stimulate some ideas. The bullet points are examples of moral judgements, but you may or may not wholly agree with the values which are embodied in them, i.e. your 'moral' view may differ.
- The unit you have just read gives you some ideas of what we mean when we talk about morality and where our moral values come from, which you can use directly in your answer. Try to consider as wide a range of sources as you can for your ideas about what you believe to be 'right' and 'wrong' – both primary and secondary. For example, you may well believe that moral laws are God-given, but the question requires you to focus on how you learn to make judgements.
- When you have thought about the question, allow yourself 15 minutes to write your answer. Turn to page 262 for some possible points.

One of the major characteristics of modern society is the way in which our existence is dominated by technology. The beneficial effects of this can be seen in such areas as housing, transport and the media. However, this technology often brings with it very difficult ethical questions. This is particularly true in the field of medicine where inventions such as life support or kidney dialysis machines give doctors apparent power over life and death. Two particularly controversial areas are cloning and abortion.

Cloning

To clone is simply to make an exact genetic copy of an existing organism. It happens naturally in many plants (if you bury a potato it sprouts clones of itself), and even a few animals. Significantly, it does not normally happen in mammals and humans, except for 'identical' twins, whose condition is due to a natural genetic aberration. Dolly, on the other hand, was a sheep created by taking cells from the udder of a ewe and 'reprogramming' them to create a new embryo, by a process known as nuclear transfer, and implanting the embryo in another ewe.

This was a biological revolution as it had been thought impossible to grow a mammal from body tissue. Also it raised the daunting question about the possibility of cloning human beings, particularly since cattle and mice had recently been cloned. Cloning raises a fundamental question about the relationship between technology and society. The fact that something is possible does not mean that it is necessarily desirable. Other factors have to be taken into account, particularly in relation to the amount of benefit and/or harm using a technology might produce.

The overwhelming reaction from most people is not just that it should not be done, but also a fear that someone might try. Statements opposing cloning human beings have issued from numerous national and international organisations, including the UN, the European Parliament, and the United Kingdom Human Fertilisation and Embryology Authority.

Ethical concerns
- Cloning runs counter to the evolutionary need to maintain a basic level of genetic diversity and variety in nature. It appears to attack the fundamental idea of individuality. Cloning selects the genetic composition of some existing individual and then takes part in an intentional, controlled act to produce an identical copy. The crucial point is not the genetic identity but the human act of control of it. The most fundamental ethical case against human cloning is that no human being should have their complete genetic makeup pre-determined by another human. We can reject their upbringing, but we cannot change our genes.
- In most of the recent controversial cases, for example the failed attempt to clone a young boy in order to provide a compatible donor for his own bone marrow (see 'Did you know?' box on the next page), the person cloned would appear to have been created not as an end in themselves but rather as a means of benefiting someone else.

- No one knows the psychological effects of discovering that one was the twin of a parent or sibling. Would that person simply be a copy of someone else who already exists and not really an individual in their own right? Since we have no sure way of knowing in advance, we surely do not have the right to inflict, knowingly, that risk on another person.
- There is the physical risk in the light of the animal cloning experience. It took 277 attempts and 29 implantations to produce one healthy Dolly. Significant pregnancy difficulties have been a common feature of cloning work in sheep and cattle, involving deformation and premature aging. In addition, while the production of cloned human embryos may provide stem cells which can reproduce themselves and replace those that cause Parkinson's disease or premature aging, for example, the medical procedures used have the potential to become mere 'spare part surgery'. Embryos would be discarded if surplus to requirements, and they might come to be valued merely as collections of usable organs rather than as potential human beings.

Abortion

This is a highly emotive and controversial subject. There are three issues central to the abortion debate:

- Should a woman have the right to do what she wants with her own body?
- Does a fetus have the same rights as someone who is already living independently?
- Is a fetus a person?

Most religious and moral codes agree that, in principle, human life is sacred. However, they differ in how far they are prepared to put aside this principle in particular circumstances. The Roman Catholic Church, for example, would not allow abortion on the grounds of rape or incest, but would allow it if it were clear that the mother would definitely die otherwise. This is the *natural law position* – the idea that human life is sacred and that pregnancy and the creation of human life are natural processes and ultimately part of God's will.

Objections to abortion often seem to concentrate exclusively on the act of abortion itself and to ignore the circumstances in which an abortion was considered. This raises the question of whether actions should be judged by the result they produce or by the motives from which they were done. This can be difficult to decide. For example, how would you assess the result of an abortion if it took away the life of the unborn child but made the mother happy?

Some Churches and other organisations would allow abortion in cases of rape, incest or where bringing the pregnancy to full term would seriously damage the health or threaten the life of the mother, or where the deformity of the fetus precludes any chance of survival.

Competing rights

Many moral issues seem to centre on the problem of competing rights. Those opposed to the *1967 Abortion Act* have argued amongst other things, that the phrase 'risk to the physical or mental health of the mother' is too vague and allows abortions to be granted for trivial and irresponsible reasons. If abortion involves the taking away of human life, then the argument that the mother doesn't want the child, or can't support it, is not sufficient to justify it. There are far more couples waiting to adopt newborn babies than there are babies available for adoption. This argument implies that the risk to the health of the mother is not equal to the death of the baby. In terms of rights, what is being said is that the right of the mother to decide to have an abortion in these cases is not as great as the right of the unborn child to live. Many of those opposed to abortion see themselves as defending the rights of a fetus which cannot defend itself.

From the moral point of view, it is usually agreed that rights and responsibilities go together. Some people have argued, for example, that a couple or a single person leading a totally promiscuous lifestyle, who ignore readily available contraceptive techniques, should not be allowed to choose an abortion which involves the death of a human being and the use of expensive, hard-pressed NHS resources.

Exercising the right to choose an abortion denies the right of a fetus to live. So the freedom to make decisions carries with it the responsibility to make these decisions carefully and sensitively, as human life is involved.

Is a fetus a human being in the same sense that we apply the term to human beings outside the womb?

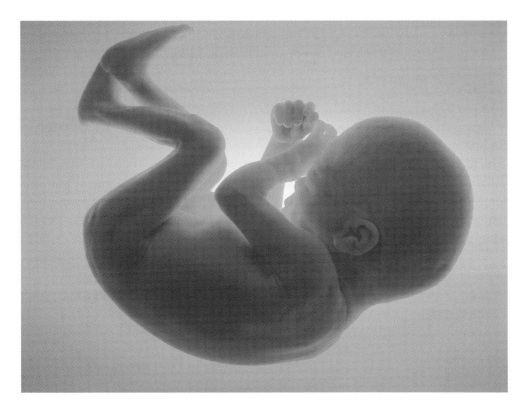

Figure 35.1 A fetus at 20 weeks

Fetuses rarely survive *ex utero* (outside the womb) before 22 weeks. (The fact that some do survive at this early stage has been important evidence in favour of the recent amendment to the 1967 Abortion Act, passed by parliament in 1990, reducing the maximum time for an abortion from 28 weeks to 24 weeks.)

Euthanasia

Euthanasia is a compound of two Greek words – *eu* and *thanatos* – meaning literally 'a good death'. The word is generally understood today to refer to the 'mercy killing' of a person by another, either with or without the person's consent. There are two important features to remember about euthanasia:

- It involves taking someone's life.
- It is done for the claimed benefit of the person whose life is being taken, usually because he/she is suffering from an incurable or terminal illness.

Historically, all civilised societies have moral principles about the taking of human life, but there have been considerable variations concerning when it is permissible. Infanticide and suicide were all accepted and widely practised in Greek and Roman times. However, the growth in influence of Judaism and Christianity in the western world led to the view that human life was sacred and that only God had the power to take it.

The legal position

At the moment, euthanasia is illegal in this country. Despite fairly recent bills debated in the House of Lords in 1969 and 1976 in support of it, the bills were defeated, mainly on the grounds that it seemed to be too difficult to draw up adequate safeguards to protect a possible recipient of euthanasia from unfair pressure or abuse. However in 1993, the Dutch parliament made law certain guidelines under which doctors could carry on administering lethal injections to consenting, terminally ill and suffering patients without fear of prosecution – a practice in which some Dutch doctors had already been engaged for several years.

Modern life-support systems make such decisions very difficult. The initial positive decision by a doctor to place someone on a life-support machine in order to improve the chances of survival, may become a more controversial issue under the following circumstances:

- removing someone when there is no possibility of improvement
- removing someone when life is only being maintained by the machine, for example a serious brain-stem injury
- removing a seriously deformed and/or very premature baby.

Without modern life-support machines, the question of survival for the examples mentioned above would not arise. However, a doctor can now be sued for switching off a machine, an action which is seen as life-threatening or life-taking. On the other hand, without the opportunity of being on the machine in the first place, the patient would certainly have died. Medical ethics often discusses these issues in terms of *proportionality*. This involves balancing the amount of benefit accruing to the patient in relation to the amount of pain, suffering, cost, inconvenience, etc.

About death

A modern philosopher, Peter Singer, has argued that the growth of our capacity to keep people alive has forced us to reconsider what we mean by 'the sanctity of life' and what we mean by death. It is now generally accepted that *brain-stem death* (when there is no chance of the brain recovering the use of its functions) is real death. This means that bodies that appear to be warm, pulsating and breathing can be technically dead, and may be given no further medical support, but may be kept functioning until vital organs can be removed for transplants.

Case studies

Baby John was born prematurely at 27 weeks with an infection and breathing difficulties and placed on a ventilator, initially for a month. However, he remained very ill and handicapped, suffered from convulsions and breathing problems, which did not improve. His long-term prospects for a reasonable quality of life were described as non-existent. He was severely brain-damaged, blind and deaf and in constant pain.

In a court case, the judge ruled that the baby should be treated with antibiotics for his chest infection but that his doctors were not obliged to put him back on the ventilator. This decision was based on two principles:

- It would not serve the child's best interests to give him treatment that would prolong his suffering and produce no benefit.
- There is a difference between normal care (i.e. antibiotics) and extraordinary care (i.e. life-support machines).

In September 1992, Dr Cox was found guilty of deliberately killing a 70-year-old patient, Mrs Boyes, who was terminally ill with rheumatoid arthritis, in terrible pain and who had asked Dr Cox to help her die. Mrs Boyes could not be relieved from her pain or cured and the injection given to her by Dr Cox was deliberately designed to end her life.

The court ruled that Dr Cox's action was illegal because it was 'deliberately designed to take a life'.

Tony Bland was in 'a persistent vegetative state' from 1989 until 1992, after the Hillsborough football disaster. His body continued to function but there was no possibility of the recovery of consciousness because of his severe brain damage.

The court ruled that doctors could discontinue ventilation, nutrition and hydration by artificial means.

According to Michael Keeling, a writer on Christian ethics, these three cases raise many of the difficult questions surrounding euthanasia, for example, deciding which of the following actions is legally or morally permissible:

Activities

2. Using an example from any recent television series you may have watched, discuss the difficulties faced by someone thinking about abortion.

3. Why is abortion described as an issue about competing rights?

4. What arguments would you use to defend/oppose the actions of the doctors in the cases described in the above case studies?

5. Discuss the view that the legalisation of euthanasia would put unfair pressure on doctors and incurably ill elderly patients.

6. Should the decision to end someone's life be a medical or a moral decision and who should be involved?

- Withdrawing sustenance, which will inevitably lead to death (Tony Bland).
- Not using 'extraordinary' or disproportionate care to keep a baby alive where the cost or difficulty of the care outweighs the possible benefit (Baby John).

Arguments for euthanasia

- Mature human beings should have the right to choose what to do with their own lives.
- Human beings should have the right to end a life that may consist only of pain, incurable illness, loss of dignity, dependence on others and loneliness.
- Euthanasia avoids the situation of being a constant physical, emotional and financial burden on others.

The points mentioned above refer to *voluntary euthanasia*, where the patient can choose for him/herself. When a patient is in a coma, so seriously ill that they are incapable of making a decision, or in the case of an incurably sick baby in an incubator, then someone else has to choose to terminate their life. This is known as *involuntary euthanasia*. This raises the problem that the responsibility for the death now lies with someone else and also the problem of how you stop a helpless patient from being murdered by greedy relatives who then claim that they were carrying out the wishes of the victim. In Holland, they have introduced the idea of 'a living will', a legal document prepared in advance, which states clearly what is to be done if the patient becomes incapacitated.

Arguments against euthanasia

- Voluntary euthanasia has been condemned by many church and civil organisations, including the *World Medical Association*.
- Where euthanasia is legal, compulsory termination of life has been used by some governments, such as Nazi Germany, to remove those who embarrassed the state, either through political opposition or because of so-called racial, mental, physical or social deficiencies.
- The practice of euthanasia would undermine the trust that patients have in the medical profession to always act in the interests of preserving life.
- If you allow exceptions to the principle that human life is sacred, you weaken the principle itself.
- The evidence gained from *the hospice movement* in the past few years has also shown that people can experience terminal illnesses in a context of love, dignity and painlessness, surrounded by their family. This evidence attacks the view that euthanasia is preferable to letting a terminal illness take its natural course.
- Many religious people would argue that because the right to life is God-given, the value of human beings is constant, whether rich or poor, strong or weak, handicapped or normal. No human life can be sacrificed merely for the economic or political welfare of either states or individuals. However, individuals may decide to sacrifice themselves in exceptional circumstances. It is never permissible to take innocent life.

It is now possible to clone human beings. To what extent should we always do what science enables us to do?

(12 marks)

AQA B January 2003

EXAMINER'S ADVICE

- This question is from AS Unit 1 set in January 2003. From 2005 onwards there will be four short essays like this for you to answer from a choice of six, with each title taken from the five different areas of the specification. Note also that they will be worth 15 marks each, instead of 12. It is absolutely essential to give equal time and attention to each of your four answers, so as not to lose vital marks. See page 1 for more information about this paper. There are other questions from this paper at the end of Units 9, 18, 23 and 28.

- This is another 'to what extent/how far' question, which implies that you have a spectrum to consider here from 'not at all' to 'always'. The likelihood is that you'll want to argue a position based on 'some science we should not do', but there are fundamental questions to ask about the differences between acquiring scientific knowledge and understanding, the means of acquiring them, and then the purpose for which they may be used. The question takes us full circle, back to the first unit of this book about scientific progress.

- The question is also a more general one, focusing on science and not just on cloning humans. As a result, as well as considering the ethical issues related to this area of scientific knowledge, you should range wider. The more examples you can bring to bear on the broader question the better, although as this is a short essay they should perhaps be references rather than developed examples. Try to think of some positive outcomes from contentious science, as well as negative ones, but remember also that the central question is about ethics – the 'right' thing to do.

- When you have assembled your arguments, allow yourself just 15–20 minutes to write your answer, then turn to page 262 for possible arguments for and against the question.

Answers to examination questions

Unit 1

Fact:

- We can now screen for genetic disorders and nip much congenital disease in the bud.
- *Medical advances* have done much, in all sorts of ways, to add to the quality of life (vaccines, antibiotics, hip and knee joint replacements, hearing aids, heart pacemakers, etc.).
- *Transport developments* have enabled us to be more mobile than ever before (the car and its contribution to independence, light-rail systems, low-cost flights in large capacity jets, etc.).
- *Household appliances* have facilitated domestic work (programmable washing machines, microwave ovens, online shopping, etc.).
- *Media,* new and old, have added hugely to the possibilities for 'education, information and entertainment' (Lord Reith's great original dream for the BBC).
- *ICT* has enabled us to communicate instantly with almost anyone, anywhere, to access data, and to keep and retrieve records in increasing volume.
- The nature of *work* has changed in that we work fewer hours at tasks that are more humanly rewarding, less manual and arduous, and that are cleaner and safer.

Belief:

- All the above benefits are available only to the middle/higher classes in 'western' industrialised countries.
- Victorian 'progress' was bought at the expense of the colonies and of the working classes.
- We must question whether material progress is enough, when there has been so little evidence of moral progress (e.g. the genocides of the twentieth century, the mutually assured doctrine (MAD) of nuclear 'deterrence', our tolerance of fundamental inequalities).

- New technologies throw up ethical problems that we are ill-equipped to resolve. We seem to live permanently on an increasingly slippery slope.
- There are as many signs of regress as of progress – we are using up resources unsustainably, and we may be changing the climate in ways to which we cannot readily adapt.
- What do we mean by 'progress'? It is a subjective idea, since there are no benchmarks against which to measure it objectively.

Unit 2

Points might include:

- Questions to which scientists are seeking answers are usually thought of as answerable in quantitative, objective terms.
- On the other hand, Gorst refers to questions ('fundamental questions') to which scientists cannot hope to supply all the answers. These are often questions artists are interested in.
- Artists cannot answer these questions objectively, or conclusively, but they can cite evidence based on human experience, and appeal to shared perceptions.
- Writers and, to a lesser extent, painters engage with the world we inhabit and recognise. They have an interest in being 'true to life' or expressing 'universal truths'.
- Music is different and engages in a more 'self-referential reality', where form is of more significance than 'content', but the shared emotional experience is still important.
- Many – perhaps most – artists would reject the notion that they are seeking or have a responsibility to find 'answers'. They might simply argue the case of 'art for art's sake' or challenging our thinking.

Unit 3

Prospects for change:

- Cultural gatekeepers are not the sole agents of social change.

- American politicians may say publicly that they believe the Biblical account of creation, but this doesn't necessarily affect their behaviour or attitude to science and technology.
- The right-wing will not be in power indefinitely in the USA. Liberal values have not been indefinitely snuffed out by the Republicans' ascendancy.
- Social change happens whatever the complexion of the government. Change is bottom-up and makes demands that democratic governments cannot ignore forever.

Barriers to change:
- Machine politics always throws up establishment politicians dependent for their survival on conservative forces.
- The more complex a society becomes, the more likely it is that pragmatism will replace ideology, and status quo will be favoured over change.
- Ruling groups strive to be self-perpetuating – aspirants to power are assimilated to the existing culture of power and influence.

Unit 4
Advantages:
- Wind turbines do not cause air pollution and will reduce the use of fossil fuels.
- Winds are stronger in winter which coincides with peak demand for electricity.
- After the initial expense of building a wind farm the production of energy is relatively cheap.
- Wind farms provide a source of income to farmers and may attract small industries to rural parts of UK.
- The technology is supported by 'green' movements – a safe method of providing energy.

Disadvantages:
- Wind does not blow all the time, and at present electricity generated during storms cannot be stored for use during calm periods, except in batteries.
- Groups of 30-metre tall turbines spoil the scenic attractions of the countryside/coast.
- 7,000 turbines are needed to produce the same amount of electricity as one nuclear power station. Could this be the end of 'our green and pleasant land'?
- It could be perceived as just a fad (pushed by the Green Party). A larger, more overall solution is needed.
- It creates some noise pollution.

- Wind farms require fewer people to run than conventional power stations.

Unit 5
Points might include:
- It would be politically impossible to cease to import oil, or to refine it for well-established and popular uses. We are essentially selfish, and are inclined to look to our own convenience above that of generations to come.
- We simply do not have the alternatives in place yet that would run on alternative, renewable fuels. It is unlikely that we would be prepared to surrender our current standard of living for an indefinite long-term advantage.
- Other gases, methane for example, make a contribution to global warming that curbing the use of oil will do nothing to mitigate. Our whole way of life threatens the environment, not merely greenhouse-gas emissions.
- The need to minimise all emissions of greenhouse gases, including carbon dioxide, is one of which we are aware – but knowledge is only a minimum requirement.
- Climate change is already with us. We owe it to populations living in low-lying areas to take their needs into active account – and this will tax all our humane sympathies and imagination.
- Non-oil-burning transport technology (e.g. alcohol in Brazil) is well advanced, but it needs an economic spur to be put to widespread use. It may be that 'market' values will correct our selfish passion for 'growth'.
- Oil has many uses – in the making of paints and plastics, for example – that argue for not burning it as a fuel. Do we value the status quo above the life-style that conservation would require?
- It is fundamentally immoral to put the future at risk for our own short-term convenience. How far will we prove to be altruists, when, for example, the Maldives or Bangladesh go under the waves?

Unit 6
Could be frightening:
- Do we want knowledge of what will happen to us? For example, would we like to know if we were likely to develop Parkinson's Disease?
- Would people abort pregnancies if relatively minor defects showed up in a fetus?

- 'Designer babies' could be 'ordered' to avoid certain personality traits and behaviour patterns.
- Employers and insurers could become interested in learning the results of tests.
- *Brave New World* rears its ugly head, i.e. playing God with nature.
- Human beings could become a species that can alter its own destiny.
- Cloning and its ramifications are not yet clear.
- Big business could control gene therapy.
- Genetic food production may be impossible to control.

Need not be frightening:
- Knowledge itself is not dangerous – it is what people do with that knowledge that is crucial.
- Even if some people misuse the information, is this a good enough reason to say it should not be acquired?
- Without the knowledge we may not be able to reap the potential rewards.
- The acquisition of knowledge is endless – we could not stop it if we wanted to.
- GM food is a way of feeding the world.
- It may become easier to clone organs than to transplant.
- It could bring about the eradication of hereditary disease.

Unit 7
(a) (i) 556/27662 × 100 = 2.01 or 2 per cent
    (ii) 1810/4 = £452.5 millions or £453 millions
(b) • The North East is not an agricultural region.
- The South West is noted for its mixed dairy and arable farming.
- The East is a major cereal-growing region.
- The South East (not London) is densely populated, so the agricultural workforce – though the second highest – is the smallest as a proportion of the total.
- Many other factors determine the nature of farming.
(c) • There is no indication of which regions are covered by the data.
- The table does not include information regarding farm size or workforce.
- We are not told the ratio of converted land to unconverted land. The proportions for all years may be minuscule.
- There is no clear definition of 'organic' farming.

(d) Arguments might include:
- Awareness of problems caused by Foot and Mouth and other related diseases in cattle has encouraged a more discriminating pattern of feed consumption.
- EU policy may have an effect on what a farm produces. Some farms may convert to organic farming because of enhanced financial/subsidy rewards.
- There has been greater demand for organic food as supermarkets respond to consumer trends.
- There is greater national awareness of the health implications involved in organic food, therefore an increased market.
- Advertising and TV programmes may have generated a greater demand for the products.
(e) Valid:
- Modern agriculture needs capital funding. Expensive machinery may be unaffordable by small farmers.
- Smaller farms are often family concerns, and the farm may have no future if the younger generation moves on.
- If there is an increasing demand for organic food, small farms may not be able to afford the initial outlay.
- Government policy on agriculture may not be beneficial to small farms, in the light of European directives.
- Larger farms may be more likely to trial GM crops.
- Supermarkets may determine cost/profit.

Not valid:
- Small, labour-intensive farms produce more per unit area than large, capital-intensive farms.
- Many small farms may be able to 'trial' new products.
- Large farms which specialise cannot 'keep up' with new products because of the major outlay to change, whereas smaller farms may be able to change more efficiently.
- Smaller farms may be used to pilot GM crops.
- Smaller farms may be family-run and therefore farmers may be more committed to succeeding.
- Small farms occupy a niche market, for example Farmers' Markets, or in the more specialist organic sector.

Unit 8

Defence of the motion might use the following arguments:

- Much sport had its origin in games – these are about competition and enjoyment.
- The most admirable aspects of sport – skill and sportsmanship – may not be compatible with an emphasis on record-breaking.
- Record-breaking tends to push athletes to take dangerous risks with their bodies.
- The same pressures encourage the taking of performance-enhancing drugs, which contaminate sport.
- The enjoyment of spectators is prejudiced when the accent is on technology and split-second margins.
- Sport is for the participation and enjoyment of all not just the elite.

Opposition to the motion might be based on these points:

- Sport is all things to all people. There is a place for the stopwatch in those sports that are based on competitive racing.
- Records are an objective to be aimed at – there need to be some objective standards of judgement in competition.
- Athletes themselves need to know how close they are, at any one time, to their personal best. Keeping and breaking records is motivating.
- We keep records in all sorts of pursuits and circumstances. They appeal to our 'need to achieve'.
- Breaking records is not only about time-intervals – a pole-vault record will certainly involve skill.
- Even team sports will aim at statistical records (very much emphasised by media pundits), for example number of points scored by a particular team.

Unit 9

Benefits might include:

- People may live longer and continue to have rewarding lives, for example organ transplants, intensive baby care.
- Major diseases can be eradicated in due course so that the whole world can benefit.
- Part of the Hippocratic oath sworn by doctors states that lives should be saved as far as humanly possible.
- Patients can be kept alive until further advances produce cures.

- Advances in technology lead to improved identification of diseases and treatment, for example scanning.
- Further advances could lead to improved treatments and reduced waiting times for other conditions.

Drawbacks:

- The cost of major life-saving treatments may be prohibitive.
- Who prioritises who is to be treated?
- The quality of life of many 'saved' patients can be very low, for example some stroke patients, permanent vegetative state patients, premature babies.
- Equally, there may be a long-term impact on the families of patients being 'kept alive'.
- There may be a high opportunity cost. Money spent on medical research and very expensive treatments could be better used, for example to alleviate poverty in the third world.

Unit 10

(a) (i) Percentage change in trains more than five minutes late, September 1998–99:

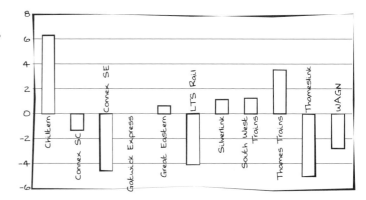

(ii) Conclusions could include:
- There is improvement with some operators, for example Chiltern.
- Only two have noticeably improved, four have appreciably worsened.
- There is a trend towards more lateness.
- There are large variations between operators, for example Gatwick Express – no change, Thameslink – almost doubled, Chiltern – almost halved.
- It is difficult to draw conclusions with such huge operator/regional variations and only over one year.

(b) Cause for concern because:
- There is no real improvement for commuters.
- Government policy does not appear to be working.
- Privatisation strategies are called into question.
- There is a trend towards more lateness.
- Lateness causes stress for commuters, and negative economic consequences for employees and employers.

(c) Information is of limited value because:
- Variations in size between companies make comparisons meaningless, for example Chiltern and Connex South East.
- Can we generalise from this data to assume that things are the same in all conurbations?
- The figures give a snapshot at a particular moment in time. How do we know that things have not improved (or got worse) now?
- Has overcapacity dropped because of improvements, or because commuters are using other forms of transport?
- Other types of knowledge are needed to give a fuller picture before overall conclusions can be drawn.
- No definition of 'rush hour'.
- We don't know about possible special incentives/offers and what effect they may have.

(d) You might agree because:
- More roads should mean fewer people on the railways.
- More roads and cars could mean raising more money via tolls, taxes, etc.
- More roads mean better communication inside the city.
- Better communications with suburbs would improve lifestyle.
- More roads could mean less overcrowding, and so fewer trains needed.

You might disagree because:
- More roads do not lead to better communication, for example extra lanes on the M25 have made little impact.
- There are negative environmental effects – pollution, greenbelt destruction.
- People using roads and trains could be a different clientele.
- More roads will encourage more suburban traffic into the centre, thus exacerbating the problem.

- More roads will disturb existing street and housing patterns.
- The problem is far more complex – issues of sustainability and integration of a comprehensive transport system must be explored to alleviate the problem.

Unit 11

Much will be lost:
- The number of host sites has risen exponentially.
- A minority of these, that would have been preserved in the past, are worth preserving for posterity – but cannot be.
- Historians will have lost much of the information on which to base their accounts of the present day.
- Much communication within and between government departments is electronic. This (as the 'Garbagegate' affair demonstrates) is the very stuff of history.
- If scientific data are being lost, it will not be clear how important conclusions were arrived at.
- We have the actual toys and games of past ages in our museums. There will be no hard evidence of what today's children did at their computer screens.
- Much social and cultural expression is now electronic. If websites are lost, much of the rich tapestry of cultural interaction will be impoverished.

Little will be lost:
- We still have the press, Hansard, government white papers, etc. – vast amounts of printed material – by way of a record of the business of government.
- There can be too much information. What is currently only in electronic form is probably of least value.
- Huge numbers of books (fiction and non-fiction) are published annually. What is worth saying is worth printing.
- Scientific data and conclusions that have long-term value are preserved in scientific journals and conference papers.
- The quantity of sites is probably in inverse proportion to their quality. We will do posterity a favour if we 'lose' them. Who would choose those to survive?
- If we lose much that is currently in electronic form, there is an equivalent to this ephemeral material in printed form (magazines, concert programmes, advertising, publicity) in sufficient quantities to satisfy the most omnivorous historian.

Unit 12

(i) Analysis of problem:
- Phone companies are exploiting young people's desire to keep up with the latest fashion trends in phone covers.
- Covers are being sold at a large profit to all those in the chain, including retailers, suppliers and manufacturers. What were originally cheap items have become quite costly.
- Having saturated the mobile phone market, phone companies created a market for the covers. This shows deliberate and aggressive manipulation of the market.
- Young people are a particularly impressionable sector of the market and are more likely to fall victim to fashion trends and to aggressive marketing strategies.
- Their parents could be said to be victims too, but they give in too easily to 'pester-power'.
- Suppliers source the covers in countries where labour is cheap.
- The popularity of mobile phones is a symptom of western consumerism. It is easy to run-up sizeable personal debts.
- Promotion and advertising are accepted even though we know they are partial and economical with the truth.
- Wide-spread use of mobile phones, particularly by young people, is adding to crime.
- There is also concern about health risks associated with mobile phone use.

(ii) Source of problem:
- Young people are letting themselves be seduced by fashion trends and manipulated by marketing strategies. They are not passively being manipulated as they put pressure upon themselves and their peers to conform to the latest trends.
- Parents succumb to pressures from the phone companies, and from their children, by giving the money to buy the covers.
- Phone companies are responsible for aggressively marketing phones and covers with little thought to the habits of consumers that they are helping to foster.

- Retailers are making what seems an unreasonable profit from the sales of covers, which would be much cheaper if they were available direct from suppliers.
- Big business (film, popular music and publishing companies, etc.) cash in on their image and make very large profits.
- Government has a responsibility to ensure that economic exploitation does not occur and that young people are protected from profiteering.

(iii) Short-term measures:
- Manufacturers could be more socially responsible, for example by reducing profit margins, limiting the range of covers produced and not producing covers based on the latest films/celebrities.
- Manufacturers could be prevented from exploiting cheap labour abroad by conforming to International Labour Organisation protocols.
- Manufacturers could spend less time developing new covers and more on improving the security of the product against theft.
- Parents could act more responsibly, giving guidance to their children and restricting their spending.
- Government could regulate the sale of mobile phones to young people to protect them from exploitation.

Long-term measures:
- Young people could learn to be more resistant to marketing and peer pressures. They should be taught to think more independently and resist fashion trends.
- Schools could educate students, for example as part of the Citizenship/General Studies curriculum, to be sensible consumers, making reasoned choices about how they spend their money and resisting peer and marketing pressures.
- Schools should lead public opinion in a drive to limit the use of mobile phones in schools and to discourage misuse and theft.
- The Consumer Association and/or government could investigate the problem and bring in appropriate legislation.
- Safety campaigns could be introduced on the health implications and possibility of theft.

Unit 13

(a)

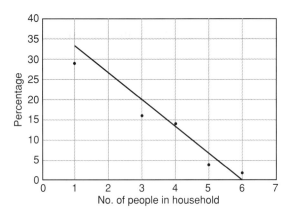

(b) (i) Examples of points:
- Overall the trend is to smaller households.
- Households with just two people have increased steadily.
- Single person households have doubled.
- Households with three people and above have decreased.

(ii) (204800 − 170440)/1170440 × 100 = 20.1595, 20.16, 20.2, 20 per cent

(c) Examples of points:
- The data are only of value to Camden.
- The age group data are not very revealing. 16–59 is a very wide range.
- There are no up-to-date figures for the 2001 census.
- There is no information about households with more than one car.
- There is little information about the type of housing or location.

(d) Examples of points:
- Cost implications for both authorities and the individual.
- Increase in house-building.
- Impact on the environment, for example further use of Green Belt.
- Other infrastructure requirements, for example roads, schools, shops, employment.
- Increase in the number of smaller housing units required.

(e) Fact:
- Population growth shown in the tables suggests that we need to plan for the future.
- Government has allocated extra funds (2002) to encourage more house-building.

- High-rise housing cuts down on travel times for workers in cities.
- Some cities and towns do not have as much room for expansion as others.
- There are many undeveloped and derelict sites in major cities, and high-rise housing make the most efficient use of this space.

Opinion:
- Families would probably prefer not to live in high-rise housing.
- Although there may be empty spaces in cities, it may not be possible from a planning viewpoint to build in that location.
- Local groups in the city/town centres may petition against proposed building.
- Some people prefer to commute to work, rather than live in the centre.
- High-rise flats are out of scale with other older buildings.
- High-rise estates have failed in the past and have contributed to increased crime and social deprivation.

Unit 14

Suggestions for what could be done might include:
- Providing extra EFL/ESL support to ethnic minorities in schools, as well as for adults, to ensure that it isn't language that is the problem.
- Training careers advisors to be 'colour-blind', and to counteract any stereotyped notions of careers suitable for particular ethnic groups.
- Funding initiatives such as Excellence in Cities, designed to provide learning and training opportunities, raise self-esteem, etc.
- Giving support to race-relations training in the public services in order to check on 'institutional racism'.
- Keeping immigration/asylum procedures drawn as tightly as is consistent with compassion.
- Working on aid and trade policies that take account of human rights so as to reduce the desire of overseas populations to emigrate to the UK.
- Enforcing quota systems where these are appropriate, and raising awareness among employers of their legal obligations.
- Making the disadvantaged in general aware of the benefits that they can claim, and of the services that they can access.

Unit 15

(i) Analysis of problem:
- There are elements of basic training in the army and fire service which some women are physically less able to perform as well as men.
- Women in the army suffer more injuries than men during basic training. In the fire service both sexes have been injured.
- The rate of injuries for women in the army is increasing at a greater rate than for men. It is not only women who suffer injuries though – men do too. This suggests that the basic training may be too intensive.
- Inability to complete basic training may mean women cannot safely meet the requirements of the job. They are effectively being denied access to an army/fire service career because of their physical build. This, in itself, is discriminatory and exactly what the law seeks to avoid.
- The situation has highlighted a conflict between two pieces of legislation – equal opportunities and health and safety.
- The services were set up for men, ignoring the needs of women.
- The overall problem is a mismatch between the requirements of legislation and the way it translates into practice. The law requires equality of opportunity but this is not working in the practices and provision of basic training, for example inappropriate nature of equipment (fire suits).
- Discriminatory practices against women are in operation.

(ii) Source of problem:
- The services are responsible for implementing legislation, but they are also responsible for ensuring health and safety of all their members.
- Women and men have different physical strength capacities. The services have a responsibility to be realistic in their expectations of different genders.
- Women have a responsibility to reach the same fitness levels/be able to handle the same equipment as men if they expect to do the same job. If they are paid equally, they should perform equally.
- Individuals have responsibility not to endanger themselves or others.
- Government is responsible for ensuring that laws complement each other (Health and Safety/Discrimination laws) rather than cause confusion.

(iii) Solution:
- Organisations should adopt a policy of positive discrimination, for example redesign equipment to suit women's stature.
- The services could be more flexible in their interpretation of discrimination laws – a common sense approach is needed.
- Rules and regulations could be changed to make more allowance for physical differences, for example specialist roles.
- Women might be failing the basic training but that does not necessarily mean they cannot do the job. The requirements for basic training could be reviewed.
- Bad publicity needs to be counteracted to encourage more women to join these services, for example recruitment campaigns, otherwise the situation will never change.
- Anomalies between different pieces of legislation should be rectified by government.
- Equality within the services should be actively encouraged, for example better team working, culture change.

Unit 16

Prison appropriate:
- Taking away freedom is a valid and appropriate punishment.
- Society is safer because certain offenders have been locked up.
- It is only an acceptable sentence for certain types of crime/criminal.
- It can be seen as a deterrent.
- Rehabilitation through education can be successful.

Prison not appropriate:
- Every crime is different – blanket punishments do not work.
- It is difficult for prisoners to put something back into the community.
- It is impossible to make restitution for what they have done in prison.
- Reforming offenders does not generally work in prisons, i.e. most re-offend.

Unit 17

Threat:

- Leaders of such groups are not elected, so have no real constituency or authority.
- Many are single issue groups, narrow or limited in scope, that don't represent the whole picture.
- They are not accountable, i.e. they can fulfil their aims and ignore consequences, for example Animal Liberation Front.
- Some see direct action as the only way to get things done – for example fuel protesters (September 2000) – which can lead to a breakdown of the democratic process and potential anarchy.

Not a threat:

- They keep elected groups, both locally and nationally, on their toes.
- They ensure a range of interests is represented in the public consciousness.
- They act as a 'watch dog' to restrain business and commercial interests.
- Many are formally constituted groups and are consulted by Government on policy matters, for example the NFU during the Foot and Mouth crisis.
- They can ensure that power is not monopolised by relatively small ruling 'clique' or minority.

Unit 18

Agreeing with statement:

- As long as people do not break the law they are free to do what they want, for example go where they want, wear what they wish.
- Freedom of speech, freedom to movement, etc. are enshrined in the law of the land.
- People cannot be arrested unless there is a suspicion that they have committed an offence.
- Whilst there is a pressure to conform within society, there have always been those who live their lives differently from the norm.
- People over 18 can vote for their representatives, use this to change a government, or simply abstain from the process.
- In free societies, people can be original and creative so innovation can be more likely, for example in technology, culture and arts.

Not agreeing with statement:

- In an increasingly integrated society it is difficult for an individual's actions not to have an effect on

others, for example a person who fails in a suicide bid would trigger many different agencies.
- It is not a free country – wealth buys elements of freedom, the poor are far more limited.
- There is increasing surveillance of people's movements, from CCTV cameras to proposed identity cards.
- The state has the right to interfere inside a person's home, for example in cases of suspected child abuse or other breaches of the law.
- The 'nanny state' has ensured that individual decision-making is less of an option, for example restrictions on what can be done with property.
- The pressures of advertising ensure that many feel that they have little choice in purchasing goods, for example designer gear.
- All citizens have a 'moral' duty in civic society, not merely to obey the law, but to take responsibility as voters, as jurors, as good neighbours, as parents, etc.

Unit 19

Still have power:

- Mr Plowden has local power as a magistrate.
- He represents the county to the Queen.
- The Plowden family business creates wealth.
- Their views on agricultural matters may be listened to and command respect.
- The family name may be enough to ensure an editor would print an article or letter.
- Political and celebrity power passes. As a landowner with a stake in a locality, power and influence will endure.

No longer have much power:

- Agriculture is no longer a way of life that creates much wealth – and wealth does not confer power by itself.
- Land value cannot be realised easily for non-agricultural purposes.
- The rural lobby has less of a voice in national affairs than it had.
- The Plowdens employ only 23 people, so it is only a modest-sized business.
- Power has shifted to financiers, footballers, actors, media pundits and the like.
- The Plowden family is rather tucked away in remote rural spot. London is the locus of real power.

Unit 20

Possible points:

- FPP voting system does not encourage popular participation. In many constituencies, the result is almost a foregone conclusion. It is only in marginal constituencies that individual votes count for much.
- People do not feel like stakeholders when one government after another comes to power on a minority vote or when a majority is so impregnable that even parliamentary votes are a formality.
- Politicians make promises before they are elected that they neglect when in power, and they claim success in power that may be exaggerated.
- Politicians lose voters' respect when they try to score points off each other in parliament and in election campaigns.
- Young people have too little knowledge of the party policies (not well served by education and by the press) to make informed judgements.
- They have found other ways of registering their views about what politicians say and do, for example direct action or wielding influence in their professional lives.
- Many simply opt out, either because they have their lives to lead or because the mood of the times is cynical at best and anarchistic at worst.
- More direct ways of registering views might be more appealing – postal or online voting, single-issue referenda, or consumer-style polling in supermarkets.
- Compulsory voting would only promote a deeper cynicism and refusal. It could only be contemplated in the context of radical reform of the whole process.

Unit 21

Valid:

- Tabloid coverage of sleaze amongst the Royal Family and politicians, for example Charles and Camilla, Prince Harry, Charles Kennedy.
- Public response to Royal Family's handling of the death of Diana.
- Growth in satirical programmes.
- Church leaders are perceived as being of far less relevance/importance today. For example, does the population take note of the Archbishop of Canterbury's statements?
- The concept of the police or judiciary always being correct has been seriously threatened by cases such as the Guildford Four and Birmingham Six.

- There is a lack of deference towards professions, for example teachers have moved down the social scale.
- Greater accountability is expected by the public.

Not valid:

- Some politicians and authority figures are still revered and listened to, for example the Queen and Nelson Mandela.
- Perhaps we look for other authorities, for example sports and entertainment stars like Jonny Wilkinson and Bob Geldof?
- Is society any more lawless? There is still a large 'silent' majority who respect police, doctors, educationists, etc.
- An increasing realisation of rights has led to a new alignment in society with less automatic deference, and with respect for authority having to be earned.

Unit 22

Points that might be included:

- Reference to the school's results/position in the league tables – perhaps acknowledging that all local children can attend regardless of their abilities and attainment – and some comments on the area which the school serves.
- Special curricular strength for which government funding has been secured, for example specialist school status.
- Mention of committed, highly-qualified and talented staff who bring special expertise to the school.
- Links with local companies that contribute to enhanced facilities, work-placements and other benefits.
- Reference to the success of students in achieving places at a variety of universities and following worthwhile careers.
- Values of the school, for example emphasis on pastoral care, achievement, discipline, perhaps on church affiliation, or special ethos.
- Involvement in extra-curricular sporting (and other) activities, providing team-building and other benefits.
- Opportunities for students to serve on the school council and exercise 'citizenship' responsibility.
- Links with the local community, for example on shared facilities, and opportunities for involvement of various sorts.
- Active parental involvement in the affairs of the school.

Unit 23

Does depend upon those who view it:

- If a person enjoys/values a piece of art, then it is valid in their eyes.
- Art appreciation can be very personal – a piece is enjoyed because it captures a moment, rekindles memories, has a close association, etc.
- The definition of art changes over generations. For example, early twentieth century abstract art had observers asking 'what is it?', as if it had to be something.
- The winners of prestigious awards, such as the Turner prize, are not always supported or appreciated by members of the public.
- Art critics can mould people's opinions about the quality of a piece of artwork.

Does not depend upon those who view it:

- There are techniques which experts can explain which identify whether a piece of work is 'good'.
- Most people view artwork at exhibitions when it has already been valued.
- Tours of art galleries give information about pieces which can guide opinion.
- Knowledge of history of art will help to explain how certain pieces of work came to be created.
- Media can generate support or opposition to new artworks.

Unit 24

Does have the right:

- Lord Elgin purchased and protected the Elgin Marbles by removing them – i.e. idea of stewardship – many other items were destroyed.
- Pollution and acid rain in Athens have damaged the Parthenon.
- The British Museum has prime expertise in the conservation of artefacts. Lord Elgin donated them for a reason.
- Centres of excellence like the British Museum build up examples of specific types of artefacts from different places, rather than just showing copies.
- The Victorians set up many museums and collections so that the public could learn about history and other cultures.
- Such collections allow access to major collections of artefacts and associated materials for academic study and research.

- Major world galleries and museums attract worldwide visitors – they are international centres.
- Many other states have purchased and retained artefacts from abroad.

Does not have the right:

- Many of these items were taken in colonial days when the UK had huge power and influence.
- The vast majority of states now have excellent museums so that items would not be damaged by being returned.
- Cultural and religious value has been lost by country of origin.
- The items were donated to the British Museum. It is morally and legally questionable as to whether we should retain them.
- Campaigns to restore Jewish art from Nazi collectors have been successful. Is this not the same?

Unit 25

Concerned:

- Film-making is very expensive and requires heavy risk investment.
- Relatively few companies, holding monopoly positions, decide on the trends and types of film being made.
- It is difficult for small independent film-makers to produce and distribute innovative work.
- There is a danger of films becoming formulaic, as with the all-action movies of the 1990s.
- The media's attention on 'Tinseltown' downgrades films made elsewhere worldwide.
- It provides another example of US cultural domination.
- The constant exposure to Hollywood advertising creates a vicious circle.

Not concerned:

- More 'Bollywood' films are made than Hollywood films.
- Film-making is becoming very much a worldwide industry, hence Hollywood domination could lessen.
- We have been satisfied with the diet from Hollywood for the last 90 years.
- Many films produced elsewhere, for example in the UK or Australia, are successful, for example *Billy Elliot, Shakespeare in Love, Muriel's Wedding*.
- A number of low-budget movies do succeed, for example *The Blair Witch Project, Fahrenheit 9/11*.

Unit 26

(a)

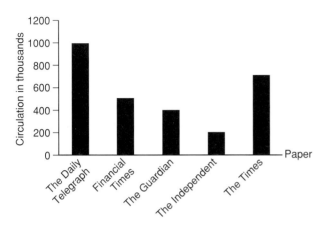

(b) (i) 9000/4 = 2,250 thousands or 2,250,000
(ii) 500/11,820 × 100 = 4.23, 4.2, 4 per cent

(c) Possible points:
- Table 2 suggests that there is a high demand for websites as the information is given in millions.
- Tabloid newspapers have the highest newspaper share, presumably because of their style of reporting.
- It is difficult to compare the column inches of newspapers read with pages visited on websites.
- Most of the data presented have their own limitations.
- The timescales involved are not clear or easily comparable.

(d) Possible points:
- Information is given for only one month.
- Information is given only for accessing commercial sites.
- No information is given about type or identities of users.
- There is little specific detail about some of the sites accessed. The finance site has the highest average minutes per visitor, but we don't know what for.
- The average number of minutes per visitor seems low.
- No details are provided about volume of transactions or money spent.

(e) Valid:
- Increased use of the Internet and ICT in general may mean fewer people are getting information from books.
- Table 2 suggests that the Internet is used frequently for news items.
- The Internet offers a faster route to accessing global information.
- The Internet may be cheaper in the long run.
- Unwanted information can be discarded more quickly and easily.
- A younger generation is being programmed to read screens rather than books.
- Links to other sites are an advantage.

Not valid:
- The type of information required may be of an individual nature and may only be accessible in 'hard copy'.
- Books are more 'mobile' than computers.
- Internet information cannot be regarded as being as sound and reliable as the printed word.
- Printed systems do not crash and have viruses.
- Not everyone can or wants to access the Internet. Older generation has been brought up to use books and they are still just as much in demand.
- A valuable and practical medium will be lost if we lose books.

Unit 27

Do share this view:
- Many news stories seem to emanate from intrusive journalism of an unsavoury nature.
- Many of the items in the Code of Practice can be manipulated for newspapers' own ends, for example comment, conjecture and fact.
- Various newspapers have been censured for offering to pay witnesses/defendants in major trials for their stories, after the verdict is reached.
- The trial of several Leeds United footballers had to be halted because an article was published by a relative of the victim before the verdict.
- Little seems to happen if the guidelines are breached. Is censure sufficient to deter?
- Long telephoto lenses and 'stalking' by paparazzi still seem to be common.
- There is a tendency for the media to pre-judge, for example child murders/abuse, etc.

Do not share this view:
- Some recent royal 'scandals' have arisen from legal embarrassments, upon which the press has every right to report.
- Intrusion is necessary to expose wrong-doing, for example Watergate, Jeffery Archer.

- Given the less intrusive reporting of the lives of Diana's children since her death, the process of self-regulation has and does work.
- If Code of Practice is ignored, then another option is legal sanctions, with the associated threat of restraint and heavy fines.
- Newspapers check the legality of everything they print nowadays to avoid the possibility of being sued.
- Newspaper owners do not want to end up in court constantly because of bad publicity and financial penalties.
- Celebrities often seek publicity themselves.

Unit 28
Possible reasons:
- Mergers will lead to branch closures which in turn will lead to a reduction in service and job losses.
- Less choice and reduced competition mean familiar high street names disappear and with them standards of service.
- Economic theory shows that monopoly power can cost more and does not always bring benefits – privatisation has had the effect of creating private monopolies instead of state ones.
- Firms in competition for sales will ensure cheaper prices and better service in order to retain customers.
- Conglomerates may be less responsive to consumer needs/demands.
- Monopolies do not have to worry about quality of performance or service and can set higher prices if there are no rivals.
- The government's Monopolies and Mergers Commission was set up to ensure that proposed mergers are in the public interest. It can veto proposals.

Unit 29
Fair:
- All members of society should make contributions to the well-being of that society.
- Many taxes are progressive, i.e. linked with ability to pay, such as Income Tax. Council Tax is progressive on property value.
- Everyone receives basic return on items such as healthcare, social security and pensions.
- Some taxes changed to become more equitable, for example Council Tax replaced the Poll Tax.
- We have choices on some indirect taxes by deciding which items to buy.

Not fair:
- Some taxes are regressive and take no note of ability to pay, for example VAT, car tax.
- Taxes are universal and the income from them cannot necessarily be directed to the areas that the taxpayer may necessarily want.
- Many people do not want to pay for services they do not require.
- There should be only minimum taxation. People would then be able to purchase what services, etc. they require.
- Many elements of the tax system ensure that the rich get richer and poor get poorer, for example tax 'havens', indirect taxation, etc.
- The present tax banding benefits highest earners.
- More affluent members of society can afford financial expertise to be able to reduce tax liabilities, for example inheritance tax.

Unit 30
Beneficial:
- Specialisation can lead to mass production and economies of scale.
- Consumers gain through lower prices.
- The country gains through efficient use of resources.
- It encourages co-operation and goodwill between states.
- Protectionism can lead to less choice and higher prices.
- Is also inefficient because of reduced competition.
- One state adopting protectionist measures can lead to other states following suit – to the detriment of all.

Not beneficial:
- MEDCs are likely to benefit more.
- Protectionism improves the country's balance of payments by increasing exports and reducing imports.
- It can also protect the country's exchange rate.
- It can raise revenues from customs duties.
- It can restrict 'dumping' of goods from overseas competitors who export at low prices to establish a position in the market.
- It can safeguard domestic employment and industries, particularly 'infant' industries not yet strong enough to compete with established overseas firms, for example EU/USA agricultural subsidies.

Unit 31

Reasons for giving, or not giving, aid:

- To ensure that an ally remains 'on side' (e.g. US aid to Egypt) or that a balance of power is maintained (e.g. US aid to Israel). Aid might be withheld by way of punishment (e.g. Libya, Cuba).
- To enable a country to purchase a donor's exports (e.g. 70 per cent of US aid) or combat the failure of a country's currency.
- To assist oppressed minorities by targeting aid, for example to women, to ethnic and regional groups (e.g. Andean Indians, Shi'ite Muslims in Iraq).
- To relieve suffering (e.g. in southern Africa) and discharge historical responsibilities (e.g. Dutch aid to Surinam, British aid to Montserrat, etc.).
- Aid may be refused if the recipient is corrupt or its market economy is weak (e.g. Zimbabwe, Somalia).
- It may be refused if there is a danger of its being commandeered by the ruling party and/or the military.
- It may be refused to a repressive regime (e.g. Zimbabwe, Burma, Iraq).

Should we judge other donor countries?

- The UN target does give a benchmark for applauding those countries that give more than 0.7 per cent of their GDP, and for being critical of those (including the UK) that give less.
- It is reasonable to distinguish between disinterested aid, given to alleviate suffering, and self-interested, tied aid – and to question whether the latter counts as aid at all. Not to condemn is to condone?
- Global poverty can only be mitigated by a global aid policy. Donors should play by the same rules if social justice is to be done.
- It is understandable that a country like Greece, which is relatively undeveloped in EU terms, should give less perhaps. Nor has it had an empire that conferred post-imperial responsibilities.
- On the other hand, the Scandinavian countries have not been imperial powers in any conventional sense, so their aid-giving is admirable in comparison.
- In a 'global village' we all have responsibility for each other. We should not permit levels of suffering elsewhere that we would not permit within our own borders.

Unit 32

Continue to have power and influence:

- Constitutionally, the monarch is head of the Church of England, and is anointed by the Archbishop of Canterbury.
- Senior bishops still sit, and have voting rights, in the House of Lords.
- The media still provide a ready forum for the archbishops and bishops when they express a view on national matters.
- Many religious leaders speak on 'Thought for the Day' on Radio 4. The Chief Rabbi, the leader of the 'Muslim Parliament', etc. speak with the authority of their communities and are listened to.
- As 'faith-communities' grow in size, so their leaders are influential, particularly in marginal constituencies.

Have lost power and influence:

- The established church has lost ground, and there is increasing talk of disestablishment (separation of Church and State).
- Leaders of faith-communities may be listened to, but more as the spokesmen of ethnic or ideological groups, less as religionists.
- As churches grow less formal (house-churches and the like), so their leaders are less publicly conspicuous.
- Scientific explanations have gained ground at the expense of myth and belief-based/theological explanations of life and phenomena.
- People think of the life to come less, and rather more of how technology can enhance life now.
- 'Power and influence' seem to be wielded nowadays more by celebrities and media personalities.

Unit 33

Points in support might include:

- Science has turned old beliefs into superstitions and caused people to reject them.
- Belief and conduct are shaped now by prevailing norms as they are represented in the home, in school, and in the media.
- Coverage of religious affairs in the media has shrunk.
- The views of religious leaders are canvassed only for their media value as 'soundbites', the more controversial the better.
- Religious studies and collective worship are vestiges, protected by legislation and custom, of a once fundamental component of education.

- Church-going is at an all-time low, and it remains to be seen whether religions new to Britain will survive more than a generation or two.

Points in opposition might include:
- Science will never have all the answers. It will never satisfy those who ask 'why?'
- There will always be a place for a spiritual element in education.
- Institutional religion may be at a low ebb, but personal religion is (perhaps, in consequence) more prevalent.
- Religious belief now takes post-institutional, non-conventional forms. It may or may not involve a god or 'providence'.
- Immigrant religions have bedded into British culture and for followers their influence is much stronger.

Unit 34
Possible points might include:
- People obtain the basis of moral judgements through primary socialisation, i.e. the norms and values of the family grouping in which the individual is raised.
- Moral judgements can be linked to the attitudes of society at a particular period of time, for example attitudes to women by the Taliban.
- Individualistic attitudes can prevail. What affronts one person does not offend another, for example nude bathing.
- The laws of a country relating to a particular moral dilemma will give a lead, for example controversies over assisted suicides.
- Moral judgements are also influenced through secondary socialisation, for example school, work place, media. People are influenced by peer group pressure, friends, colleagues, etc.
- Religion still plays a major role in guiding moral judgements.

- Culture, literature, media, etc. continually examine moral dilemmas and force observers to consider various options.
- Individual personal experience can also affect attitudes.

Unit 35
Arguments for:
- Science is morally neutral. Only the application of science by humans is open to abuse.
- Progress has been ensured throughout history by following scientific discovery and knowledge, for example the steam engine, electricity, vaccination, rocket propulsion, contraceptive pill.
- Unknown cures and remedies can only be discovered through scientific progress.
- Who has the right to tell humankind which areas of science can be explored and which not?
- Most scientific discovery, or technology, has been put to good purpose.

Arguments against:
- Values and ethics are important constraints, for example the Hippocratic Oath, conventions against germ warfare.
- There are religious constraints – 'playing God', going against nature.
- Some applications of science must be prohibited, or licensed, to prevent abuse, for example sex determination, weapons of mass destruction.
- Human cloning as such appears to confer no social/individual benefits. The process is exceedingly complex, with unknown outcomes, and could be harmful physically and emotionally.
- We should not do what the vast majority of thinking people would be against, or what the law (ultimately democratically defined) condemns.

Index

abortion 242–4
abstract art 177
acid rain 38
Act of Settlement (1701) 145
adversarial politics 142
advertising 205
aesthetic evaluation 162–7
ageing population 113
aggression 62–3
agnostics 227
agriculture 50–5
   CAP (Common Agricultural Policy) 210–11
   developments in 51–3, 204
   subsistence 50–1, 215
AIDS (Acquired Immune Deficiency Syndrome) 68, 69
air pollution 39, 76
air travel 72, 75–6
American Declaration of Independence 129, 136
Amnesty International 130
amniocentesis 47
analogy, arguing from 6
anarchy 135, 136
The Angel of the North 172, 173
animals
   cloning 43, 241, 242
   psychology of animal behaviour 57–8, 59–60, 62, 63
   rights and welfare 38, 128
antioxidants 70
Aquinas, Thomas 124, 239
Archimedes 9
architecture 176–7
Arctic climate change 38–40
argument, types of 5–6
Aristotle 9, 129, 140, 239
the arts
   and aesthetic evaluation 162–7
   and censorship 162, 188–9
   and creativity 175–9
   government sponsorship 165–6
   and science 87–8
astrolobes 76
atheists 227
authoritarian governments 140
authority
   arguing from 5–6
   and power 134

Babbage, Charles 80, 89
Bacon, Francis 15
balance of payments 204
ballet 87, 170
banks
   European Central Bank 212
   use of computers 82
Baroque art 165
BBC (British Broadcasting Corporation) 166, 181–2, 188
   radio 181
behaviourism 56, 60, 62, 156
Bentham, Jeremy 129, 238
Big Bang 11, 24, 27
Bill of Rights (1689) 145
Bin Laden, Osama 234
biological diversity 36
biological psychology 56, 60–2
biotechnology 50, 51, 52
birth rates 112
Blair, Tony 184
Bland, Tony 245, 246
blasphemy 189, 191
Boyle, Robert 10
brain-stem death 244, 245
Brandt Report 215, 218
Bretton Woods Agreement 194
British Constitution 145–51
   and devolution 146–7, 148–50
   need for reform 146–7
   and regionalism 150
Brown, Gordon 205
Buddhism 224, 226, 238
buses 74
Bush, George W. 221
business use of computers 82

CAD (computer-aided design) 81
CAM (computer-aided manufacturing) 81–2
CAP (Common Agricultural Policy) 210–11
capitalism 90, 107, 108
cars 30, 72, 73, 74–5, 76
censorship 90, 187–92
   and the arts 162, 188–9
   forms of 187
   and gatekeeping 190–1
   and the press 187–8, 190, 192

censorship – *continued*
  and television 188
chamber music 165
Christianity 129, 224, 226, 238, 244
    and science 27, 28, 36–7
    and Western culture 169
CIM (computer-integrated manufacturing) 81
citizenship 131–2
civil disobedience 124–5
civil laws 124
Civil Rights Movement 125
classical music 164, 169–70, 175
classless society 114–15
cloning 43, 66–7, 241–2
coercion, and power 134
cognitive psychology 56
command economies 201–2
Common Agricultural Policy (CAP) 210–11
Competition Commission 195–6
computers
  history of 80–1
  uses of 81–4
Comte, Auguste 106
consequential ethical theories 238
Constitution
  British 145–51
  EU 211–12
consumerism 196
Copernicus, N. 9, 17, 25, 176
Council of Ministers (EC) 209–10
creationism 26, 28, 36–7
creativity 175–9
crime 118–22
criminal law 124
culture 168–74
  education and the transmission of 154
  French culture 171
  high 164, 169–72
    government sponsorship of 165–6
  popular 164, 165, 166, 172–3
  and religion 232
  and science 87–92
  subcultures 119, 120
  Western 168–9
cyberspace 83

Darwin, Charles 16, 17, 23–4, 28, 37, 63
death rates 112
deductive arguments 5
deforestation 31
democracy
  and censorship 187, 190
  and government 140–1
  and power 137
demographic trends in the UK 112–14
deontological ethical theories 238
Descartes, René 37, 90, 176, 230
desertification 217
determinism 237
developmental psychology 57
deviancy 118–22
devolution 146–7, 148–50
dictatorships 140
direct action 125, 126–7
DNA 17, 43–4, 45, 46–7
dreams 62
Durkheim, Emile 232–3
duty 130–2, 238

economic issues 199–208
economic theories 194–8
ecosystems 35–6
ecumenical movement 227
Edelman, Gerald 68
Education Act (1998) 155
educational issues 152–9
  and cultural transmission 154
  fees in higher education 156–7
  functions of schools 152
  gender gap 155–6
  illiteracy 216
  systems of education 152–5
  traditionalists and progressives 154
Einstein, Albert 11, 19, 24, 26
electric telegraph 76
Elgin Marbles 174
embryo technology 67
empirical knowledge 15, 230–1
employment 202–3
energy 29–34
  human conversion of 30
  law of conservation of 29–30
  transforming into electricity 30–3
environmental issues 35–41
equality
  and government 136
  of opportunity 116
  and social change 114–15, 116
  and wealth distribution 115, 218, 220
ethics
  ethical issues 241–7
  ethical theories 237–40
  of genetic engineering 47–8, 66–7, 241–2
  see also morality

ethnic minorities, in the UK population 110, 112–13, 114
ethology 63
EU (European Union) 209–14
    Constitution 211–12
eugenic programmes 47
euro (European currency) 212–13
Europa 25, 27
European Central Bank 212
European Commission 210, 212
European Court of Justice 210
European Parliament 210, 241
euthanasia 243, 244–6
evolutionary theory 16–17, 23–4, 25, 28, 37
exchange rates 194
exobiology 26–7
Expressionism 165
extraterrestrial life 25–7
extremophiles 25, 27

families, and social change 113, 114
FAO (Food and Agriculture Organisation) 52, 219
fertility drugs 67
films 171, 172–3, 188–9
first-past-the-post electoral system 143
fiscal policy 201
FMS (flexible manufacturing systems) 81, 82
food production 50–5
fossil fuels 30–2, 76
free market/libertarian thinkers 136
free will 237
freedom of expression 141
freedom of information 83, 84, 136, 190
French culture 171
Freud, Sigmund 233
Friedman, Milton 197
functionalists
    and religion 226, 232–3
    and society 106–7, 108

Galileo Galilei 10, 22, 23, 90, 176
Gandhi, Mahatma 125
GATT (General Agreement of Tariffs and Trade) 204
gay rights 128
GDP (gross domestic product) 204, 215
gender gap in education 155–6
gene therapy 44–7
genetic engineering 42–9, 66–7
    ethics of 47–8, 66–7, 241–2
genetic modification (GM) 51–2
genetic screening 13
genomes 17, 44
geo-thermal energy 32

germ-line therapy 42–3, 47, 66
gerontology 69–70
Gibson, William 83
global economy/politics 219–20
global village 89
global warming 38–40
globalisation 142, 219
governments
    and democracy 137
    and politics 140, 141–2
    purpose of 135–6
    sponsorship of the arts 165–6
gravitational motion 10–11, 73
Greek science 9
green tourism 76

Habeas Corpus 145
Harvey, William 10
HDI (Human Development Index) 219
heart surgery 69
Heisenberg uncertainty principle 25
heliocentric theory 9–10, 23
Hinduism 225, 232
histograms 99
HIV (human immuno-deficiency virus) 67
Hobbes, Thomas 129, 136, 239
homophobia 130
homosexual marriage 238, 239
House of Lords 147–8
Human Genome Project 42–4, 66
human rights 129–30, 135, 137
hunger 50, 216
hydroelectric power (HEP) 32–3
hyperinflation 203
hypotheses 15

illiteracy 216
IMF (International Monetary Fund) 219
immunology 67
Impressionism 88, 165, 177
in vitro fertilisation 67
income tax 200, 207
inductive arguments 5
industrial location 202
inflation 201
installation art 164–5
interactionism 107, 108
Internet 82–3, 83–4, 89, 204
Islam 27, 225, 228, 234, 238
Islamic science 9
Israel 234, 235
ITC (Independent Television Commission) 182, 183, 184, 188

Jesus of Nazareth 224
Judaism 27, 28, 225, 238, 244
justice 123, 124, 130
justified arguments 6

Kant, Immanuel 130
Kelly, Dr David 191
Kepler, Johannes 10
Keynesianism 196–7
King, Martin Luther 125
knowledge, types of 2–4, 230–1
Kohler, Wilhelm 59–60
Kuhn, Thomas 8, 11

LAN (local area networks) 81
Landsteiner, Karl 67
laws 123–7
    civil and criminal 124
    and civil disobedience 124–5
    and justice 123, 124
    need for 123
    privacy laws 189, 190
    and punishment 124
Le Corbusier 176–7
LEDCs (less economically developed countries) 215, 217–18
legal aid 136
lieder 165
literature 170
Locke, John 129, 135, 152–3
Lorenz, Konrad 62–3

Maastricht Treaty 211, 212
McCartney, Sir Paul 175
Machiavelli, Niccolo 135
mainframe computers 81
malnutrition 50, 216
market economies 195, 201
marketing 205
Mars 25, 26
Marx, Karl
    and education 154
    and government 135–6
    and Marxist sociology 107, 108
    and religion 233
mathematics 93–103
    bearings 100
    calculating percentages 96–7
    calculating probability 97
    calculating volumes 97–8
    inequalities 100–1
    mean, median, mode and range 93–4
    networks (critical path analysis) 99, 101

ratios 99
scale 99–100
scatter graphs 95
media 180–6
    bias 183
    censorship 187–8
    influence 183
    ownership 184
    the press 89, 180–1, 185, 192
    radio 181
    television 87, 89, 173, 181–2
medical developments 66–71
medieval science 9
memory, psychology of 57
meritocracies 114, 136
migration 112, 113–14
minority rights 128
mixed economies 202
mobile phones 91
modern art 177–8
monarchy (Britain) 141, 146, 151
Monet, Claude 177
monetarism 197
money, and exchange rates 194
moral rights 128
morality 237–40
    and religion 238
    see also ethics
motor cars 30, 72, 73, 74–5, 76
MRI (Magnetic Resonance Imaging) 62
Murdoch, Rupert 184
music
    classical 164, 169–70, 175
    popular 172
    and science 20, 87

National Curriculum 132, 156
NATO (North Atlantic Treaty Organisation) 89, 211
natural law 129–30, 239, 242
natural rights 129–30
natural theology 21, 26
networks (critical path analysis) 99, 101
neurology 68
New Towns 112
Newton, Isaac 10, 11, 22–3, 24, 37
Northern Ireland 149

Obscene Publications Act 187–8
observation 108–9
OECD (Organisation for Economic Co-operation and Development) 204
Official Secrets Act 189

oligarchies 136, 142
opera 87, 169–70, 172
organic farming 52–3, 204
ozone layer 38

painting 87–8, 172
paradigms 8, 11
Parliament Act (1911) 145
Parliament (Britain) 141, 142, 143
Paul, St 129, 231
Pavlov, Ivan 58, 59
PCs (personal computers) 80, 81
peace movement 125
phenomenologists, and the nature of society 107
philosophers, and the nature of society 108
photography 87–8, 89
plate tectonics 17–18
Plato 129, 152, 239
PLCs (public limited companies) 195
PLO (Palestine Liberation Organisation) 234–5
Plowden family 138–9
poetry 170–1
politics 140–4
    in Britain 140–1
    electoral systems 143
    and government 140, 141–2
    two-party system 141, 143
pollution 76
pop art 172
Popper, Karl 16
popular culture 164, 165, 166, 172–3
popular music 172
population 37–8, 217–18
    demographic trends in the UK 112–14
positivists, and the nature of society 106–7
poverty 215–22
power 134–9
    and authority 134
    and coercion 134
    and government 134–7
PR (proportional representation) 143
the press 180–1
    and censorship 187–8, 190, 192
printing technology 87
prisons 118
privatisation 197
    of public transport 74
proportional representation (PR) 143
Protestantism, and capitalism 90
psychodynamic psychology 56, 62
psychology 56–65
    and religious belief 233

Ptolemy 9
public transport 73, 74
punishment 124

quantum physics 24, 26

racism 114
radio 181
rail transport 72, 73, 74, 75, 78–9
rational knowledge 230
Rawls, John 124, 237
referenda 142
regionalism 150
relativity, theory of general 19, 24, 26
religion 224–36
    and abortion 242
    and education 154
    and the environment 36–7
    and euthanasia 246
    and everyday life 227–8
    fundamentalism 26, 227, 233
    major world religions 224–6
    and morality 238
    religious beliefs 230–6
    and science 21–8, 48
    symbolism and ceremony in 226–7
    and terrorism 234–5
Renaissance 22, 172
Representation of the People Acts 145
representational art 177
representative government 141
responsibilities 130–2
revealed theology 22
Riemann, Bernhard 11
rights 128–33, 168
    and abortion 242–4
    animal rights 38, 128
    defining 128
    and duties 130–2
    human 129–30, 135, 137
    natural 129–30
road safety 77
Romanticism 165
Rousseau, Jean-Jacques 136–7, 153–4, 239
rural development issues 204
rural drift of population 113–14

scale 99–100
scanning techniques 68
scatter graphs 95
schools see education

science
    and creativity and innovation 176
    and culture 87–92
    history of 9–10
    progress in 8–13
    and religion 21–8
scientific knowledge 3
scientific method 15–20
Scottish culture 168
Scottish devolution 143, 148–9
sculpture 172
sexism 130
Shakespeare, William 171, 175, 176
Sikhism 225–6
silicon chips 82
Singer, Peter 245
Single European Act/market 141, 211
Skinner, B.F. 60
sleep homeostasis 60–2
Smith, Adam 195
social change 112–17
social class 114–15
social contract theory 239
social psychology 56
social surveys 108
socialism 136
society
    defining 106
    nature of 106–11
Socrates 124, 129
solar energy 33
somatic-cell therapy 42
sonnets 165
southward drift of population 112, 113
Soviet Union 89
space travel 72–3, 73, 76
speciesism 130
statistical studies 108
steam engines 30, 72, 73
Stephenson, George 72, 73
structuralism, and deviancy 119
subcultures 119, 120
subsistence farming 215
supercomputers 81
supply and demand, law of 195
surgery 69–70
Surrealism 165
surrogacy 67
sustainability 52, 53
Sutcliffe, Peter 231

tariffs 204

taxation 199–200, 207
technology
    and culture 88–9
    and transport 72–3, 76, 77
television 87, 173, 181–2
    censorship 188
Ten Commandments 123–4, 131
terrorism, and religion 234–5
Thatcher, Margaret 184, 197
theatre 87, 166
theology 21–2
Thoreau, Henry David 124
totalitarianism 136
traffic congestion 74–5
transformers 76
transplants 69, 70
transport
    history of 72–3
    issues 73–7, 113
    and society 88–9
truth 3, 6
tuition fees 156–7
Turner Prize 172

unemployment 110, 202–3
United Nations
    FAO (Food and Agriculture Organisation) 52, 219
    UNICEF 219
Universal Declaration of Human Rights 129, 130
universal rights 128
universal suffrage 136
university tuition fees 156–7
urbanisation 37–8
utilitarianism 237–8

vaccination programmes 66
valid arguments 6
VAT (value added tax) 200

Wales 143, 148, 149
Warhol, Andy 172
Watt, James 30, 72, 73
wealth, distribution of 115, 218, 220
Wegener, Alfred 17
Western culture 168–9
white-collar crime 119
Wilson, Tuzo 17
wind generators 33, 34
Wittgenstein, Ludwig 24
World Wide Web (WWW) 81, 82

youth crime 119–21